APPRENTICESHIP FOR ADULTHOOD

APPRENTICESHIP FOR ADULTHOOD

———◆———

Preparing Youth for the Future

Stephen F. Hamilton

THE FREE PRESS
A Division of Macmillan, Inc.
NEW YORK

Collier Macmillan Publishers
LONDON

The Free Press
A Division of Macmillan, Inc.
866 Third Avenue, New York, N.Y. 10022

Collier Macmillan Canada, Inc.

Printed in the United States of America

printing number
1 2 3 4 5 6 7 8 9 10

Library of Congress Cataloging-in-Publication Data

Hamilton, Stephen F.
    Apprenticeship for adulthood: preparing youth for the future/
Stephen F. Hamilton.
        p. cm.
    Includes bibiliographical references.
    ISBN 0-02-913705-5
    1. Apprentices—United States. 2. Apprentices—Germany (West)
3. Occupational training—United States. 4. Youth—Employment—
United States. 5. High school graduates—Employment—United
States. 6. Vocational education—United States. I. Title.
HD4885.U5H36 1990
331.25'922—dc20   89-23541
                                                      CIP

For our sons
Peter, Joseph, and Benjamin

Contents

Preface   *ix*

Acknowledgments   *xi*

1. The Future of Youth and Work   *1*
2. The Perilous Transition from School to Career   *19*
3. Discovering Apprenticeship   *39*
4. Academic Schooling: General Preparation for Work   *69*
5. Vocational Schooling: Specific Preparation for Work   *91*
6. Cloudy Futures: Why the American System Fails   *119*
7. Principles for Practice: Specifications for Reinventing Apprenticeship   *135*
8. An American-Style Apprenticeship System   *153*

Notes   *187*

Index   *219*

Preface

In *Coming of Age in Samoa,*[1] Margaret Mead taught us that as young people grow up their behavior follows patterns that are determined as much by culture as biology. Even allowing for subsequent criticisms of her work, she demonstrated that adolescent storm and stress are not inevitable. Urie Bronfenbrenner made a related point in *Two Worlds of Childhood,*[2] contrasting the Soviet Union's careful orchestration of social institutions to nurture exemplary citizens with the United States' tendency to give families and schools responsibility for rearing children and then undermine their capacity to do so successfully. Both conveyed the message that the difficulties we face in this country of fostering competent and responsible youth are self-inflicted. They are the darker side of some of our most cherished beliefs.

Current interest in cross-national comparisons of school performance suggests that the message of these two classics may be getting through. When American youth learn less in school than their peers in other countries, and when they use more drugs, commit more crimes, and have more babies, then this behavior cannot be attributed simply to their youthfulness; it must have something to do with the conditions surrounding them. The message is hopeful because it implies that improvement is possible, but cautionary because it means that effective change will be deep-rooted and difficult to accomplish.

This book has a narrower theme, but it echoes the same message. It is about the transition from adolescence to adulthood of youth who do not enroll in higher education. Contrasting that transition in the United States and West Germany reveals how difficult it is in this country and how it could be eased. I went to West Germany because what I had read about apprenticeship there and in the other German-speaking countries suggested that it constituted the most highly developed system of experiential learning in the world.

Experiential learning is a way of harnessing learning outside of schools to make schools more effective. Although various forms of experiential learning gained prominence during the school reform movement of the late 1960s and early 1970s, nearly everywhere they failed to move beyond the marginal status of special programs. The publication of *A Nation at Risk*[3] in 1983 marked a new era of school reform that turns inward toward the classroom as the only venue for learning, not only rejecting experiential learning but also denying the power of family, peer group, workplace, and neighborhood either to reinforce the school's lessons to the advantage of some youth or to contradict them to the disadvantage of others.

Happily, a lively debate over the quality of secondary education has persisted far longer than expected and has fixed attention on some issues raised in that report by the National Commission on Excellence in Education, notably employers' fears for the quality of their workforce, particularly as the youth population is becoming less white and less middle-class. More questions have also been raised about whether the Commission's recommendations for excellence are compatible with equality.

This continued ferment has altered the style as well as the content of this book. What began as an academic treatment of the socialization of noncollege youth for adulthood in the United States and West Germany became an argument in favor of establishing a system of apprenticeship in this country. I trust that the argument is well grounded, but it is frankly stated at the beginning rather than cautiously drawn as an implication at the close of a dispassionate investigation. My hope is that citing authorities and acknowledging scholarly debates in footnotes will lead other scholars to find this argument both persuasive and generative of further research without deterring the policymakers and practitioners in education, business, and government who have the power to make the proposed changes.

Acknowledgments

A sabbatical leave from Cornell University combined with a Fulbright Senior Research Fellowship gave me the opportunity to spend a year in West Germany. The Fulbright-Kommission in Bonn was exceedingly helpful, as were faculty and staff of the University of Regensburg during a two-month stay there for an advanced German course.

My host as Guest Professor at the University of Munich was Professor Rolf Oerter. His staff became my colleagues and supporters: Dr. Eva Dreher, Dr. Michael Dreher, Dr. Rainer Schönhammer, Frau Fischbach, Frau Lehman, and especially Dr. Irene Burtchen, who gave many hours of her time to help us settle into daily life in a new country. Rosemary Oerter was a gracious hostess who became a colleague as well.

The Deutsches Jugendinstitut provided a first-rate library and wonderful colleagues. The late Dr. Georg Kärtner and his colleague, Dr. Peter Wahler, shared their valuable contacts with two firms and a vocational school, where I began my observations. Dr. Sibylle Hübner-Funk, Dr. Rudolf Pettinger, and Dr. Sabine Sardei-Biermann became advisers and friends. Herr Reichel, of the Chamber of Industry and Commerce for Munich and Upper Bavaria, found medium-sized firms where I could observe apprentices working in offices.

Dr. Paul Baltes, director of the Max Planck Institute for Human Development and Education in Berlin, helped me locate German scholars with interests related to my own. Visiting the Institute at his invitation made it possible for me to meet Dr. Wolfgang Lempert, whose own work and good advice were crucial to my study. Many other German scholars were generous in their assistance. A partial list includes Professor

Carl Graf Hoyos, Dr. Hans Specht, Professor Walter Heinz, and later Professor Klaus Hurrelmann, and Professor Rainer Silbereisen.

Because their identities are not revealed in the text, I cannot personally thank the many people in training firms and vocational schools who allowed me to look over their shoulders and ask questions. They are the ones who taught me how apprenticeship works.

Ray Rist and Peter Katzenstein encouraged and assisted me from the planning stages to reading draft manuscripts. Urie Bronfenbrenner also assumed those tasks in his role as the consummate mentor.

My wife and our three sons approached the year in Germany as an adventure. We were constantly assisted in overcoming the stresses of that adventure by colleagues, friends, and neighbors, especially the Froelichs, the Felkners, and the Simon-Weidners. My wife hastened to complete her doctoral thesis before taking charge of preparations for our trip and then reorganizing the household in Regensburg and in Munich. That she managed also to pursue some of her professional interests testifies equally to her energy and her intellectual curiosity. After our return, she became the primary proponent of the book that has emerged. Without her aid and comfort I could neither have started nor completed this project. Thank you, Mary Agnes.

1

---◆---

The Future of Youth
and Work

Inexorable demographic forces are rapidly changing the United States' workforce, just as surely as economic and technical forces are changing the nature of the work to be done. The great challenge facing the nation is to prepare a changing population of young people to do new kinds of work. Failure imperils economic health, social progress, and democracy itself.

By the turn of the twenty-first century, the proportion of white male workers will be smaller than ever before; more workers will be women, blacks, and Hispanics. A larger proportion of workers will have grown up in poor families. As a result of new technology and the continuing shift from manufacturing to service industries, many jobs will demand high levels of technical knowledge and skill, and most will require well-developed social skills. At the same time, others will be simplified to the point where unskilled workers will replace well-paid skilled workers.

Current forms of education and training, which in the past have adequately prepared white males to fill available jobs, cannot survive unaltered the simultaneous transformation of work and the workforce. During the 1980s, a school reform movement was motivated by the premise that making all schools as effective as the best traditional schools would meet the challenge. Improving schools is a necessary but not a sufficient response to new demographic and economic realities. Along with better schools, a new institution is needed to connect schools to workplaces and to provide young people with clearer paths from school to work: apprenticeship. The ancient practice of teaching crafts by means of practical activity in a one-to-one relationship has traditionally prepared boys

to do men's work in many cultures, including our own. The most successful contemporary apprenticeship is the German dual system, which has
been progressively modernized to prepare both boys and girls for twenti-
eth-century business and industry. Although the United States can adapt
some of the principles from that system, a truly viable American apprenticeship must be reinvented to suit a different economy and educational
system, and a distinctive set of societal values.

Apprenticeship has always done more than teach a specific trade.
Learning to work means learning to be an adult. When Freud was asked
what a healthy person ought to be able to do well, he replied succinctly:
"lieben und arbeiten" (to love and to work).[1] Work is a central human
function. The capacity to engage in paid employment is a hallmark of
adulthood. Being a productive worker calls for many of the same qualities
as being an active citizen and a nurturant family member. Fostering
young people's growth in one of these adult roles improves their ability
to fill the others. Although the focus here is primarily on preparing
youth for work, it is by extension about preparing youth for adulthood
as well.

Many of our noncollege youth now exist in a kind of no-man's-land.
The labor market presents serious barriers to these young people, who
are typically denied entry into adult jobs until they are in their twenties,
even if they have graduated from high school.

Vivian Glenn is underemployed. An 18-year-old high school graduate
with better-than-average grades, Vivian comes from a stable white working-class family and has demonstrated in a series of jobs, beginning
with babysitting when she was 13, that she is dependable and willing
to work hard. Yet after completing a two-year high school vocational
program she has been unable to find a job as a medical office assistant.
Six months after graduation she is still working as a part-time sales
clerk in the drugstore where she worked after school and on weekends
while a student.[2]

Vivian's case is far from unique. Regardless of their credentials, teenage
workers are concentrated in low-skill jobs. Forty-four percent of 16- to
19-year-old workers are employed in retail trade, compared to less than
14 percent of workers over 25. Even after they have completed their
schooling, teenagers are much more likely to be part-time workers than
adults.[3]

New high school graduates are simply not a prime commodity in the labor market. Employers who can afford to be selective, those with career-entry positions to offer, prefer to hire young adults with no better educational credentials than teenagers. In two or three years Vivian will be a good candidate for such a job. For now she is considered too immature.

During the floundering period between high school completion and the early to mid-twenties, young people are frequently unemployed. Although many find short-term jobs, poor and minority youth, especially those in large cities and in depressed regions of the country suffer prolonged unemployment.[4] Employment opportunities for recent high school graduates are largely limited to the "secondary labor market," low-skill and low-paid jobs with little security and no prospects of advancement. Ironically, these are the same jobs open to high school dropouts and high school students working part-time. Dropouts are less likely to get a job than high school graduates; in fact, they are twice as likely to be unemployed. But when they are employed, dropouts' jobs are indistinguishable from those of high school graduates. Only when young adults move into the "primary labor market" of career-entry jobs does a high school diploma begin to pay off in more attractive work opportunities.[5]

This striking pattern of teenage floundering has gained prominence over the past 25 years as a result of a growing youth population and the shift from a manufacturing to a service economy. By the mid-sixties, the postwar baby boom had substantially increased the supply of young people. The ratio of youth (aged 14–24) to adults increased by 39 percent in the 1960s.[6] Meanwhile, the number of low-skill, highly paid factory jobs was declining, being replaced—and displaced from the cities to the suburbs—by low-paid service jobs, notably in retail sales and food service. Young workers' real earnings have fallen precipitously as a result: by 25 percent for males aged 20–24 from 1973 to 1986.[7]

Although this pattern of constrained employment opportunities and lack of career direction has complex causes and far-reaching implications for our economy and our society, employers, career guidance specialists, and economists attribute it merely to youthful immaturity. Young people, we are told, are like that. They do not know what they want and are not ready to settle down and make commitments. This explanation improperly blames individuals for a systemic failure. In fact, changing jobs frequently is rational when available jobs offer no avenue of upward mobility. The best way a young person can improve earnings and upgrade the level of work is to find a new job.

At best, this floundering period is a very frustrating time for young people and their parents, who together assume they are responsible for the failure to find a real job. It is also a waste of "human capital." Society has invested in young people's education, but then limits them to jobs that do not require that education, and often fail to inculcate the work attitudes and behavior employers seek, leading to longer-term waste, especially among minority youth who remain longer in the youth labor market.

If it were true that teenagers are, by nature, too immature to hold responsible jobs, then we would see the same pattern of delayed career entry in other countries. However, the experience of West German young people is quite different. After completing three-year apprenticeships, youth in West Germany successfully assume "adult" jobs around age 18. They are inherently no more responsible than American youth; their advantages are training and opportunity.

Anna Heberer is only a few months away from the completion of her apprenticeship in a large West German manufacturing firm. At age 17 Anna has worked in the firm's accounting, purchasing, inventory, production, personnel, marketing, sales, and finance departments, and studied those functions in school. She is very enthusiastic about the recent news that the company will give her an additional 18 months of training in electronic data processing before hiring her as a regular employee. She is already skilled and reliable enough to have substituted for two weeks in cost accounting during her supervisor's vacation.

Apprenticeship enables ordinary German teenagers to begin careers at the same age that their U.S. counterparts are being turned out of school to sell candy, flip burgers, and pump gas.

West Germany's system can aid our thinking about how to integrate high school graduates into the labor market. The system vividly demonstrates that the floundering period results from educational and labor market conditions, not from any inherent irresponsibility or instability of youth. Rather than eschewing young employees, West German employers prefer hiring 15- and 16-year-olds as apprentices in order to instill in them the kinds of attitudes, work habits, and skills they require. The success of the German system suggests that some kind of apprenticeship might improve the transition of U.S. youth from school to work.

The best kind of apprenticeship system would bridge school and career, adolescence and adulthood. In the United States, college functions as such a bridge for more privileged youth. About half begin the passage to adulthood by enrolling in college, but less than half of college entrants graduate.[8] The education of the quarter who succeed in earning a four-year degree is very costly to society. Although college students and their parents pay for their education, they also enjoy a subsidy from federal and state governments and from private sources averaging $5,000 per student each year. In contrast, even when tax support for postsecondary vocational education is included, the subsidy available for the education and training of young people not enrolled in postsecondary education amounts to less than one-seventh the per capita amount allocated to college students.[9] Noncollege youth have been consistently overlooked and undertrained. Although some enter military service, which can provide job training, experience, and time to mature, enlistees are predominantly male and constitute only a minority of 16- to 24-year-olds. In 1985, only 4.9 percent of white males and 6.8 percent of blacks in that age-group were in uniform.[10] Thus, a large number of late adolescents are receiving no public support during their transition to adulthood.

Since the 1960s, employers have managed to meet their workforce needs by this haphazard system. But now that period has passed. As the youth population declines, employers will be forced to consider younger applicants for career-entry positions. What will happen to make young people readier to assume them? Some young people are already reasonably stable and responsible. They should have little difficulty handling a career-entry position if they can find one. However, changes in the nature of the youth population that will accompany its declining size make this a troubling question for a growing proportion of youth. We face the specter of high unemployment coexisting with a labor shortage because too many potential workers are deemed unemployable.

White males have traditionally been the most "employable" segment of the population; they enjoy higher levels of education and earnings than any other segment. But they are becoming scarce. Now 47 percent of the workforce, they will account for only 15 percent of new entrants by the year 2000.[11] Who will take the demanding and rewarding jobs formerly reserved for white males?

As the baby boom generation matures and faces retirement supported by a far smaller cohort of workers, pressure will mount for older workers to remain active. Two-thirds of today's workers will remain in the workforce until the year 2000 or longer. By then, the average age of workers will rise from 36 to 39. Longer life expectancies combined with the smaller number of workers mean that more workers will remain employed beyond the traditional retirement age. They will be joined by 600,000 immigrants, who are expected to make their way to the United States by the end of this century. Women will be a major source of workers, accounting for two-thirds of new entrants to the workforce from now to the year 2000.

Nevertheless, assuming that severe economic problems do not slow the demand for workers, employers will also have to turn increasingly to young people. One would expect the floundering period to diminish as the total number of youth shrinks, reducing competition in the labor market. Between 1980 and 1996 the number of youth aged 15–24 will decline by 21 percent, from 43 million to 34 million.[12] After 1995, the youth population will begin to increase again, but by the end of the century it will only return to the level of the early 1980s.

The happiest result of a smaller youth cohort would be reduced youth unemployment rates. Youth unemployment generally mirrors overall unemployment, but at a higher rate—in recent years 2.4 times as high as the rate for workers over 25. Surprisingly, improvement in the youth unemployment rate continues to lag behind improvement in the overall unemployment rate, suggesting that a declining youth population will not, in fact, ease the transition from school to work by itself.

One factor that accounts for persistent youth unemployment is the number of young workers who come from minority families. Although the majority of poor youth are white Anglos, black and Hispanic youth face a greater probability of living in poverty than white Anglo youth. Racial and linguistic bias continues to stifle their opportunities for education and employment. Our schools have not fully developed, nor have our workplaces fully utilized, the talents of black and Hispanic people.

The black youth population is declining less rapidly than the white. Thus, as a proportion of the youth population, blacks will increase from 13.7 in 1980 to 15.2 by 1996. Hispanic population growth is harder to predict because it is heavily influenced by immigration, but Hispanics are expected to constitute 11 to 13 percent of all youth by 1996, up from 7.5 percent in 1980. As the white labor force grows by 15 percent by the year 2000, the black labor force will grow by 29 percent (3.7 million), almost 17 percent of the total labor force increase. The Hispanic labor force is projected to grow even more rapidly, by 74 percent (6 million), accounting for 29 percent of the total increase. The challenge will be to find productive employment for these growing numbers.

One-fourth of all minors, white as well as black and Hispanic, live in poverty. Poverty interferes with the ability to acquire educational credentials and the work attitudes and behavior employers reward. Continued high divorce rates and out-of-wedlock births mean that a quarter of all children grow up with only one parent, almost always the mother. Families headed by single mothers seldom escape poverty. Because families move in and out of poverty, more than a quarter of all youth entering or hoping to enter the labor force will have spent some or all of their childhood economically disadvantaged. In general, youth from such families perform less well in school and in the workforce than youth from middle-class, two-parent families. Two-fifths of our youth will have faced the double disadvantage of minority status and poverty.

A range of problem behavior is generally associated with poverty and racial discrimination, although it is also found among white middle-class youth. Unless the association between problem behavior and disadvantaged youth is attenuated, a growing population of disadvantaged youth will mean that more would-be workers will be hampered, if not disqualified, by such problems as school failure, premature parenthood, drug and alcohol abuse, and delinquency.

At present one-fourth of all youth fail to graduate with their high school class. However, some succeed in graduating late and others earn their high school equivalency (GED) certificate by passing an examination. About 15 percent of 20-year-olds have not completed high school or acquired a GED. Sadly, some youth with high school diplomas are unable to read, write, and calculate well enough to follow instructions, fill out forms, or make change. They too are victims of school failure despite having graduated. Having a diploma helps an applicant get a job, but having the skills the diploma is supposed to represent determines earnings.[13] Youth without basic academic skills are seriously handicapped in the labor market.

Premature motherhood is a major impediment to high school graduation and employment for young women. An astounding 40 percent of all young women become pregnant before the age of 20; 20 percent bear children while in their teens. The total fertility rate for white teenagers (14–19) in the United States is 221 per 1,000 females; for blacks it is 515.[14] Most of these pregnancies and births are out of wedlock. Less than one-third of live births to teenagers are legitimated by marriage and those marriages are highly unstable.[15]

Although declining drug use among U.S. youth has been one of the few positive social indicators in recent years—annual surveys of a national sample of high school seniors show a steady decline in the use of marijuana and hashish since 1978 and a recent decline in the use of cocaine, but not crack—drug use continues to hamper the school and job performance of frightening numbers of young people. Fully 57 percent of 1985 seniors said they had used an illicit drug at least once, 42 percent within the past year. Moreover, 92 percent had used alcohol, illegal at their age in most states, and 66 percent had used it within 30 days of the survey, suggesting regular use by about two-thirds of all seniors. These usage rates are particularly distressing because they exclude youth who have dropped out or are truant on the day of the survey, a group that can be assumed to use alcohol and other drugs at an even higher rate because drug abuse is often associated with truancy and dropping out.[16]

Even more distressing, young people who become involved in crime seriously jeopardize their educational and employment opportunities. The peak age for property crime arrests in the United States is 16, for violent crimes, 18. Juveniles (under 18) are responsible for almost a quarter of all crimes; youth (under 25) constitute two-thirds of all those arrested for property crimes and half of those arrested for violent crimes. In 1984, 625,000 U.S. juveniles were incarcerated in detention centers and correctional facilities.[17]

The number of youth recognized as having serious problems indicates the presence of much larger numbers who demonstrate the same behaviors, but at a less serious level, where they still manage to cope with them. The figures on drug and alcohol abuse are the best testimony to this tip-of-the-iceberg phenomenon. While only a small proportion of youth can be considered addicted, a much larger proportion use dangerous substances, exposing them to the risk of addiction and other complications. Similarly, the incidence of pregnancy reflects widespread sexual activity among unmarried youth, much of it without protection against either pregnancy or sexually transmitted disease.

School failure, premature parenthood, drug and alcohol abuse, and criminal behavior interfere with young people's preparation for work by diverting them from more constructive activities and signaling to potential employers that they are poor prospects as workers. Such serious problem behavior constitutes a major barrier to educational attainment and to employment for many youth. As they move toward adulthood all youth must learn to cope with sexuality, with the availability of drugs and alcohol, and with temptations to break the law. Unless we can give more youth the will and the means to resist self-destructive behavior, it will continue to harm far too many, to the detriment of our economy and society as well as the young people themselves.

Poor and minority youth are, as always, the most frequently and severely afflicted; advantaged youth have more resources to draw upon in resisting and recovering from self-destructive behavior. The number of "disconnected youth" who, because of poverty, discrimination, or alienation are neither in school nor at work has been estimated at 1,250,000 white, 750,000 black, and 375,000 Hispanic 16- to 19-year-olds. This group accounts for the greatest share of high school dropouts, teen pregnancies, delinquency, and drug abuse. Their lack of involvement in either school or work is a vicious circle that condemns them to a life of marginality. While these problems have been identified before,[18] they have only recently been tied specifically to the projected needs of the labor force.[19]

Simply put, the declining youth population will, if economic conditions do not worsen drastically, require that employers dip into this pool of currently "disconnected youth" to find their entry-level workers or suffer from a serious labor shortage because there will not be enough high school graduates who have avoided these problems to meet employers' needs. For their own self-interest, employers must help schools and communities find ways of "reconnecting" these youth so they will be ready to assume constructive roles in the labor force when places open up for them.

While our haphazard system of preparing youth for work sufficed in a period when youth and women were entering the workforce in record numbers, it is no longer capable of meeting employers' needs or the needs of young people. Steadily increasing numbers of young people are diverging from the white middle-class pattern. Opportunities for education and training must adapt to changes in the youth population. Forms of education that are reasonably effective with advantaged youth will not automatically enable disadvantaged youth to achieve the same goals. To overcome the many barriers they face, poor and minority youth need more support than even good conventional schools can offer. A carefully planned apprenticeship program can provide that support.

Even if few changes were anticipated in the youth population, employment training would have to be adapted to workplace realities that are constantly being altered by economic and technological forces. Semiskilled manufacturing jobs that pay enough to support a middle-class life-style are no longer available.[20] Most of the growth projected for the U.S. labor force to the year 2000 will occur in the service sector,[21] which is large and diverse, including occupations ranging from physician to custodian. Although many service jobs are unskilled and low-paid, many jobs in medical care, finance, and communications pay more than semiskilled blue-collar jobs. Nevertheless, those young people who were formerly able to find high-paying, blue-collar jobs that required little formal education now need at least a high school diploma to get a good job in the service sector. Unless more young people can succeed in earning one, they will fail to achieve their aspirations and impede the nation's prosperity.

Service-providing firms tend to be smaller, offering fewer opportunities for advancement and steadily increasing earnings. Hence employee turnover in service firms is usually high, implying a need for employees who are flexible and capable of continued learning.[22]

These same qualities will also be important in the manufacturing sector, which will continue to employ substantial numbers of workers despite its contraction. The types of jobs available in manufacturing to workers without college degrees, however, will change. Mass production, which has characterized such basic industries as steel and automobiles, will become less and less prevalent. Based on single-purpose equipment and semiskilled operatives, this form of manufacturing has been relegated increasingly to developing nations with cheap labor. Ironically, those countries have gained their advantage in mass production with the aid of large firms based in the United States, West Germany, and Japan— the very nations they are displacing—which have designed and built their efficient, state-of-the-art plants. The future of manufacturing in the developed nations appears to be in "flexible specialization," that is, workers with highly developed craftlike skills who use multi-purpose equipment to turn out a wide variety of products in short production runs.[23] Steel making illustrates this phenomenon best. Large-scale steel plants producing general-purpose sheets, bars, and rods have essentially disappeared from the United States. Korea and Brazil are now among the world's leading steel makers. But the steel industry lives on in the United States in small mini-mills that produce high-priced specialty steel in smaller quantities. Workers in such industries must be capable of adapting readily to new production processes and varied tasks.

Flexible specialization in manufacturing generally entails greater participation by workers in decision making. When production processes are altered frequently and tasks redistributed among highly skilled workers, experienced workers' knowledge is critical.[24] They are increasingly asked to participate in quality control and group decision making that were previously reserved for specialists. A productive worker under these circumstances needs social skills and good judgment in addition to technical skills.

Many early advocates of such worker participation argued that efficiency and productivity would follow workers' involvement in decision making, but they were generally dismissed as impractical visionaries.[25] Hardheaded managers with their eyes on the bottom line were not interested—until they recognized that Japan had displaced the United States in manufacturing a wide range of products for domestic and international markets. Only when investigators searching for the secrets of Japan's success returned with accounts of quality circles and other procedures for tapping workers' knowledge and creativity did workplace democracy begin to sound like smart business. Although some investigators concluded that the value placed on group consensus in Japanese culture rendered these practices unworkable in the United States, others pointed out that quality circles were invented in the United States, and, like the videocassette recorder and so many other inventions, fully exploited only in Japan.

The relationship between these changes in the workplace and the need for higher academic achievement is debatable. Some experts claim that credential inflation has accompanied the expanding supply of educated applicants: employers now demand a college degree from applicants for jobs that previously required only a high school diploma, while the actual educational requirements of the position have remained unchanged.[26] Second, the argument goes, even though the highest rates of *growth* will occur in jobs requiring relatively high levels of education, the categories of jobs that will continue to employ the greatest *number of people* will demand no more than a high school education, and often less.[27]

These two points do not invalidate the goal of assuring that all youth earn a high school diploma; they do, however, warn that improving the educational level of the populace does not by itself alter the occupational hierarchy, either in terms of relative prestige or in terms of the academic demands associated with lower-level jobs. Even if everyone earned a high school diploma, there would be no guarantee that everyone would be able to find a job that required a high school diploma.

Moreover, education has purposes beyond preparation for work. Because education has civic and humanitarian value as well as economic worth, a better-educated citizenry must remain a societal goal, independent of the needs of the labor market. Workers with high school diplomas can be labeled "overeducated" only for the kinds of jobs that now exist and are anticipated if no changes are made in the way workplaces are organized. It is plausible, however, that if workers obtain higher levels of education, workplaces will be transformed to take advantage of more thoughtful and more skilled performance by workers. If jobs now require less than a high school education of workers, then the jobs should be changed to make them more satisfying to high school graduates.

What do youth need to know and be able to do in order to assume productive adult roles as workers, citizens, and family members? What is the proper balance between education and socialization which are equally appropriate for all future adult roles and specific training preparing youth for particular roles? Employers, who have been among the most vocal critics of secondary schooling in recent years, might have been expected to call for improved vocational education, to provide them with workers trained to do specific jobs. Surprisingly, they have advocated more rigorous academic education instead. The entire thrust of the reform movement associated with *A Nation at Risk*[28] has been to increase requirements for academic courses, to make those courses longer and tougher, and to test frequently what students have learned from them.

Surveys of employers, notably one done by the Committee for Economic Development,[29] consistently find that they are more interested in applicants' mastery of basic academic knowledge and skills than in their possession of job-specific training. The fundamental demand is for workers who can read, calculate, and write. Most employers can find applicants with acceptable reading and math skills, but would like them to be even better. Acceptable writing skills are rare. Beyond the level of basic academic skills, employers seek competence in problem solving, a skill made more critical by changes in the nature of work. Employees who assume responsibility for a wider range of activities must be able to do more than routine tasks. Manufacturing workers, for example, increasingly do their own quality control inspections and jointly reorganize their production processes. Service workers handle a larger variety of customers' concerns in order to avoid frustrating customers by passing them along an endless chain of people, each of whom can deal with only one part of their situation.

Chief executive officers of large corporations have become leading proponents of improved academic education, complaining of job applicants' meager academic competence and testifying that they must invest heavily in remedial education before beginning to train new workers for specific jobs. Even more ominously, they have warned that poor academic skills limit their firms' responsiveness to new competitive demands and new technology. Without trainable employees who are also flexible and capable of contributing to group decisions and quality control, those employers must either relocate or consolidate; they cannot expand.[30]

Vocational education, which aims to prepare youth for specific jobs, has, in contrast, been either ignored or explicitly rejected in many recent reform recommendations. When former Secretary of Education William Bennett outlined his ideal high school curriculum by describing a mythical ''James Madison High School,'' vocational courses were listed only as electives.

The recommendation of *A Nation at Risk,* repeated in many other reports, is that all youth, including the noncollege-bound, must acquire knowledge and skills in language, mathematics, science, and citizenship in high school at levels now attained only by those entering better colleges. Amid the debates that accompanied this recommendation, its underlying assumption was insufficiently appreciated, namely, that all youth are capable of acquiring education at a level that was reserved for a small elite only a few decades ago. The belief that a first-rate high school education is fundamental to full participation in contemporary society is a welcome expansion of what it means to be a citizen in a democracy and what a democracy owes its citizens.

By asserting that high school graduation is universally attainable, educators and policymakers have shaken off the feelings of helplessness that afflicted many of them for nearly two decades, when they became convinced that schools were impotent to overcome the disadvantages of racial discrimination and poverty in students' families and neighborhoods.[31] When nonschool influences are accepted as decisive, then one is faced with a choice between radicalism and resignation: society, not only schools, must be radically restructured;[32] if that is not possible, then we must resign ourselves to the negative consequences of inequality.[33] Affirming that schools can effectively educate all youth is a far more optimistic stance, but it is merely whistling in the dark if we ignore all that we have learned about the influence of factors beyond the schools' control.

The most hopeful message of the new school reform movement is that schools can be improved and that those improvements matter. Its blind spot, however, has been the assumption that students will respond uniformly to newly toughened schools and school programs. When school and nonschool influences on youth are perceived ecologically, as factors that interact in complex patterns without one necessarily determining the other, then two more constructive possibilities emerge. First, schools can be structured to accommodate the differences among students that result from differences in their families and communities and to compensate for the disadvantages of inequality.[34] Second, education can continue within the family and the community, and especially the workplace, rather than stopping at the schoolhouse door.[35]

In its enthusiasm to reject the assumptions and practices of school reformers in the 1960s and 1970s, which were intended to make education more accessible to young people from a wider range of family and community backgrounds, the school reform movement of the 1980s ignored the effects of nonschool influences on student performance, boldly asserting that all youth should be taught the same material in the same way. A rash of requirements issuing from state departments of education spell out in minute detail what teachers and students should do, not just what students should learn. Apprenticeship is based on a different assumption: that youth can be effectively prepared for adult roles only when schools recognize the educational implications of the different contexts in which students live their lives and when the task of educating them is shared with other institutions, especially workplaces. This argument accepts the validity of the current emphasis on academic learning but takes into account as well what we have learned about the influences of race and class on schooling, using this knowledge to inform action rather than to justify inertia.

In addition to having academic knowledge and skills, young people need to be punctual, diligent, responsible, and receptive to supervision. Employers emphasize these qualities most in selecting new employees from applicants without college degrees. The German word *Arbeitstugende,* meaning the virtues of work, nicely captures this domain. Worker virtues are a special concern with respect to disadvantaged youth, who are often judged deficient for not having learned how to cope effectively with workplace demands in their families, schools, and neighborhoods.[36] In the 1960s, some radical school reformers argued that trying to inculcate worker virtues amounted to an imposition of "middle-class values." When worker virtues are yoked to passivity and subordination, they deserve to be stigmatized, but when viewed as elements of personal competence, they are as important to athletes and musicians, union organizers and political activists as they are to managers, engineers, accountants, and assembly line workers.

The school reform reports may have neglected this form of learning to avoid seeming to stereotype disadvantaged youth as undisciplined. Such stereotypes are certainly to be avoided, but there is just as certainly a need to recognize that worker virtues are essential to all workers. Middle-class youth who have coasted through school, spending most of their time watching TV, listening to music, and having fun with their friends also need stiffer challenges if they are to develop worker virtues.[37] The best chance of motivating young people to internalize worker virtues and other forms of responsible behavior is to convince them that by doing so they can improve their own future prospects. Too many youth, especially disadvantaged youth, have sound reasons to doubt that responsible behavior will yield substantial future benefits.

Changes in the workplace require two new worker virtues: skills in social interaction and the ability to continue learning. Neither is unprecedented, but both will be in greater demand because of the workplace changes identified above; just showing up for work on time, working hard, and doing what the boss says will no longer suffice. Even relatively unskilled workers in both service and manufacturing jobs must have sufficient social skills to deal with co-workers and customers.

Technological change and the increasing premium on flexibility require workers to be ready for a lifetime of learning. Knowing fundamental facts and academic skills is a necessary basis for continued learning, but it is not sufficient. Youth also need to acquire habits of thought and conceptual frameworks that foster further learning, not just the ability to memorize isolated facts for an examination. Curiosity, problem-solving skills, and thoughtfulness—"higher-order skills"—are also required.[38]

This prescription for what youth need in order to face the future was derived from analyses of labor market needs and proffered by business leaders and an archconservative presidential administration. Yet it sounds remarkably like the liberal vision of universal education for broad humanistic purposes. Some of the same people who excoriate John Dewey and blame all the weaknesses of American education on him and his followers are now staunchly opposed to narrowly utilitarian job training for the same reason he opposed it. Perhaps this ideological convergence is part of the reason the momentum of school reform has persisted far longer than anyone had reason to predict in 1983. At any rate, it creates an opportunity to restructure the educational system to accommodate both individual growth and economic needs simultaneously.

But serious differences remain among those who would improve education. However, they are differences about means more than differences about purpose. Alongside widespread agreement that more young people should be achieving levels of academic competence heretofore achieved only by the most talented and most privileged, controversy remains over how best to achieve this worthy end.[39]

The "first wave" school reform reports agreed that the way to improve academic learning is to make secondary schools more rigorous by requiring that all youth take more demanding academic courses and more of them. Unfortunately, this prescription rests on an inadequate diagnosis of the problem. Schools cannot effectively teach academic material to all youth in the same manner. Nor will increasing schools' academic demands necessarily make them more effective at teaching worker virtues. Too many youth simply do not take school seriously. Some who feel this way drop out physically; many more drop out mentally—they attend classes steadily enough to avoid expulsion and pass most of their courses, but they neither put in nor take away much of value. Mental dropouts include college-bound students who go through the motions of learning and get good enough grades without expecting or gaining much from the exercise.

Reform efforts focused only on improving schools academically ignore other powerful influences on the preparation of youth for work, especially family, community, and work experience. We need better schools, but if we stop with that we will still fail to improve the academic learning and the employability of all youth.

Too many youth fail to learn even in undemanding classes, not because they are incapable but because they lack motivation to perform well in school.[40] Convincing youth that academic learning will make a difference in their future is the most powerful motivation; it is best accomplished by relating learning to work. Ironically, by correctly emphasizing academic learning as the best preparation for work, the current movement to improve schools for the sake of increasing the country's international competitiveness has slighted the potential educative power of work experience. Exploiting the workplace as a learning environment contributes to the democratic and humanitarian aims of education that are easily overlooked when education is seen primarily as an engine of economic development.

A comprehensive apprenticeship program can simultaneously supplement schooling as an alternative environment for learning and motivate youth to learn more in school by relating learning to work. The traditional image of a boy learning a craft at the feet of a master fails to capture the vitality and variety of the contemporary practice of apprenticeship in West Germany, where the institution has been successfully transformed to meet contemporary needs, serving white-collar as well as blue-collar occupations and girls as well as boys. German apprenticeship, however, cannot simply be transplanted intact to the United States. It must be more flexible and reflective of American values and traditions. An effective contemporary apprenticeship system should contain the following essential features:

1. exploit workplaces and other community settings as learning environments;
2. link work experience to academic learning;
3. give youth constructively ambiguous roles as, simultaneously, workers with real responsibilities and learners; and
4. foster close relationships between youth and adult mentors.

In this form, apprenticeship can motivate youth to perform well and behave responsibly by giving them a clear vision of adult opportunities and the paths leading to them, and by interacting harmoniously with constructive influences from the family, community, and peer group.

Because the contemporary labor market demands sound academic learning rather than specific job training, the new apprenticeship must be released from its bonds to narrow vocational training. While they are in junior high school or middle school, youth should be able to enter into apprenticeships for exploratory purposes, for example, in mentoring programs, career exploration, and community service projects.

By the time they reach high school, some youth will be ready for apprenticeships designed to prepare them for work, but that preparation should be broad, leading to a wide range of future occupations. Apprenticeships designed to train youth for specific jobs may be appropriate too, but even so their primary purpose and effect must be to teach academic subjects and worker virtues, in addition to a single job. Apprenticeship, by this definition, will be a means of preparing youth for work that uses people and activities outside the school to motivate youth to learn in school and to teach them lessons they fail to learn there. When specific job training is included, it is as a means to broad educational ends.

Distinguishing ends from means is often useful, but it is dangerous to treat the two as literally separable; they are in fact closely intertwined. Work here is treated as simultaneously an end and a means of youth development. Work experience contributes to young people's learning and maturation, which, in turn, enable them to be more productive workers.

When apprenticeship is defined in terms of the four essential features listed above, then the term becomes somewhat metaphorical, referring not only to a formal on-the-job training program but also to a range of less intense and broadly focused educational experiences outside of school classrooms. The final chapter distinguishes between exploratory apprentice-like opportunities for youth and arrangements that could be recognized by the U.S. Department of Labor's Bureau of Apprenticeship and Training as true apprenticeships. But, for the most part, the term "apprenticeship" is used broadly here to designate a coherent approach to a number of issues that have previously been considered separately: namely, the reform of secondary schools, the reform of vocational schooling, corporate investments in human resources, the prevention of youth problem behavior, experiential education, and youth community service.

The system of apprenticeship proposed here can integrate these issues, show their relationships to one another, and solve a multitude of problems that have previously been considered independent and incommensurable. We need an apprenticeship system to enhance the ability of schools, families, and communities to help all young people make a safe passage to adulthood.

2

◆

The Perilous Transition from School to Career

American youth who do not graduate from college move gradually over a period of years from being full-time students who are not in the labor force to being full-time workers not enrolled in school. They enter career-level jobs even later. In previous decades, sufficient numbers of youth successfully made the transition and eventually assumed responsible work roles. That time has passed. To assure that the smaller, more diverse, and more disadvantaged youth cohorts of the 1990s are prepared to do the work of the new decade and the new century, their transition must be made smoother and more efficient.

Vivian Glenn's inability to find a better job after high school graduation than the one she held as a student demonstrates that the typical transition from school to career of noncollege youth begins during, not after, high school. High school students' part-time jobs are the first stage of the transition. Far more than in West Germany or any other developed country, American secondary school students work part-time, after school, on weekends, and over school vacations. Working is now literally the norm for high school students: more than half do so at any given time.[1] With the addition of another quarter of students who say they are looking for work, three-quarters of U.S. high school students may be said to be in the labor force.

Even allowing for some exaggeration resulting from students' rather casual labor force participation, employment is undeniably widespread among high school students. Because youth move in and out of the labor market easily, a much higher proportion is involved in employment at some time over the course of the school year than during a given week, which is how most surveys record labor force status. Adding summer work, reported by 90 percent of white male seniors,[2] only a small proportion of high school students have never been employed before graduation.

This has not always been true. Employment of high school students has grown steadily since the mid-1960s, unexpectedly coinciding with rising prosperity among American families. Labor force participation by 16- to 19-year-old males enrolled in school increased by one-third between 1960 and 1977, while remaining stable for males of the same age who were out of school. The participation rate for female students increased over the same period even more than it increased for out-of-school females. These increases reversed the trend of the first half of the century toward reduced labor force participation by youth as more of them enrolled in school. Sixteen-year-old male high school students are 5 times more likely to be employed today than in 1940; female students of the same age are 16 times more likely to work.[3]

During the first half of the century, high school students worked when they had to. As a result, employment was more prevalent among poor youth. This has also reversed. Students from low-income families are less likely to be employed than those from middle-income families. Young people who live in suburbs are more likely to work than those living in either urban or rural locations, even after other factors such as race and family income are controlled.[4]

Black youth from low-income families living in cities are least likely to be employed while in high school. Although black males have increased their school enrollment substantially, they have been unable to combine enrollment with employment as whites have.[5] Wage rates and hours worked are also lower for poor and minority youth. Sadly, those young people who most need to contribute to family income by working are least able to find jobs.

What accounts for the increase in employment among high school students? It is not simply that high schools enroll a larger proportion of the youth population for a longer time. During the first half of the century, youth employment declined steadily as high school enrollment rose. Clearly it is not that more young people face financial hardships requiring them to earn money for subsistence. The majority of teenage workers say they take jobs to earn money for recreation and clothing and to gain experience. Only a small minority say they work to help support their families.[6]

Rising demand for youths' labor is the most compelling answer to the question. It also explains the distribution of work among youth and the types of jobs youth take. Unskilled jobs in the first half of the century were concentrated in factories and on farms (though employment on farms shrank steadily). As factories have been automated and more manufactured goods imported, the service sector has become the largest source of unskilled and semiskilled jobs. Retail trade has moved from the center of cities to suburbs and, simultaneously, store hours have been extended. Many office jobs have also moved from city to suburb. Together, these trends have created a host of new jobs for unskilled part-time workers. Along with married women, high school students have been drawn into the labor market to fill these jobs, especially high school students who live in the suburbs and possess the social skills needed to serve customers. Because young people, like adults, never have enough money to satisfy their wants, the opportunity to earn extra money has lured students into the workforce.

High school students are confined by their age, their uncompleted education, and their part-time status, to a limited set of jobs, notably retail sales, food service, clerical, and unskilled manual work. Most are employed in one of three economic sectors: wholesale and retail trade; service and recreation; and agriculture, forestry, and fishing. Their occupational titles are predominantly: operative; service worker; laborer; sales worker; and farm laborer.[7] Forty-four percent of 16- to 19-year-olds are employed in retail trade, compared to less than 14 percent of workers older than 24. The category "service worker," which includes low-skill jobs such as custodian, contains 25.7 percent of all employed teenagers but just 10.5 percent of workers older than 24.

Young people's work experience follows a logical progression. Most high school sophomores work at casual jobs such as baby-sitting or lawn mowing. Seniors are far more likely to have regular part-time jobs in stable workplaces. After they turn 20, young workers begin to resemble adults in their propensity to work full-time and in the types of jobs they hold. Generally, 20- to 24-year-olds look more like adults than like teenagers. Males in particular move into manufacturing industries and skilled occupations. Workers older than 24 move into occupational categories requiring higher levels of education, notably professional and technical, and managers and administrators, because many have graduated from college.[8] Black youth remain in the youth labor market longer than whites and move only gradually into more stable and desirable jobs; too many never make the move.[9]

Youth jobs have low entry requirements and offer little training, indicating how unskilled they are. One study found that only 14 percent of the jobs held by 16- to 21-year-olds required a high school diploma.

Forty-six percent of those jobs offered no more training than a short demonstration.[10] The kinds of jobs for which employers hire workers without college degrees and then provide extensive training are precisely the kinds of jobs youth are least likely to get: skilled trades, health-related work, and factory jobs.[11]

If part-time and summer jobs constitute the first stage of the transition from school to career, the second stage occurs when work takes precedence over schooling, most often at the completion of high school. Beginning a career is the third stage. Careers—defined as employment in positions requiring some specialized knowledge and skill, paying enough to support an independent adult or family, offering reasonable security and benefits, and providing opportunities for progressive advancement—are seldom open to teenagers. Graduates of four-year and, to a lesser extent, two-year colleges can reasonably expect to find careers in this sense immediately after completing their educations. High school graduates who do not attend college typically begin their careers at about the same time as their classmates who went on to college. During the second stage, between graduation and career initiation, they remain in the secondary labor market, holding the same kinds of jobs they held as students.

Young people's jobs are different from adults' jobs. They are neither as demanding nor as rewarding as career jobs and neither their occupants nor employers expect that they will be long-term. Youth are not alone in jobs like these, which some economists call secondary labor market jobs. Many adult women and minority group members also work in jobs that pay little more than the minimum wage, offer no fringe benefits, demand few skills, are insecure, and lack advancement opportunities. In jobs such as these, employers' principal method of discipline is firing. Their investment in recruiting and training workers is minimal. High turnover is expected. The best way for a worker to improve working conditions and earnings is by finding another job; seniority and past performance count for little.

According to the theory of dual or segmented labor markets, there are substantial barriers between the primary and secondary labor markets. These barriers retard the movement of certain groups of people into more desirable employment. One way to describe the barriers segmenting the labor market is to invoke the familiar legend of the stock boy who works his way up to become president of a giant corporation. There are chief executive officers in corporate suites today who began their careers in the mailroom, but this is becoming much rarer and more difficult.[12] The population's rising level of education, combined with growing economic and technological complexity, lead firms to seek junior executives among MBAs,[13] or at least college graduates, instead of among their bookkeepers, sales staff, or unskilled workers. Rather than constituting a continuous "internal labor market," where hard work and native wit can open any door, such firms create discontinuities by requiring educational credentials for entry into the upper levels of their hierarchies; these requirements constrain the advancement possibilities of employees in the lower levels because few are able to acquire added educational credentials.

Not all economists accept segmented labor market theory because of the difficulty of specifying which jobs, and how many, are in which segment. On the same grounds, some economists question the validity of the claim that there is a youth labor market. However, teenagers' work experience is quite distinct from that of adults; so long as the youth labor market is not expected to be perfectly distinguishable from the adult labor market, it is useful to describe the context in which young people begin their post–high school working lives.[14]

In this distinctive youth labor market, unemployment is more than twice as high as among adults, and it declines steadily as a function of age. Short-term unemployment does not have negative consequences on the subsequent employment and earnings of youth. In fact, young workers who change jobs frequently, thereby experiencing short spells of unemployment between jobs, earn more both in the short term and in the long term, because advancement in the secondary labor market comes from changing jobs rather than being promoted within a firm.[15]

Youth unemployment is high in part because young people readily move into and out of the labor force. Many of them use passive job search strategies; they report that they want to work but that they have done nothing to find a job. This suggests that there is a large pool of potential workers among youth, who are ready to take a job if they happen to learn of a suitable one but who are not counted among the unemployed. There are also youth who are accurately described as "target earners," who work long enough to buy a car or stereo or a plane ticket and then quit, withdrawing from the labor market rather than entering the ranks of the unemployed.

Youth behave differently from adults in the labor market because most are able to rely on their parents for food, clothing, and shelter. But semidependency alone cannot explain the fact that most American young people have not begun careers two or more years after terminating full-time school, particularly in view of the contrast between this pattern and that found in West Germany, where career entry begins with apprenticeship and is accomplished around age 18.

The determining force is not the attitudes and behavior of youth, but U.S. employers' practices, which systematically relegate youth to the secondary labor market. Primary labor market employers prefer to wait for young people to compile a work history, and to hire 20- and 30-year-olds who have outgrown their presumed youthful instability. Significantly, employers responding to surveys do not say that older applicants are more skilled than teenagers. They continue to expect to have to train their new workers. The difference that maturity is said to bring is in reliability, responsiveness to authority, and willingness to work hard—worker virtues.[16]

The youth labor market is not rigidly segregated, occupied exclusively by young people, and containing every young worker. But the majority of high school graduates experience a "floundering period" lasting from two to five years following high school graduation when they are unable to enter a career, when the jobs they do neither recognize nor reward their educational credentials. There is little disagreement and no cause for alarm in describing the labor market for youth who are enrolled in high school as limited to dead-end jobs. Most young people are not stuck in such jobs; they succeed in moving on to better jobs as they grow older. The critical issue is whether work experience in the youth labor market enhances the maturation and the employability of young people who do not enroll in higher education and specifically whether it is adequate preparation for the work of the future.

Little research has investigated how well the secondary labor market prepares young people for adult work roles. However, what evidence there is, combined with what is known about the nature of the work young people do, suggests the following generalizations about the impact of youth work experience:

1. young workers gain few technical skills;
2. youth jobs do little to reinforce school learning;
3. some youth develop worker virtues, especially social skills; and
4. sometimes the effect on worker virtues is perverse.

The first two conclusions may be inferred from the nature of youth jobs. Because those jobs neither require nor offer training in job skills and academic knowledge, they cannot be expected to enhance them. Studies that have actually looked at what young workers do and what they learn confirm this expectation.[17]

Strengthening worker virtues is the most beneficial effect attributable to youth work experience. The strongest evidence supporting this attribution comes from a longitudinal study following young men from 10th grade through their mid-twenties. By the age of 25, subjects showed a convergence of attitudes about work. Regardless of previously expressed attitudes, they tended to say they were willing to work hard for good pay, even under less than desirable circumstances. Though they did not collect evidence to test the connection, the authors inferred that the young men's intervening work experience made the difference.[18]

Less direct evidence comes from economists' studies of the effects of youth work experience. Typically, economists relate the extent and regularity of employment while in high school to subsequent employment and earnings. At first glance, the effects of part-time work experience appear quite positive. The more young people work during high school, the more they are likely to work and earn during the year following high school.[19] One explanation for this finding is that high school seniors who are employed are more likely to have a post–high school job lined up, namely, the one they already have. This is especially true for students with more adultlike jobs in such fields as health care, manufacturing, and the skilled trades.[20] A closer look, however, raises questions about the value of this association.

First, it may simply reflect the fact that students with the capacity to find and hold a part-time job while in school also work more after graduation because of that capacity, not because they changed as a result of their work experience. In this case, higher postgraduation employment and earnings are not an effect of work experience so much as a manifestation after high school graduation of worker virtues acquired in the family and at school.

Second, the association may not reflect real differences between youth with more and less part-time work experience but instead employers' preference for applicants with experience. Experience, according to this explanation, does not change the young person; rather it sends a positive signal to potential employers regarding her or his reliability.[21] The difference results from selection bias among employers more than real variations among young workers.

The third and most compelling reservation about the economic impact of high school work experience is that it appears to fade. Longitudinal studies following young people for several years after graduation show a short-term benefit in terms of higher employment and earnings during the first few years after high school but then a dropping off of that advantage, presumably because, as noted above, educational credentials gain importance among young adult workers.[22] A high school student wondering whether and how much to work would be best advised that work experience may be beneficial, but not if it interferes with educational attainment, which has a much more powerful and longer-lasting effect on subsequent employment.

Unfortunately, increasing involvement in work has, by some accounts, come at the expense of young people's commitment to school. Negative consequences of working on school performance have been found when students work more than 15 or 20 hours per week. Many teachers blame the prevalence of student employment for declining academic achievement, saying that they cannot give substantial homework assignments when many of their students work after school.[23]

Ellen Greenberger and Laurence Steinberg were the first developmental psychologists to undertake a large-scale study of work experience's impact on adolescent development. Their provocative findings included, in addition to the negative impact of work on school performance, a greater likelihood for employed high school students to engage in some forms of undesirable behavior, including using more alcohol, tobacco, and marijuana, lying and stealing on the job, and displaying increased cynicism about work-related values.[24] These perverse effects on worker virtues have not been found in other studies, but few have looked for them as closely. The authors' conclusion that work has a negative impact, on balance, cannot be firmly established by one study, but their findings constitute a warning that the kind of work most youth do is not necessarily conducive to the attitudes and behavior primary labor market employers value.

By conducting systematic observations in selected subjects' workplaces, Greenberger and Steinberg found an explanation for the contrast between their findings and the much rosier expectations of advocates of youth work experience, an explanation based on the distinctive nature of the youth labor market. Contrary to the assumption that adolescent workers establish close working relations with adults, learn new skills, and apply knowledge from the classroom, their observations showed adolescents spending only 11 percent of work time with an adult supervisor, 7 percent reading, writing, or computing, and experiencing about one instance of instruction per hour. Twenty-five percent of all the observed adolescents' work time was devoted to two tasks: cleaning and carrying things. They found adolescent workplaces dominated by peers rather than benevolent adults and by repetitive, low-skill tasks rather than opportunities for learning.

Critics have pointed out that Greenberger and Steinberg's results may be seriously biased by the location of their study in Orange County, California, an unusually affluent community. However, even among these relatively privileged youth, they found some benefits to adolescent work experience. Working appears to add to young people's store of practical knowledge, knowledge about working and financial matters. These gains were greatest among the students with the poorest school records. Measures of pride in work accomplished showed gains for workers, and working girls expressed greater feelings of independence. Most of the positive effects were found even when students had engaged in only small amounts of work—10 hours per week or less—while the negative effects followed from large amounts of work—15 hours per week and more.

The authors expressed some surprise that their subjects almost unanimously said their work experience had been valuable to them, given the rather unstimulating conditions they observed. But this is a common finding of studies that ask young workers to reflect on the value of their jobs. A study of youth employment in the fast-food industry found that youth believed they had learned how to deal with customers and co-workers, how to be responsible on the job, and how to manage money.[25] The role of high school student is so passive and unrewarding that even limited amounts of responsibility are challenging and satisfying in contrast. When money is the ultimate measure of value, young people conclude that anything they do is important if someone is willing to pay them.

With the exception of negative consequences for school performance, Greenberger and Steinberg's findings can be extrapolated from high school students to graduates because recent graduates do the same kind of work. Paul Osterman demonstrated the looseness of the connection between that work and adult careers in a study that combined large-scale data analysis with individual interviews. One of his interview subjects illustrates the common pattern.

After dropping out of high school, "Jim" held a string of unrelated unskilled jobs—in a shipping company, a chemical company, for a paper box manufacturer, driving a truck, and as a shipyard laborer. When he was interviewed at age 22 he had been a machine operator for an electronics firm for more than a year and planned to keep this job, explaining that previously he had only been interested in earning money but now he had "a sense of responsibility."[26]

In view of his haphazard path through the secondary labor market, Jim can hardly be said to have made a "career choice" in the sense of a conscious decision about what specific line of work he wished to pursue during his working life. He may have had a preference for manual labor that influenced his searches and the opportunities he accepted, but, like most young people, he could not select a specific career at high school graduation that he could expect to follow for a lifetime. Instead, he accepted an unrelated series of jobs that became available, applying criteria such as pay and location, and if there was more than one possibility, type of work.

The sequence of jobs young people hold during the first few years after high school often reveals no consistency and has no logical connection with their subsequent career. Young people who do not attend college seldom find themselves in a lifetime career by following a rational process of selection based on an optimal fit between their interests and talents and the nature of the job. Rather, their "choices" are seriously constrained by labor market conditions and represent an accommodation to those conditions rather than an optimal match. It is misleading even to call it a matter of choice. Noncollege youth look for work; choosing a career is a privilege associated with higher education.[27]

Primary labor market employers have become accustomed to using age as a proxy for reliability. To curtail the costs of training new employees who soon quit for another job, they have simply rejected teenage applicants, waiting until they have a few more years' work experience before offering them career-entry positions and investing in their training. If we were deliberately to create a system for supporting young people's transition to adulthood, it would not include so long a period of secondary labor market work experience. Secondary school reform rose to prominence in the 1980s because some business leaders foresaw that the baby bust and associated changes in the demography of youth would inevitably confront them with a challenge they had not faced in decades—more jobs than they could find qualified applicants to fill. Under these conditions, they can no longer ignore teenagers, simply allowing them to season in the secondary labor market. They must begin hiring applicants they previously dismissed as too costly to train because of their age, educational attainment, or family background.

Employers will have to turn to this labor pool unless serious economic decline or the accelerated exportation of jobs sharply curtail new hiring. In the more prosperous parts of the country they are already feeling the pinch. Some fast-food restaurants must now pay well above minimum wage to attract workers. Retired people are beginning to appear in jobs formerly monopolized by teenagers. Assuming that substituting elderly, female, and immigrant workers can reduce but not eliminate the impending labor shortage, employers must learn to incorporate workers they formerly considered unemployable. To date their response has been to demand improvements in schools. They must now consider as well their own direct investments in the broader education and training of youth. Apprenticeship in various forms represents a strategic investment because it simultaneously meets employers' training needs and contributes to strengthening schools.

West German employers have a strong tradition of investing in the training of young workers. They view apprenticeship as essential to their own and the nation's prosperity. At the same time, it is a critical component of the West German educational system. A close look at one apprentice reveals how apprenticeship can fulfill both of these functions in an industrial economy.

Rolf Kemmler is a colleague of Anna Heberer, who was briefly introduced in Chapter 1. Both are apprentices at Brandt, a large industrial firm known worldwide for its high-quality manufactured products. Brandt enjoys such prestige that it receives more than a thousand applications each year for about 40 apprenticeship positions in management. A separate program trains manual workers. Brandt's apprentices are a highly select group. Their school grades are good, they have performed well on the test devised and administered by the company, and they have made a favorable impression in personal interviews. However, an internal document specifying the process of selecting apprentices listed an unexpected criterion: "It is recommended that no top students (*Spitzenschüler*) be taken." The document explained that such students are likely to leave the firm in order to enroll at university. Brandt expects to recoup its investment in training through its employees' competence and commitment. The director of the company's managerial training unit added another reason for this policy when asked about it: high achievers in school are often overly individualistic and competitive; they do not make good team members.

Continuing to describe the selection process, the director volunteered that the selected group contained only conforming or adapted (*angepaβt*) young people, no rebels. This is not an explicit criterion, he said, but the screening process naturally yields such a group. Rolf, Anna, and their colleagues were socially adept, articulate, well dressed and physically attractive. In contrast to many young people riding the subways and strolling the sidewalks, they eschewed torn blue jeans, punk hairdos, and earrings worn by males. They were well groomed and clothed in the style of young corporation men and women.

A firm of Brandt's size—it employs 40,000 people—can commit resources to apprenticeship and offer special types of programs that are beyond the reach of smaller firms. For example, like some other large firms, it has a special program for young people who have qualified to enter a university but chosen apprenticeship instead. It prepares them for positions that would otherwise be offered to university graduates. For its apprentices, Brandt has a full-time professional training staff, a suite of classrooms, and a typing laboratory equipped with the latest audiovisual aids.

The training director moves apprentices through more than ten major divisions. He can choose from 120 different placements, each supervised by an employee who has volunteered and is qualified to train apprentices on the job. The learning needs of apprentices determine placements, not the need for assistance in a particular office.

When he was observed, Rolf Kemmler was assigned to Brandt's cost accounting division, located in the futuristic headquarters building, in an office with spectacular views across the city and beyond. Rolf is 18. He had planned to enroll in a specialized vocational school following the *Realschule* (technical middle school; see Chapter 3) to earn the *Abitur* (college entrance certificate) and eventually go into advertising, but he applied for apprenticeships at three major firms and was accepted by all of them. He is pleased with his choice of Brandt because it is more interesting and challenging than *Realschule*. Unlike school, he says, something new happens every day and everything is not worked out in advance. Right now he is helping Herr Stein design a computerized inventory control system. They are constructing a diagram or flow chart of the new system.

Rolf uses a template to draw boxes on the diagram, which has been drawn on several separate sheets of paper. Herr Stein helps him sort out the sheets and piece them together to make the proper connections. As Rolf continues to draw, Stein asks about his schedule over the coming few months, especially when he will be away for vacation and when he will attend *Berufsschule* (the part-time vocational school that apprentices attend).[28] Rolf then types labels on the diagram, corrects them, and makes clean photocopies. Together, Rolf and Herr Stein go over each sheet. When each is correct, Stein slips it into its own transparent cover in a notebook, taking care to get the order right. Rolf makes copies of the final versions. When he returns, Herr Stein takes us to the computer terminal a few steps away where he logs on, calls up some numerical tables and prints them. Returning to his desk, Stein cuts out a section of the printout, shows Rolf how to fit it into the diagram, and then tells him what other sections to cut out and glue onto the diagram. As Rolf makes another copy of one page, Stein returns to the terminal and changes some of the numbers in a data file. He then sends Rolf to the central computer room with a message to rerun a job.

Stein himself was trained as a precision mechanic in a large electrical firm. He was fortunate, he says, to work with engineers and designers in the development division, constructing prototypes and models. This gave him the opportunity to teach, because when a new product was introduced he would explain how to construct it. He learned about computers as his firm began to use and to manufacture them. He moved into accounting as a computer expert. Then he moved to Brandt in order to work with a person from IBM to develop and install a new computer system, the first of its kind in West Germany.

Stein and Rolf continue to work on the diagram, cutting its component pieces from the separate sheets and then gluing them together on a large sheet of paper. As this task is completed, Herr Stein explains that the diagram must now be refined and specified in greater detail. Each box contains a set of procedures to be built into a computer program and they must spell out what is to be done before the programmers can do their job. This will take another two months. A program has already been written for one box and needs only slight improvement. It will serve as a model for the others.

Stein asks Rolf to get the diagram printed half size. Rolf protests that it will be hard to read and says there is a copier that can reproduce it without reducing its size. Stein points to places where boxes can be squeezed together and, in the process, loses track of two connections. Rolf points them out to him. As a result, Stein then discovers an error and corrects it by adding a box and then connecting it to the adjacent boxes with arrows. In response to Rolf's question, Stein explains what the new box he has drawn represents, then goes on to say it is necessary to lay out all of the parts as they have done, precisely to reveal such gaps as he just discovered.

Rolf and Herr Stein check their schedules again, Stein emphasizing that they will have to teach everyone how to use the new system, which will be a whole new job, and that holidays and vacations must be taken into account as they plan. Pushing back from his desk, Stein says, "Alright, take a deep breath."

Rolf was not a designer of computer systems. His tasks included routine typing and copying. Yet he was deeply involved in a complex and challenging project under the guidance of a grandfatherly mentor who openly relished both his work and the chance to tell others about it. This apprenticeship, and these few hours of it, cannot be considered typical. Both approach the ideal. But as an ideal type, Rolf's apprenticeship exemplifies some of the West German system's best features.

Brandt's accounting department certainly served as a learning environment for Rolf. He had numerous opportunities for learning, not only about the technical aspects of the job at hand but also about how to relate to people in any job. Second, that learning was reinforced by the lessons taught in his *Berufsschule* about inventory control systems and constituted a clear application of broader academic competencies, including reading, writing, problem solving and logical thinking. Third, he accomplished real work, but was primarily a learner rather than an errand boy. Finally, Herr Stein acted as a mentor to him, demonstrating interest and support for him and his career.

Two other points about this apprenticeship deserve special notice. Managerial jobs are not traditionally associated with apprenticeship. Rolf's managerial work was clearly a long distance from craft work in a small shop. Herr Stein's own career is also revealing. Although the West German system is excessively rigid in some respects, Stein's progress from manual worker to high-level executive proves that the system allows for upward mobility and job change. Indeed, some American observers have argued that one of the strengths of West German industry in contrast to U.S. firms is the prevalence of top executives who have worked their way up from the shop floor and, as a result, understand production thoroughly.[29]

This portrait of Rolf and his apprenticeship also illustrates that West Germany's system is not just for marginal or "at-risk" youth. Exactly the opposite is true. More than 60 percent of all 16- to 18-year-olds are apprentices, making it the most prevalent form of upper secondary education. Apprentices typically train for three years, spending one day each week in a vocational school and the other four on the job. About 20 percent of 19- to 21-year-olds enroll in higher education.[30] Full-time secondary and postsecondary vocational schools are an alternative or an augmentation to apprenticeship, but apprenticeship is the most common experience for West German youth and their primary bridge from school to career.

The opening of the 1984 annual report on vocational education issued by the German federal minister for education and science succinctly states many key characteristics of the West German apprenticeship system. The first sentence refers to "the dual system," which is the combination of apprenticeship with part-time vocational schooling.

> 1983 was a record year for vocational training in the dual system.
> Never before in the Federal Republic of Germany have so many youth
> found an apprenticeship as in 1983. This is the result of a joint effort
> of all participants in the vocational training system—the companies,

employers' organizations, labor offices, chambers, unions, and public administration.

Such a unified joint effort is also necessary in 1984 in order to assure future training and vocational opportunities for youth, to strengthen the competitiveness of the economy, and to fulfill the social obligations of the society.

When these words were written, the greatest challenge facing the dual system was a shortage of apprenticeship places resulting from the conjunction of large numbers of baby boom youth attaining school-leaving age and a sluggish economy owing to worldwide recession and Asian competition. The report's stress on the record number of placements was intended to assuage public concern about the large number not placed, concern expressed in regular newspaper and magazine articles about jobless youth and the need for apprenticeship places. The minister's report must also be read as a partisan document, justifying the policies of the conservative Christian Democratic party in power and denying the claims of its more leftist rival, the Social Democratic party, that fundamental changes in the vocational training system were needed to deal with the shortage.

The third sentence's reference to a joint effort (*Gemeinschaftsaktion*) accurately enumerates the diverse actors in the apprenticeship system. The *companies* are ultimately responsible for apprenticeship. They provide the bulk of the places, pay apprentices' stipends, and bear the costs of apprentice training. The interactions between *employers' organizations* and *unions* cannot be understood by assuming that they parallel the U.S. situation. Union membership is far more widespread in West Germany. Unions are seen as making an essential contribution to the polity by playing an active role in the vocational training system and in other aspects of economic and social policy. Likewise, employers' organizations (comparable to the U.S. Chamber of Commerce and National Association of Manufacturers) are accepted as natural and legitimate means of promoting the employers' perspective. Despite frequently conflicting perspectives, unions and employers' organizations do not castigate each other as promoting special interests.

The German *chambers,* descendants of the medieval guilds, are also employers' organizations, but they are quasi-public agencies, not voluntary promotional organizations. There is a chamber with sections for small businesses engaged in manual trades, such as house painters, bricklayers, bakers, and barbers (*Handwerkskammer*). There is a chamber of industry and commerce for large businesses (*Industrie- und Handels-*

kammer). Every business enterprise is required to join and pay dues to a chamber. Any employer wishing to train apprentices must meet and maintain the standards enforced by the appropriate chamber.

Labor offices are government entities comparable to employment offices in the United States except that they are federally rather than state run. They play a much larger role in job placement than most U.S. employment offices, especially for apprentices, because employers are urged to register all apprenticeship places with them and because by law only labor offices are authorized to give youth career guidance and placement counseling. School personnel are explicitly denied that role.

Public administration, the sixth participant listed, is included not only for its regulating function, but also because it is recognized as another field of employment and, as such, provides apprenticeship places for future public employees. The post office, the government-owned railroad, the military, and other public agencies, all attempted to increase the number of young people they could train in response to the shortage of apprenticeship places.

The report's second paragraph urges continued unified (*solidarische*) joint effort, and spells out the functions of apprenticeship. The first, providing training and vocational opportunities for youth, is familiar enough, but the second and third, strengthening economic competitiveness and fulfilling societal obligations, are more ambitious. The West Germans depend very heavily upon exports for their prosperity. They compete successfully with the United States and Japan for world leadership in the export of industrial products with a third of the U.S. and half the Japanese population.[31] Apprenticeship training is widely regarded as the wellspring of the highly skilled workforce that sustains the nation's international competitiveness.

Finally, the notion that employers have social obligations to fulfill by training apprentices seems odd in the United States, where the free market philosophy is so strong that corporate obligations are limited to making money and obeying laws. The statement reflects a shared expectation that young people are entitled to vocational training as apprentices, and that the private sector must provide that training.

Apprentices' paths from training to career can be quite simple and direct. More than half remain with their training firm two years or more after the completion of training. Many of the remainder leave voluntarily to take similar positions in other firms. However, there are other paths as well, as Herr Stein's career illustrates. Some movement away from training firms is inevitable because some occupations do not have authorized apprentice training programs. Openings in those occupations are usually filled by people trained in a different occupation. Recognized training occupations, now numbering about 370, lead to more than 20,000 related occupations, some requiring further training but all based upon completion of apprenticeship.[32]

Employers pay all the costs associated with training apprentices, including their stipends. The net cost to employers is a topic of debate between employers and unions, employers insisting that they invest substantial sums and critics arguing that some employers exploit apprentices as a source of cheap labor. Although outdated, average net costs estimated in the early 1970s probably reflect current proportional outlays accurately: DM 6,692 per apprentice per year for industrial and commercial firms with more than 1,000 employees: DM 5,050 for industrial and commerical firms with less than 1,000 employees; and DM 2,582 for craft firms. All other occupational sectors listed had lower net costs.[33] Inflation and fluctuating exchange rates make an exact dollar conversion impossible, but it is safe to say that the net expense, subtracting apprentices' productive work, was as much as $3,000 per apprentice each year for large industrial and commercial firms, somewhat less for smaller firms, and half as much or less for craft firms.

West German firms not only accept this burden, they actively oppose unions' efforts to transfer more responsibility for vocational training to tax-supported schools. The unions favor such a transfer to strengthen public control over the training system.

Private companies invest so heavily in training young people who have no obligation to remain with their training company partly because of social tradition. Perhaps the most vivid demonstration of that tradition's force was the passage in 1976 of a law empowering the federal government to levy a new payroll tax if sufficient apprenticeship places were not provided, the money raised thereby to be spent on alternative, primarily school-based, vocational training programs for those young people unable to find apprenticeships.[34] Although the tax has never been levied and the law was subsequently revoked on constitutional grounds, the number of apprenticeship places was increased, suggesting that the threat was effective. The need for a threat reveals the private sector's view that their obligation is bounded, but the ability of the *Bundestag* to pass such a law over the employers' objections demonstrates the power of the belief that an obligation exists.

Although this obligation falls on the private sector as a whole, not all companies train apprentices. About 10 percent of companies engaged in industry and commerce and about 40 percent of craft firms train apprentices.[35] The difference reflects levels of investment: because it costs less for craft firms to train, more of them do. In addition, small craft firms rely on apprencies as cheap helpers. Hence, self-interest plays a part in determining which companies bear the obligation. One way in which training serves a company's self-interest is that a company that trains apprentices is, in effect, certified as doing high-quality work, because the public is aware of the machinery for controlling the quality of apprenticeship training. Manufacturing firms describe their apprenticeship programs in their glossy annual reports. Plumbers and cabinetmakers display signs in their shop windows announcing that they train apprentices.

A full-page ad for Lufthansa in *Der Spiegel,* the West German equivalent of *Time* magazine, graphically depicts employers' interest in training. It shows four apprentices clustered around a jet engine attending raptly to an adult worker's instructions. Lest there is any doubt about what is happening, the words "Lufthansa Training" are visible on the fuselage in the background. The caption reads, "Whoever wishes to go high needs a solid foundation" ("Wer nach oben will, braucht eine solide Basis"). The double meaning is obvious to any German reader: (1) These young men, who wish to make something of themselves as airplane mechanics, need the solid foundation of apprenticeship training; (2) You, the airline passenger, who wish to fly, need the solid foundation provided by Lufthansa's high-quality aircraft maintenance, which is assured by first-rate training.

Large firms like Lufthansa and Brandt train apprentices because they expect to employ the people they train and to recoup that investment in productivity. Such firms train no more young people than they expect they will need to fill their upcoming vacancies. Small firms, in contrast, often train more apprentices than they can take on as regular employees and depend upon them as a source of inexpensive labor, an expression of self-interest that may result in lower-quality training.

West Germany's apprenticeship system demonstrates that with opportunities for training, relevant school learning, and access to adult jobs, young people are capable of assuming adult work roles much sooner than is common in the United States. American youth who do not attend college face a perilous transition between the conclusion of their full-time schooling and the assumption of adult careers. Although the habit of primary labor market employers rejecting recent high school graduates' applications will surely change as the number of new entrants to the labor market declines, they must also begin to address the challenge of preparing for employment young people who in the past could safely be ignored. Reinventing apprenticeship will enable young people who in the past have been considered unemployable to make better lives for themselves and contribute to the common good.

Apprenticeship in the United States must fit into an educational system in which prolonged school attendance is the norm but school performance, especially by poor and minority youth, is inadequate. Adapting to these conditions requires a thorough understanding of the U.S. educational system and the ways in which it differs from West Germany's.

3

———◆———

Discovering
Apprenticeship

Apprenticeship is not completely alien to the United States, but such minuscule numbers of American youth serve formal apprenticeships that it cannot be counted as an institutional bridge to adulthood. Since the end of World War II, when returning veterans were given preference, U.S. craft apprenticeship has been predominantly for young adults rather than youth. The median age of U.S. apprentices is 25,[1] compared to 18 in West Germany. A follow-up study of the nationally representative High School and Beyond class of 1980 sample found that only 5 percent of all U.S. high school graduates had enrolled in some form of apprenticeship immediately after graduation and only 1 percent said they were still enrolled three years later.[2]

Over the past decade, the number of apprentices in the United States has remained between 250,000 and 300,000. Eight hundred occupations have recognized apprenticeship programs, but a mere 30 occupations enroll more than three-fourths of all apprentices; the construction trades alone enroll more than half.[3] The United States would have to enroll 7 million apprentices to match the proportion of youth who are apprentices in West Germany, multiplying the current number by 28.[4]

Although craft workers such as plumbers, electricians, carpenters, and masons continue to learn their skills by means of apprenticeship, they are far more likely to acquire them informally. Among craftsmen in the National Longitudinal Survey between 1966 and 1976, only 11 percent said that apprenticeship training was the most important source of their skills. Four percent attributed their skills to other types of formal on-the-job training (e.g., short-term traineeship). In contrast, 60 percent said they had acquired their skills mostly informally.[5] One explanation for these small numbers is the fact that completing a program gives a worker little advantage in the labor market. Dropouts and workers with no apprenticeship training at all are often able to compete with certified journeyworkers, which reduces the incentive to enter or complete an apprenticeship.

To make matters worse, American apprenticeship is almost entirely the domain of white males, despite serious efforts at affirmative action. Although this is frequently attributed to union practices, apprenticeship programs sponsored by corporations have this same limitation.[6] Many large corporations operate apprenticeship programs to train skilled workers for such tasks as machine repair (millwrights), carpentry, painting, electrical work, and pipe fitting. Typically, entrance is limited to experienced unskilled and semiskilled workers with sufficient seniority, which results in the same overrepresentation of white adult males found in union programs.

Although formal craft apprentices are rare, some other programs manage to bridge school and work for small numbers of U.S. youth. They fall far short of the West German system in size and depth, but they show how some of the key features of West German apprenticeship already thrive in this country. Such apprentice-like programs include the Job Corps, Summer Training and Education Program, community service, Foxfire programs, Experience Based Career Education, cooperative education, and informal apprenticeships.

The Job Corps is the costliest, longest-lived, and most effective of the federal government's employment training programs for youth. These three distinctive characteristics are more than coincidentally related. Established in 1964, the Job Corps continues to enroll the neediest of low-income youth between the ages of 14 and 21. During the most recent period studied in depth (1977–81), enrollees were 70 percent male, 75 percent minority, and between 85 and 90 percent had not graduated from high school. More than 90 percent came from families below the poverty line or receiving welfare. Thirty-eight percent had been arrested and 19 percent convicted of crimes.[7]

The Job Corps's high cost, about twice that of other federal employment programs per enrollee, result from its intensity and comprehensiveness. It transports youth away from their home communities, feeds and houses them, and provides them with an array of medical services, counseling, and educational opportunities along with employment training. The program's long life and centralized control—relative to other federal programs, which have had more local autonomy—have enabled it to accumulate and replicate effective practices. Nonresidential programs, for example, have been tried and, for the most part, rejected as less effective. The strong conservation emphasis in many early camps has likewise been substantially reduced as camps offering training linked to local labor market needs have demonstrated greater success.

The program's ability to absorb new practices and to respond to the results of evaluation studies has undoubtedly contributed to its effectiveness. Evidence indicates that placing disadvantaged youth in a new environment with new norms and expectations is critical, as is the comprehensiveness of services. The teaching of actual skills is but one part of a total program, whose pieces mesh to produce its results.

Those results are evident in a follow-study of Job Corps participants compared with nonparticipants from similar backgrounds over a period averaging four years beyond termination.[8] Participants worked an average of three weeks more per year and earned 15 percent more each year than nonparticipants. Twenty-seven percent more received high school diplomas or equivalency certificates. More participants enrolled in vocational and technical schools and enlisted in the military services. Participants were involved in fewer serious criminal activities; they received fewer welfare payments and less unemployment insurance. The magnitude of participants' advantage over nonparticipants correlated with the amount of time they spent in the program.

Employing a variety of assumptions and formulas, the researchers estimated that the program's benefits exceeded its costs by about 45 percent, and that society's investment in the program was paid back within three years, primarily in the form of higher productivity by better trained workers and of reduced costs of crime. Nevertheless, effective as it has proved to be, the Job Corps does not work for about half of all enrollees, who leave before the program has had any impact.

These favorable results from studies of the Job Corps contrast with evaluation results for less intensive programs and programs for younger youth. In general, subsidized employment has been found more effective among out-of-school youth than among those still enrolled in school.[9] Since the Neighborhood Youth Corps was established by the Economic Opportunity Act of 1965, a series of federal programs has employed high-school-age youth in poor urban neighborhoods during the summer. Motivated in part by fear of the damage that could result from riots, they have been referred to more than once as "fire insurance." Given the short duration of these programs and the make-work nature of too many of their jobs, they have demonstrated few dramatic or enduring effects.[10]

The Summer Training and Education Program (STEP) is a new and promising approach to serving this younger population that has been developed by Public/Private Ventures, a research and development organization. STEP's unique feature is requiring attendance in summer school as a condition for receiving a summer job. Such a requirement was suggested by research indicating that learning loss over the summer was a major contributor to the reduced school achievement of disadvantaged children and youth. In an environment that seldom demands and models academic skills, disadvantaged youth apparently forget during the summer more of what they learned in school than do young people with more highly educated parents and homes with more opportunities to read and engage in other schoollike activities.[11] The STEP experiment has verified this finding experimentally by supplementing federally subsidized summer jobs for disadvantaged 14- and 15-year-olds with an educational program, which not only prevents loss, but moves enrollees ahead in their achievement test performance.[12] STEP confirms the validity and replicability of one of apprenticeship's key features: the purposeful integration of work experience with schooling.

The Job Corps and STEP prove that disadvantaged youth are not, as a group, unemployable. Provided with appropriate support and reasonable opportunity, they display willingness to learn and to work hard. Evidence that Job Corps participants do better in the workforce is all the more impressive in view of the likelihood that employers treat Job Corps experience as more of a liability than an asset. In the absence of close cooperation between programs and employers, and of programs having favorable reputations among employers, an applicant who lists work experience in a subsidized program signals employers that he or she is a less than desirable candidate because such programs are reserved for high-risk youth, and employers know it. Participation in a program can, as a result, unintentionally reduce employment prospects by labeling a young person as "at risk."

Furthermore, conditions in programs that are limited to disadvantaged youth tend to replicate the inequalities from which those youth suffer in the larger society. Disadvantaged youth are thrown together with their peers in subordinate relations to program staff while engaged in menial and sometimes meaningless tasks. A more promising approach would be to desegregate schools, workplaces, and neighborhoods so as to introduce disadvantaged youth to the peer culture and social networks of their more fortunate peers. In the absence of Utopia, programs in which conditions are carefully designed to alter power relations are more promising than conventional programs, which recreate and perpetuate the larger society's biases.

Research on less effective subsidized work experience programs indicates that simply giving youth work experience is not sufficient. Work must be combined with education, counseling, and a supportive environment, as it is in the Job Corps and in STEP. Second, even though disadvantaged youth have stronger needs that require special treatment, placing them in programs that label them as deficient and treat them as subordinate carries negative consequences that counteract program benefits. In order to be really effective, apprenticeship should not only serve all youth, but provide disadvantaged youth with extra attention and resources. Work experience should be optimally "discontinuous" with the adolescent's previous experience, meaning that it should offer new but manageable challenges to the adolescent's view of him/herself and the world.[13]

In addition to subsidized work experience programs like the Job Corps and STEP, other apprentice-like programs introduce youth to worker roles and responsibilities without paying them. Community service is the most prominent.

Young people who engage in community service take on real responsibilities to do things with and for others, while retaining a learner role. As school projects, through churches and youth organizations, young people read to elderly people, serve in soup kitchens for the homeless, tutor younger children, help out in animal shelters, collect materials for recycling, rehabilitate broken-down playground equipment, and in countless other ways volunteer their time, energy, and talents for the benefit of their communities.[14] Young people have always participated in the American volunteer ethic. Boy Scouts, Girl Scouts, 4-H, and other youth organizations have traditionally stressed community service and have regularly introduced to service young people who, as adults, became community leaders.

Partly in reaction to the self-centered striving of the 1980s, there has been growing interest in recent years in promoting community service through schools. The Atlanta city school district required community service of all high school graduates. The New York State Board of Regents added a practicum in school, government, or community service as a graduation requirement, though the requirement was softened by subsequent regulations.[15]

Civic duty and the inculcation of responsibility are the most compelling rationale for efforts such as these. As citizens, young people have an obligation to serve their communities, which service programs enable them to discharge. Moreover, studies have found such service generally brings improvement in punctuality and reliability among participants and, to a lesser extent, in young people's attitudes toward their roles as citizens.[16]

Because youth community service has been seen primarily as a means to discharge civic duties and aquire the proper social attitudes, learning, in the sense of gaining knowledge and skills, has not often been stressed as one of the benefits. Yet one study found that community service and other forms of experiential learning increased participants' problem-solving ability.[17] However, in most cases the subject matter that might be learned by means of community service is so diverse as to make it very difficult to study. One exception was an intern program in local government in which participants gained new knowledge about local government as well as more favorable attitudes toward political involvement.[18] This program demonstrated the potential of using community service as a means of instruction in some academic subjects. One source of its success in fostering academic learning was the use of didactic presentations and seminars to complement direct experience.

Community service can also be a form of career exploration, because it places young people in contact with adults outside of school and gives them worklike responsibilities. The largest study yet conducted of experiential learning programs included 33 programs, some of which emphasized voluntary service, some career exploration, and some outdoor adventure (patterned after Outward Bound). Participants in the programs that had no explicit emphasis on careers demonstrated gains on a Career Exploration Scale almost as high as those in the career-related programs, suggesting that it is the opportunity for responsible participation rather than the career focus that matters most.[19] Thus, community service may be conceived as a form of exploratory apprenticeship, well suited to younger adolescents who are not yet ready for the paid workforce.

One advantage of voluntary service over paid work is that young volunteers often take on responsibilities and participate in decisions that are considered beyond their competence in workplaces. Especially for young people whose experiences at home, at work, and in their neighborhoods are limited to subordinate roles, taking part in a voluntary project in which they help to make important decisions and in which others depend on them can have profound effects on their sense of who they are and what they can do.

Another apprentice-like program that profoundly affects young people is *Foxfire,* a magazine of local history, folklore, and crafts that has been written and published by high school students in Rabun Gap, Georgia, for more than two decades. Anthologized in a series of best-selling books, the magazine and its associated activities stand as one of the most dramatic and successful experiments in American education during the 1970s. Eliot Wigginton, the teacher who has worked with the student journalists and publishers since the beginning, has written eloquently and proselytized tirelessly on behalf of the educational principles embodied in the magazine.

Wigginton's book *Sometimes a Shining Moment* [20] gives an engaging account of *Foxfire's* birth and growth along with thoughtful reflections on its underlying principles and helpful advice on how other teachers can apply them. He argues strongly in favor of making students responsible not only for their own learning but for helping others learn and for behaving responsibly toward people in their community as well. A major theme throughout the book is compatibility between the approach he advocates and instruction in basic skills. Repeatedly he points to the ways in which producing a magazine stimulates academic learning and he describes devices teachers can use to insure that such learning is more than incidental.

The book's appearance in 1985 was propitiously timed. While marking Wigginton's twentieth year as a teacher in Rabun Gap—he continues to teach five classes a day and to live on his teaching salary, contributing all his publishers' royalties and speaker's fees to the Foxfire Foundation—it also counters the pendulum swing in educational reform away from unconventional approaches. During the 1980s there has been a tendency to attack all of the innovations of the late sixties and early seventies as part of the problem needing to be solved rather than part of the solution. The Deweyan educational philosophy embodied in *Foxfire* must be defended as Dewey himself proposed it: as a more effective means than conventional didactic instruction to improve academic learning.

Observations of a program inspired by Foxfire demonstrate the kind of learning afforded by this form of apprentice-like program. [21]

A group of girls arrive at the magazine office to work on an article about their county's history. As soon as they come in, they get to work on various tasks. Considerable time is devoted to arranging schedules so that interviews will be completed, photos developed, and other tasks completed on time. With one of the staff members, the girls then sit down and begin to read aloud from the transcripts of their interviews, outlining their article at intervals as they read. All take part in commenting and criticizing the transcripts. When the staff member leaves, they continue. At 4:30, two-and-a-half hours after they began, they decided to take a break before continuing.

———————————————

Writing, listening, photography, planning, and group decision making are among the skills fostered by experiences such as these. The relationship to English and history classes is obvious. What is different from an ordinary academic class is the motivation and self-direction evident in the girls' work. They define what they are doing as real work because it will lead to an article in a magazine rather than just a school assignment. They will lay out and edit the magazine and then people will buy it and read it.

Community service and Foxfire programs give youth real responsibilities that are combined with learning opportunities, but they do not place them in adult workplaces except incidentally. Experience Based Career Education (EBCE) demonstrates that workplaces may also serve as learning environments for unpaid youth. As its name indicates, EBCE is for career rather than vocational education. Sidney Marland, commissioner of education under President Richard Nixon, promoted career education to help give young people a sense of future direction. He sharply distinguished career education from vocational education. Unlike vocational education, which involves training for a specific vocation, career education is *about* careers and is suitable for all young people, regardless of age or future plans.

Marland proposed that career education begin in early elementary school and become progressively more thorough in the upper grades so that senior high school students would be knowledgeable about career possibilities before graduating. His vision was that information about careers would infuse the curriculum; in every subject reference would be made as a matter of course to the kinds of workers who make use of the knowledge and skills being learned.

Marland's crusade failed. Career education is no longer a major force in American education. One reason is that classrooms are not very good places for learning about careers. Only abstract and superficial information about what people do at work can be conveyed in the classroom. High school students who most need the information do not learn much that they can use by reading brief descriptions of careers, which may or may not be accessible to them because of their location or level of schooling.

Although EBCE has virtually disappeared as an identifiable movement, scattered programs persist, which embody some of the key features of a good workable apprenticeship program. EBCE students are released from classes in order to participate in a series of different workplaces.

Because they are not paid and do not remain at the same site for more than 14 weeks, students concentrate on acquiring skills and learning how to behave on the job rather than producing goods or services. Participants typically spend one year in the program, with between 20 and 80 percent of their school time devoted to on-site work experience. In its most elaborate form, EBCE uses work experience as the focus for the whole year's academic work. Seminars and tutoring sessions relate math, science, English, and social studies to the workplaces and career areas each student is exploring.

Developed as a model program by four regional educational laboratories, EBCE has been extensively evaluated. Among the consistent findings has been that students, parents, and work site supervisors almost unanimously find the program worthwhile. Students in EBCE acquire more information about careers and communicate greater self-confidence about their ability to plan for the future and achieve their goals. On standardized tests of academic learning, they show no disadvantages compared to similar non-EBCE students.[22] A study using results from 80 external evaluations of EBCE programs found that EBCE students gained more than comparable students not enrolled in the program in life skills, career-related skills, and academic skills and that programs following the EBCE model most closely produced the most favorable results.[23]

Exploiting workplaces as learning environments and relating on-the-job and classroom learning are not foreign practices. EBCE demonstrates that they can be accomplished in the United States as well as in West Germany. However, EBCE's failure to thrive also demonstrates that great effort is needed to make such opportunities widely available; employers must be willing to give young people places to learn and schools must accept work as a learning experience.

Cooperative education is the form of secondary vocational schooling that most closely approximates traditional apprenticeship in the United States. (Vocational schooling will be considered in more detail in Chapter 5.) Best established in "distributive education" classes (i.e., wholesale and retail commerce), cooperative education places students in real workplaces to complement their school instruction with supervised experience and informal instruction. Cooperative education is widely acknowledged to be one of the most effective vocational education strategies.[24] However, only about 10 percent of vocational students participate in cooperative education.[25] Although it is usually seen as a means of learning vocational skills, cooperative education has also been advocated in broad form as a bridge between adolescence and adulthood and as a means of experiential learning for general purposes.[26]

Roger Parsons,[27] aged 17, is enrolled in a vocational agriculture program at the area vocational center serving his high school and several others. (In New York State, these centers are commonly referred to as "BOCES" which stands for Board of Cooperative Educational Services.) He attends classes at his local high school in the morning, then reports to BOCES, where he meets regularly with the placement adviser. When asked about how BOCES compared to his high school, he said there was no comparison. "At school you sit around and talk. At BOCES you go out and do something. There's a world of difference."

Roger has been working at the Roberts dairy farm for two years. The farm is located about a mile and a half from his home. He is very happy with his work experience because he hopes to become a dairy farmer. He enjoys working with cows and watching calves grow. The farm he worked on before starting at Roberts has now shut down, like many others in the area. But George and Jim Roberts, the father and son who own the farm, are excellent dairymen and he believes he can learn from them how to operate a dairy farm successfully.

Roger does a variety of tasks. Milking is the most repetitive. He comes in for the early morning milking on the weekend, but on school days he helps only with the afternoon and evening milkings. In the summer he mows and chops hay and other feed crops. He likes to feed the calves. Since mastering the routine tasks, he has been learning to diagnose and treat cows' diseases.

On this visit, Roger has arrived later than usual and the afternoon milking has been completed. George and Jim Roberts greet us and give a tour of the barn and milking parlor. Roger shows the calves, which are tethered to "calf hutches," small individual sheds. He calls attention to a bull calf with red coloring, saying this has become a desirable trait among Holstein breeders, making this calf particularly valuable.

As he walks around the silos, Roger points out the equipment, describing how it is used and exclaiming at how expensive it is. Coming to the large corrugated steel tanks that hold the feed, he steps into a little shed where feed additives are stored and records kept. He explains how the feed rations are mixed, naming the minerals that are added. They are added to a carefully calculated mixture of chopped hay, alfalfa, corn silage, cotton seed, and other ingredients. Different mixtures are fed to high-and low-producing cows, dry cows, and heifers. The calves receive a different feed altogether.

Roger is up to date on a current controversy among dairy producers regarding BHT, a growth hormone that drastically increases milk output. If it is approved for commercial use, it will drive even more small producers out of business because fewer cows will be needed. Jim Roberts is an active opponent of the hormone and Roger staunchly supports his arguments. Jim says he likes to take Roger with him to meetings where dairy operators talk about such issues and to courses given by the dairy association and the farmer's cooperative.

Roger is more of a worker than a learner at this point. He has mastered the basics. But because Jim is a mentor who habitually seeks new ideas and information and enjoys involving Roger in that process, he has numerous opportunities to learn more about dairying. Jim revealed his commitment to continued learning by describing disparagingly a neighbor's ignorance of a bovine disease. Although farming is rarely considered a high-tech field, Jim clearly believed the only way he could keep his farm viable was to be knowledgeable about the latest developments in the field, a belief he consciously tried to pass on to Roger.

Roger had absorbed a great deal of information about cows and dairying, along with numerous relevant skills. He clearly understood the basic processes used around the farm and was able to perform them competently. Moreover, he appeared to understand as well some of the complexities of feed mixtures, breeding, and veterinary first aid. Feeding is especially critical on a dairy farm because profits are determined largely by the efficiency with which cows convert feed into milk.

In addition, Roger demonstrated an appropriate willingness to work hard, to stay late and get up early to take care of regular chores. Whether acquired on this job or before, his willing acceptance of the burdens associated with dairy farming is critical to his effectiveness as a worker.

The existence of cooperative education programs like Roger's and school-related on-the-job training programs demonstrates that the basic idea of integrating study with work experience is feasible in the United States. However, like formal apprenticeship, cooperative education operates on a very small scale and touches only a small fraction of those who could benefit from it.

A few programs based in schools or community organizations sponsor informal apprenticeship as a mode of career and community exploration. The Learning Web is one. Operating in Ithaca, New York, since 1973, the Learning Web matches teenagers who wish to learn a skill with adult mentors who are willing to teach them a skill they have in connection with their work or hobby. Inspired by Ivan Illich,[28] the Learning Web was founded independently of the school system as an alternative mode of organizing education. It now receives referrals and some financial support from area schools, but maintains its office on the Cornell University campus and retains a casual, noninstitutional atmosphere.

The Learning Web's "apprenticeships" are not intended as specific job training, though many youth ask for placements related to immediate or long-term employment prospects. Sites range widely, including a caterer, soup kitchen, radio station, bookstore, cooperative grocery store, seamstress, architect, photographer, child-care center, plumber, and several retail stores. It is exploratory in the manner of Experience Based Career Education, but its purpose has always been couched in broader terms, as supporting the development of youth by empowering them to make their own decisions about their learning. Ideally, Learning Web apprentices form close relations with adults, discover new resources within themselves, and learn how they can find and make use of learning opportunities in the community.

Field notes from observations of a Learning Web apprentice convey a sense of the kind of learning that can occur in such settings.[29]

Judy Griffith, 17, is apprenticed to Marti Jensen, an electronic synthesizer musician. Judy has studied classical piano for several years and has done some composition, including a piece that will be performed this spring by the high school chamber orchestra. She hopes to learn enough from Marti about synthesizer technique to be able to compose a piece in several voices. Marti was full of praise for Judy's musical talents and volunteered that she herself was gaining a more complete understanding of the synthesizer and recording equipment by teaching Judy.

The studio, in an old farmhouse, is a jungle of electronic paraphernalia. Only the keyboards scattered about indicate that the equipment is musical. The synthesizers bristle with tiny lights, toggle switches, dials, and cables.

Judy and her mentor assess the musical effect of slipping and turning various switches and knobs. They work together in a mutual learning process. Together they fiddle with a set of knobs and establish how their manipulations affect the fundamental and overtones for each note, discovering through experimentation the relations between knob settings and sounds. Much of their discussion is laced with technical terms. Marti asks Judy if she wants to undo a "set-up," an intricate series of electrical connections that she had just demonstrated, and then replicate it on her own. Judy declines, saying she prefers a review before trying it "solo." Throughout the intense hour-and-a-half, Judy takes quick schematic notes and asks questions.

Judy and Marti worked together almost as peers, even though Marti knows much more about the synthesizer. In addition to the fact that they were close in age, they were engaged in an activity conducive to this sort of relationship, exploring the possibilities of the synthesizer for their own uses, unburdened by maintenance and routine operational responsibilities. Their respect and affection for each other were obvious.

The responsibilities Judy assumed were less momentous than those of Rolf Kemmler and other West German apprentices, though as serious musicians, neither Judy nor Marti thought of their activity as anything but productive work.

Learning Web apprenticeships offer multiple opportunities to learn. Mentors are warm and caring adults as well as teachers. In a questionnaire asking Learning Web apprentices to name the five most important adults in their lives, parents came first, followed by other relatives. Half of the adults named as important were associated with the program, though not all apprentices named an adult they knew through the Learning Web. Apprentice-like opportunities cannot guarantee that each young person will acquire an adult mentor, but they appear to make it much more likely.[30]

Programs like the Learning Web, cooperative education, EBCE, Foxfire, community service, STEP, and the Job Corps demonstrate that apprenticeship's key elements are viable in the United States. They exploit workplaces and other community settings as learning environments, link work experience with academic learning, give youth responsible roles combining work and learning, and foster mentoring relationships. None, however, is sufficiently intensive, long-lasting, and integrated with both schooling and the labor market to constitute an effective apprenticeship system. Even more seriously, none is universally available to all youth who might benefit. Even cooperative education, the most widely available apprentice-like program, enrolls only a fraction of vocational students, who themselves are a fraction of all high school students.

These programs have already demonstrated their value in preparing youth for work, both directly and indirectly by motivating better school performance. They need to be expanded to incorporate more young people and articulated with each other to establish a system of apprenticeship enabling an individual to move through a coherent series of steps from more exploratory to more job-focused apprenticeships. Attention to West German apprenticeship suggests the dimensions of such a system.

The most dramatic contrast between West Germany's apprenticeship system and the preparation of American youth for work is the extent to which West German youth learn in the workplace. Apprentices typically spend four days of each week at work and one day at school for three years. The *Berufsschule* or vocational school focuses sharply on a particular occupation, providing courses in bookkeeping and business law for office workers and in applied mathematics and technical drawing for auto mechanics. All apprentices study German and social studies, but their lessons often contain material related to their occupation.[31] Integration of school with work experience is critical to the system's effectiveness.

Rolf Kemmler, whose morning's work on a computerized inventory control system was described in Chapter 2, is an apprentice *Industriekaufmann*—a middle-level office worker in an industrial firm. Comparable occupations in the United States are labeled by specific function—such as bookkeeper, personnel officer, account executive—whereas the Germans, consistent with their guild tradition, divide occupations by sector. Thus, in addition to *Industriekaufleute*, there are *Kaufleute* in banking, real estate, wholesale and retail trade, insurance, advertising, and other fields, each with a separate apprentice training program.

Kaufmann is one of the largest German occupational categories. The feminine form is *Kauffrau*, though the masculine is often applied universally. The plural of both is *Kaufleute*, "commercial people." *Industriekaufleute* is the fourth-largest occupation offering apprenticeships, enrolling 3.6 percent of all apprentices in 1985.[32] Unusual among West German occupations, it includes comparable numbers of males and females, another reason for examining it. It illustrates well the reach of West German apprenticeship into contemporary service occupations and its inclusion of females.

Large firms like Brandt offer more options for placements than small ones. Apprentices can move from one department to another in order to obtain the widest possible exposure to the firm. They can be placed under the supervision of experienced employees who have a personal commitment to teaching them and sometimes special training and talent as well. Apprentices are there primarily to learn; if they can best do so by contributing to productive work, all the better, but the work they do need not substantially offset the costs of training until after training is completed. Apprentices who have trained in large firms can easily find employment in other firms if they choose to move.

Small and medium-sized firms are less attractive and therefore less selective. They cannot employ enough apprentices to make a full-time trainer economically viable or to support facilities reserved for training. Apprentices may be pressed into service to fill vacancies left by illness, vacations, or departures and kept in the same location longer than their educational needs dictate.

Large firms, however, are not always superior to smaller ones. Smaller firms are increasingly cooperating, with government financial assistance, to create multifirm instructional shops. An apprentice in a small commercial firm may learn more functions in greater depth because the firm as a whole is comprehensible and she or he is able to work in all facets of its operations. One of Rolf Kemmler's colleagues made this point by contrasting his large training firm with the small firm his father owns. The purchasing office where he trained at Brandt buys nothing but synthetic parts, while the lone buyer in his father's small firm is responsible for all purchases of raw materials, components, equipment, and supplies. He was convinced that he could have learned more by helping the buyer in his father's firm make diverse purchases than he did in one highly specialized office of Brandt's huge purchasing department. Trainers in large firms volunteered that while they could in general offer a better apprenticeship, some small firms give excellent training.

Limitations to the quality of apprenticeship owning to size of firm are particularly noticeable in the craft sector, which continually trains more apprentices than can be hired as skilled workers. Here there is a constant danger of exploitation. Apprentices have traditionally been helpers in the skilled trades. They have carried mortar for masons, swept the shop floors at the end of the day, and fetched snack food and beverages. There is nothing inherently wrong with apprentices doing unskilled tasks; it is the proportion of learning to labor that is at issue. Especially during the 1970s, much of the drive for reform of the West German system came from the perception that too many apprentices were spending too much of their time in activities unrelated to learning.

However, that was not the case with Petra Raab, apprentice *Industriekauffrau* at Luft-tek, a medium-sized firm that manufactures and services aeronautical instruments and other precision equipment. When she was observed, Petra had passed the written examination concluding her training and had only a few weeks to wait before taking the oral part. Fully expecting her to pass—and more than 90 percent of apprentices do—Luft-tek offered her a recently vacated position in their personnel office. When she was observed, she was being introduced to this position.

A counter just inside the personnel office door provides work space for employees who come in to fill out forms and tend to other business. Petra, who is addressed as Fräulein Raab, rather than by her first name, in recognition of her new status as a regular employee, works at a desk behind the counter facing another desk, occupied by Frau Mohr. A door leads through a glass and wood partition to the office of Frau Kalb, the personnel director. Petra's task is to prepare a contract for a newly hired employee. She uses a standard contract from a notebook as her model, typing slowly with four fingers, and consults various documents to fill in specific information. Frau Mohr helps by providing details about vacation time and showing Petra where the stationery is stored.

As Petra continues with her task, a foreign worker comes through the door to the counter. He wants to bring his mother to West Germany, and must provide a statement of his wages to immigration officials. When he asks Frau Mohr whether her report of his earnings might be inflated for this purpose, she says no and sends him to Frau Kalb, the personnel director, in the adjoining office. A few minutes later, Frau Kalb steps in to ask Petra for a document but Frau Mohr finds it before Petra has a chance, gives it to Frau Kalb and then follows her into her office to join the discussion with the foreign worker.

When Frau Mohr returns to her desk, Petra asks her to read a handwritten note from a file. Frau Mohr does so, answers another question, and assures Petra, smiling, that she will soon be able to read Frau Kalb's handwriting herself. Petra continues her work for 20 minutes as phone calls are made and received and Frau Kalb moves in and out. Frau Kalb comes out of her office again and asks Petra whether she has finished with the contract. Petra says she has and is now working on something for the employee council (*Betriebsrat,* a group that represents employee interests in personnel and other decisions).

Frau Kalb explains that the foreign worker is paid on a piecework basis and never achieves his quota. Therefore, he receives only the minimum hourly wage and, she remarks, "The poor man didn't even understand why he earned so little." She leaves the man's documents for Petra to fill out.

Petra was clearly the new person in the office. She engaged in less social interaction than Frau Mohr, but was included in some joking. Frau Mohr seeemd anxious to help but also once took work from Petra's hands. Although much of Petra's work was fairly routine, she had clearly not been hired as a typist. Producing a proper contract required both knowledge and judgment on her part, and reference to a variety of documents.

The case of the foreign worker illustrated for her both adherence to legal requirements—denying his request to report higher earnings than he actually received—and sensitivity to his particular situation. Because they talked in her private office, it was unclear whether Frau Kalb attempted to explain to the man why he was failing to earn extra wages for higher productivity, but she devoted all of her attention to his situation for more than 20 minutes and expressed sympathetic concern about him. No overt bias was visible. The incident was a good introduction for Petra to some of the sensitive issues in personnel work.

Although Petra's opportunities for learning were not as rich as Rolf Kemmler's, she was being initiated appropriately into a responsible position where her work would become more demanding and rewarding with time. In contrast to office workers of the same age in the United States, what was most striking was that Petra was a personnel officer, not a clerk.

Petra's and Rolf's apprenticeships in white-collar occupations will enable them to attain an occupational level frequently filled by college graduates in the United States. Although they were employed by manufacturing firms, the kind of work they did is quite similar to what office workers do in the growing service sector. The next pair of apprentices are training for a blue-collar craft occupation: auto mechanic.

Auto mechanics in the United States and in West Germany do the same kind of work under similar conditions. American auto mechanics can learn their trade in secondary or postsecondary vocational school, in the military, or in a small number of formal apprentice programs. However, most learn informally, tinkering in their backyard, then helping out in the corner garage while pumping gasoline, and finally, if their employer judges them to be skilled enough, on the job as full-time mechanics, in most cases without benefit of formal certification. A few experienced mechanics have the good fortune to attend one of the excellent schools operated by auto manufacturers, and acquire a certificate there.

In Germany, where there is a tendency toward overspecialization, auto mechanics are divided into two separate occupations with independent training programs. Training of mechanics to work in large repair shops owned and operated by auto manufacturers is regulated by the industrial chamber. Training for mechanics in small and medium-sized independent firms is regulated by the craft chamber, which sets somewhat different standards.[33] As a result, auto mechanics in large firms train for three-and-one-half years to earn the title *Kraftfahrzeugschlosser,* while those in smaller firms take three years to become *Kraftfahrzeugmechaniker.* *Schlosser* is a general term for a worker in metal, especially one who does repairs. The term indicates an association with industry, but has no different substantive meaning from *Mechaniker.* The titles are distinguished only to reflect the separation of the training program, which follows from the different demands of employers in the two categories and, perhaps even more importantly, from the two separate chambers to which the employers belong.

In both the United States and West Germany, automobile owners complain about the high cost of repairs. However, in West Germany a customer can ordinarily count on repairs being done properly, something that cannot be assumed in the United States. The best American mechanics are probably the equal of Germany's best; it is among ordinary mechanics that the difference in skills shows up.

Like Petra Raab, Karl Oettinger had recently assumed a skilled worker's position in a medium-sized firm as he completed the final months of his apprenticeship. Karl's firm sells and services Honda and British Leyland products (Rover, Land Rover, and Jaguar), although he works only on Hondas. The main floor of the garage has bays for servicing nine vehicles. It is well lighted, and remarkably clean and quiet. The lower story has spaces for doing electrical and bodywork on five or six more cars. There is also a room where brakes and engine power can be tested and engines analyzed electronically.

Karl, 18, was enthusiastic, articulate, and self-confident. He explained that he would take his qualifying examination in two months. Confident that he will pass, his boss has already given him a locker with the qualified auto mechanics. The apprentices have their lockers in a separate room. As the newest employee, he even has the newest and most complete set of tools, a source of some envy from more experienced mechanics.

Karl is supervised by the two *Meister* (masters) who oversee the shop. One of them gives him a card listing the work to be done on a Honda. Karl stamps it to indicate the starting time for the job, then walks over to his service bay and goes to work.

After completing the routine maintenance, which includes changing the oil, adjusting the timing, aligning the headlights, and finding the source of a rattle reported by the customer, he takes the card back to the *Meister* and then returns to an older Honda he was working on earlier. Its engine has now cooled so that he can adjust the valves and the head. The head adjustment involves loosening and then retightening to the proper torque all of the head bolts, one at a time, in the proper sequence. When asked about the purpose of the procedure, he explains that it compensates for the effects of uneven temperatures on the engine's lightweight metals. He also describes two different sequences that can be used and gives his reasons for preferring the sequence he uses.

Karl was impressively knowledgeable about his work. He explained clearly why he did each task, what the specifications were (e.g., the desired level of acidity in the battery's electrolyte—his word), and why tasks were done in a particular manner and sequence. He also displayed great pride and identification with the firm and the product. He glowingly described the features of a sporty new model, stating that no German car near the price had its speed or accessories. He asserted that the firm, which he referred to as "we," would soon become the top dealer in Jaguars in the city because of a large stock and high-quality service.

He also expressed personal pride. He signed his name on the tags affixed to the engine giving the date of the oil change and antifreeze check, noting that some mechanics did not do so, but that he *wanted* to take responsibility for his work. When he mentioned that another apprentice was not in the shop today, he said the absence might be pretended illness, something he would not do. He spoke of his desire to do well on the qualifying examination, saying that the time and money he had invested in a review course would be worth it if he gained only one point because he hoped to outdo his father and older brother, both auto mechanics who had achieved high grades on the exam. His brother, in fact, became a master at age 25 and Karl plans to do the same, perhaps even advancing farther to become an engineer. Being only a journeyman is not enough for 40 years, he says. His dream occupation is designing engines, but that, he says with a smile, would be like winning a lottery—there are so few places.

Although pleased with his immediate future, Karl brought a critical view both to his training and to his occupation. The most troubling limitation of his training, he said, is its narrow specialization on one make of automobile and its overemphasis on routine maintenance. He would like to do more work on transmissions and rear axles, but they seldom need service because the cars are well made. Inspecting a 12-cylinder Jaguar engine at an adjacent bay, he said he envied the apprentice who was learning to work on it because that apprentice could easily master the tiny 4-cylinder Honda engine while he would be lost trying to service the Jaguar. He went on to say, "My occupation is in a crisis," because mechanics are trained to be able to identify a faulty component, take it apart, repair it, and then put it back in, but that may take three hours, which costs too much for labor, so instead they take it out and put in a new one. "We are becoming nothing more than parts changers," he concluded ruefully.

Karl's medium-sized training firm, nonetheless, appeared to have done a good job of preparing him for employment as a skilled mechanic. Despite the limitations he noted and the constraints on training resources in comparison to a larger shop, he had already made the transition to being a confident independent worker.

Georg Wanner, also 18, enjoyed the benefits of training in a large firm, a sales and service operation owned and operated by a German auto manufacturer. He was being trained as a *Schlosser,* under the auspices of the industrial chamber. During his first six months of training, Georg spent most of his time in a large, well-equipped training shop, learning the fundamentals of metalwork—drilling, cutting, bending, filing, soldering, lathe operation, welding, and so on. Most of these skills have no place in contemporary auto repair, as Karl Oettinger pointed out, but they are considered fundamental to all metalworking trades and they teach what Herr Bauer, the firm's apprentice supervisor, identified as the most important lessons he tried to teach his apprentices: precision, cleanliness, and order ("Genauigkeit, Sauberkeit, und Ordnung"). Herr Bauer's formulation was striking because apprenticeship is ordinarily seen as specific technical training, but his objectives were general Germanic worker virtues.

Only after his stint in the training shop did Georg begin working in the repair shop, a shop as different from a corner gas station as a shopping mall is from a neighborhood variety store. With the capacity to repair up to 200 automobiles and trucks a day, the shop is divided into sections for various types of repair. It stocks parts and specialized tools for every conceivable job.

Georg's first assignment in the repair shop was the same as for all apprentices, in the routine maintenance section, where he worked with a team of apprentices under the supervision of a skilled mechanic. When observed during his third year, Georg had spent time in several other sections and was paired with a journeyworker in the accident section, but working relatively independently. Herr Bauer was so satisfied with Georg's maturity, skill, and speed on the job and his performance in part-time vocational school that he encouraged him to take his qualifying examination early, which he will soon do.

Georg is reinstalling an engine following the completion of work on the body and frame to repair damage sustained in a front-end collision. The engine is suspended inside the engine compartment by cables attached to an overhead hoist. The auto is parked over an opening in the floor through which a mechanic standing on the subfloor below has access to its underside. Georg goes below in order to attach the drive shaft to the transmission. He calls to the mechanic working on the ground floor in the next bay who hands down the yoke that supports the shaft.

The bolt holes in the frame won't line up with the holes in the yoke. Georg complains that the bodywork was not done well. After struggling to align them for more than five minutes, he comes up to the ground floor and finds Herr Faber, the mechanic who supervises his work. While Georg installs the battery and radiator, Faber goes to the parts room and brings back some clips to hold the yoke in place while Georg bolts it on.

After exchanging assistance with the mechanic working at the next bay, Georg reattaches various electrical cables and hoses, installs the exhaust pipe, and uses a pressurized tank to fill the brake system with fluid. During this operation he gives a thorough explanation of the order in which he adds fluid to the brakes, the reason why he repeats the procedure, and the personal and environmental dangers posed by brake fluid, which, he explains, is both corrosive and poisonous.

Georg's work is diverse and complex; he performs it independently and quickly. His explanation demonstrated a thorough comprehension of the systems he worked on. He interacted with the mechanic at the next bay on an equal basis, trading favors and addressing him by his first name and with the familiar pronoun, *"du."* Yet he was not fully independent. Herr Faber was never far away. Herr Faber set out the sequence of tasks to be performed, checked on their performance, and made decisions about when to install new parts. Faber solved the problem Georg encountered in replacing the yoke; apparently Georg had not known the clips were needed. But Georg was not entirely subordinate. He declined Faber's recommendation of a special tool at one point, completing the job with another tool of his choice. He spotted an electrical wire with a section of insulation worn off and pointed it out to Faber, who agreed that it should be replaced.

This shop offered technical training of very high quality. Both in the instructional shop and in the repair shop, apprentices were constantly exposed to the message that there is a right way to work and that they must learn to work that way. The "right way" was not defined rigidly. Rather it was a matter of understanding what is required and accomplishing it quickly and thoroughly. Parts, tools, equipment, and expert advice were always close at hand. High regard for apprentices was demonstrated by a high level of responsibility. The restoration of a classic automobile was entrusted to a group of apprentices, work that is given to only the most highly skilled specialists in the United States. Here it was being done by 17- and 18-year-old apprentices.

The sharpest contrast between Rolf and Petra, the white-collar apprentices, and Karl and Georg, the blue-collar ones, was between working conditions in the two kinds of occupations. Auto mechanics spend most of their time standing on oil-stained concrete floors, their hands greasy, and their ears filled with roaring engines and clanking steel. Verbal interactions are directed primarily to accomplishing the task at hand, interspersed with masculine banter. In contrast, *Industriekaufleute* dress up in attractive clothes and work in quiet carpeted offices, usually decorated with a few personal items. Much of their time is spent in conversation with others, both face-to-face and over the telephone. The borders between work and nonwork are more difficult to trace. Male-female interaction is frequent and occasionally flirtatious.

Social skills and physical appearance are important to commercial employees, along with technical knowledge and the ability to complete tasks and solve problems. Technical skill and knowledge are the key virtues for auto mechanics. When asked about the adults they viewed as good examples, the apprentice auto mechanics who named adult auto mechanics always cited expertise as their chief exemplary quality.

The dramatic differences in working conditions and social relations between auto mechanics and white-collar apprentices raise the question whether apprenticeship is more a means of preparing youth for different kinds of employment or of sorting youth who are already different into work settings appropriate to their characteristics. The issue is whether experience as an apprentice is the major source of differences between two groups of people or whether those differences predated the experience, and are merely confirmed by the experience. Had the social graces exhibited by white-collar apprentices been acquired earlier? They surely had been. They were as evident in first-year as in third-year apprentices. Especially in Brandt, where competition for places is stiffer than in the most selective U.S. colleges, those selected were already, as the training director said, young people who knew how to fit in and how to get along with other people. The different conditions in which manual and white-collar apprentices learned their occupations matched preexisting differences between them, but probably exacerbated them as well, in addition to foreshadowing their future.

Although by most measures *Industriekaufleute* are in more advantageous positions than auto mechanics, the contrast between mechanics and office workers in Brandt should not be generalized. The latter are the elite among *Industriekaufleute*. The gap between their working conditions and career prospects and those of *Industriekaufleute* at Luft-tek and the other medium-sized firms observed is at least as great as between Petra Raab and Georg Wanner. A longitudinal study of *Industriekaufleute* and machine repairers (*Machinenschlosser*) in one firm found that both groups entered their apprenticeships assuming that the managerial apprentices had far more interesting and independent work and higher status, but after three years they saw themselves as closer to the same plane. The *Industriekaufleute* felt less privileged than when they began, the machine repairers more.[34]

The training of Rolf, Petra, Karl, and Georg illustrates the key features needed in any effective apprenticeship system:

1. workplaces and other community settings are exploited as learning environments;
2. work experience is linked to academic learning;
3. youth are simultaneously workers with real responsibilities and learners; and
4. close relationships are fostered between youth and adult mentors.

With their situations in mind, it is now possible to analyze those features in greater depth.

In striking contrast to the assumption guiding *A Nation at Risk,* that the only place young people can learn is in a classroom, the majority of West Germany's older youth spend more time *learning in workplaces* than in schools. School attendance is mandatory until age 18, but the part-time *Berufsschule* satisfies the requirement. Apprentices learn how to perform specific jobs, but they learn for broader purposes as well. Especially in large firms with many specialized positions, the apprentice's mastery of a particular job is less important than her or his acquisition of knowledge and skills that provide a foundation for further learning and for a broad range of jobs. Moreover, they are expected to internalize the appropriate worker virtues, expressed in the large auto repair firm as "precision, cleanliness, and order."

Apprentices' schooling will be described in detail in Chapters 4 and 5. Suffice it to say at this point that apprentices *learn in* Berufsschule *some of what they need to know at work,* both basic academic material and more specialized topics related to their occupation. The interaction operates in reverse order as well; when they *apply their academic learning at work,* they reinforce school instruction and gain motivation to learn what they are taught in school. The most critical point is that work is closely associated with school learning for most youth, something that cannot be said in the United States, where even students in vocational programs are often employed in unrelated part-time jobs.

The *combination of work with learning* defines the apprentice's distinctive role. Too much work and too little learning constitute exploitation by the employer, a problem in some West German firms, but predictably not a major problem in those that permitted observation of their apprentices. Too much learning is difficult to imagine, but too much emphasis on the role of learner could transform an apprentice into a pupil, one without the responsibility and the hands-on experience that are crucial to apprenticeship and, arguably, to all effective learning settings. In all four of the cases described above, young people around the age of 18 discharged responsibilities that are normally reserved for people over the age of 20 in the United States. Especially Karl Oettinger, working independently as a mechanic, and Petra Raab, involved in sensitive transactions in the personnel office, performed duties that U.S. employers believe teenagers are inherently unable to handle. They did so competently because they had been thoroughly trained, because it was expected of them, and because they had the opportunity.

Along with giving them real responsibilities, work experience places young people in *close contact with a range of adults* who are neither their parents nor their classroom teachers. Instead, those adults are simply going about the business and diversions that constitute their working lives. Some, but not all of them have explicit instructional responsibilities. In medium-sized and large firms there are typically at least two adults charged with instructing an apprentice. One is the person who oversees the apprentice's training program. At Brandt and the large auto repair firm, that was a full-time professional trainer. In the medium-sized auto repair firms it was the master of the shop. In Petra's firm it was the personnel director. Only in a small shop does an apprentice work day-to-day with a master. An adult employee was responsible for daily supervision and instruction of each of the observed apprentices. In the medium-sized auto repair shops, Karl served as an assistant to one journeyworker for most of his three years. In the larger industrial auto repair firms, apprentices moved from one section to another, learning and working with a different mechanic in each.

The term, "mentor," can be defined in many ways. In the technical sense, each of these adults plays a mentoring role by teaching and advising apprentices. However, mentors are usually defined as older, more experienced people with a broader and longer-term commitment to their protégés, people who act as parents in some respects. By this definition, not all of the adults with whom apprentices work and talk are mentors. But by virtue of being in adult workplaces and interacting regularly with adults, apprentices have more opportunities to find mentors in this sense, and adults have more opportunities to become mentors, than in the United States where young people spend most of their time in schools. Herr Stein certainly seemed a potential mentor for Rolf. The director of apprenticeship at Brandt commented one day after greeting a former apprentice in the elevator that some came back to him regularly for career advice, suggesting that he continued to perform a mentoring role for some adults. In two of the medium-sized auto repair shops observed, journeyworkers provided lunches for apprentices who had none. When 21 apprentices were asked to name the five most important adults in their lives, their responses were similar to those of Learning Web participants: all named their parents first; parents and other family members accounted for two-thirds of the nominations. Friends were the next most frequent category. Nine apprentices also listed an adult from their workplace among their five most important people. Apprenticeship does not guarantee that young people acquire mentors, but it does make unrelated adult mentors more accessible.

West Germany's apprenticeship system is more than a training program intended to teach the knowledge and skills related to a specific job. In addition to fulfilling that function, it is a form of general education and an institution for socializing youth to adulthood.

Apprenticeship is the natural way to learn a craft. References to the practice of bringing a boy into the home of a craftsman as a learner and helper in Hammurabi's Code, Greek and Roman, Chinese and Indian writings[35] suggest that it has been reinvented many times to meet the perpetual need to prepare youth for skilled work. Yet in the United States it has apparently been in perpetual decline. Writers in every era have mourned its parlous state, leading the skeptic to doubt that it ever flourished. Why did apprenticeship fail to take hold in the New World?

One reason is that apprenticeship has historically been an urban institution. Specialized crafters need relatively concentrated populations to provide them with a market for their products. Once settlement spread beyond the East Coast, America's farmsteads were scattered widely across the countryside rather than clustered around towns and villages in the European manner. Although farmers' sons in the eighteenth and nineteenth centuries often repaid their parents for the cost of their upbringing by living with and working for a neighbor for several years,[36] this was a less formal, less educational, and more purely economic arrangement than apprenticeship. Work, not learning, was its core.

Loose social controls made it easy for apprentices, and indentured servants, to run away from their masters and join the stream of internal and external migrants moving from place to place. Many skilled immigrants abandoned their crafts upon arrival to take advantage of cheap land and become farmers.[37] Persistent shortages of skilled labor prevented potential employers or customers from demanding evidence of extended training from those who represented themselves as craftsmen. As long as they could be hired to do skilled work without formal training, workers had little incentive to seek formal training.

Benjamin Franklin both symbolized and, through his widely read autobiography, perpetuated the American apprentice's career. Finding the obligations of apprenticeship too confining, he ran away and, in archetypical American fashion, worked at a variety of jobs before succeeding as a printer.[38] Boys like Franklin were able to make successful careers for themselves without completing apprenticeship.

The decline of apprenticeship was loudly mourned at the turn of the twentieth century in the writings of social and educational reformers. Although the decline was described as a new phenomenon, similar observations were made in previous eras. However, this time a new and powerful force was blamed: industrialization. Commentators in Great Britain also noted apprenticeship's decline and also attributed it to industrialization. The argument is compelling. Industrial production, depending upon machine power, mechanical precision, and repetition, rather than craftsmanship, requires fewer advanced skills than craft production. The celebrated example of Eli Whitney's introduction of interchangeable parts to the manufacture of firearms for the Union army is apt. Previously each weapon was made by a single gunsmith who made each part by hand, down to the screws and springs. By using machines to stamp out the parts, Whitney could hire relatively unskilled workers to assemble them, saving both time and money in the process.[39] When skilled gunsmiths were in less demand, apprentice gunsmiths became rarer. Moreover, rising wages for semiskilled and unskilled industrial workers attracted youth into factory jobs who might formerly have become apprentice craft workers.

But industrialization is an inadequate explanation. Apprenticeship was limited in extent and effectiveness in the United States before the onset of industrialization in the middle of the nineteenth century. Moreover, industrialization did not eliminate craft production any more than it eliminated farming; it simply gained predominance over those two more traditional modes of production. Although there were occupations that were all but eliminated by industrialization, such as handweaving, there were other craft occupations that were simply overshadowed by industrialization. Carpenters, for example, continued to build houses using craft methods, and still do. Their product was not industrialized to any large extent until much later, but they and other craft workers constituted a shrinking *proportion* of the total number of workers as industry grew.

The most decisive argument against industrialization as the cause of apprenticeship's demise, and the most important here, is the fact that apprenticeship thrived in Germany even as that country made its tremendous leap into the forefront of industrialization before World War I. Something about Germany and German apprenticeship enabled it to adapt to the same industrial conditions that British and American historians have blamed for apprenticeship's near-extinction.

German apprenticeship traces its roots to the medieval period, when the vast majority of the population lived as serfs, performing primarily agricultural labor on feudal manors. Apprenticeship was, therefore an institution of the towns, not the countryside. It was controlled by guilds, associations of craftsmen who banded together to promote their mutual interests. A major guild function was to control entry to craft occupations, in part to maintain standards of quality but not incidentally to maintain earnings by restricting competition. Too many bakers would lower the price of bread. By requiring that anyone wishing to become a baker first serve an apprenticeship under a master baker and then demonstrate his competence to the satisfaction of the guild, they achieved both goals, providing a formal means of access to the occupation in the process but not as the primary purpose.

In fact, the guilds were better known for restricting access than for opening it. They offered entry first to relatives of members and next to the progeny of the town's better sorts of people, namely the members of other guilds. Only when sufficient aspirants were not available to meet demand would they open their doors to outsiders, who were more likely to be from another town than from the town's lower orders. The easiest way for a nonresident craftsman to be admitted to citizenship was to marry the widow of a guild member. The guilds provided a form of insurance at a time when death was commonplace. Upon the death of a craftsman, his wife and children would be assured of care by another practitioner of the craft who would, by marrying the widow, assume responsibility for the family along with ownership of the shop.

Under the feudal system, lords of the manor were the ultimate authorities, untrammeled by central government. They fought among themselves, uniting only to prevent any one of their members from becoming too powerful. But the cities and towns were anomolies. Necessary for trade but mostly independent of the feudal system, they frequently managed to remain independent of any one lord. The saying *Stadtluft macht frei* (City air makes [a person] free) communicated the fact that people living in cities and towns had no feudal obligations. They were not serfs bound to their lords and the land; they were not required to spend a certain number of days doing roadwork and other forms of public service. In the absence of either feudal authority or central government, the guilds brought both social and political order to the towns. In addition to controlling entrance to occupations, they governed the towns. The *Bürgermeister* (mayor) was not only the master of the townspeople but also the head *Meister*. *Bürger* originally meant one living inside the fortification or *Burg*. Now it means both citizen and member of the middle class, a significant conflation because the middle class originated in the towns and cities. The town fathers were the masters of the crafts represented in the town. Thus the craft guilds, in addition to their commercial function, were also the principal political bodies and guarantors of social order.[40]

Guilds performed these social and political functions in other parts of Europe during the medieval period, but as early as the fifteenth century a division occurred: the German guilds maintained their power while their counterparts in England and France began losing power to merchants who were unaffiliated with guilds.[41] As England and France developed into centralized states under powerful monarchs, Germany remained a collection of minor principalities without strong central government. This political backwardness resulted primarily from the policies of France and the Vatican. Both powers protected themselves from a potentially threatening neighbor by intervening regularly to prevent centralization. Surely one of the most successful long-term foreign policies in world history, this intervention kept Germany divided until 1871 when Prussia, after defeating first Austria and then France, created a nation where before there had been a language and culture but no central government.

In the German towns during this long sweep of history, guilds played the role that governmental institutions had long since assumed in England and France. Thus, when industrialization began in earnest in Germany, a century later than in England, the guilds were still a vital institution. Apprenticeship was one of the guild functions that was transformed and adapted to industrial production rather than cast off as it was in England.

In the aristocratic German social structure, universities were the province of gentlemen. Solid *Bürger* were craftsmen and merchants whose formal education ended when they were confirmed in the church at age 14. At that point they were officially adults and qualified to enter apprenticeship. Farm children needed no apprenticeship to become adult workers; they simply went to work full-time doing the kinds of jobs they had helped with as children. Unlike Britain, where the middle class grew with industrialization and central government was gradually allowed to share and finally take over power from the artistocracy, German aristocrats maintained their social and economic distance and kept the middle class subordinate.[42] The small size and political impotence of business people, industrialists, civil servants, and professionals in Germany, as compared to England and France, and the aristocratic cast of the universities, maintained apprenticeship as the primary educational path for the vast majority of people.

Apprenticeship thrived in Germany then, for two complementary reasons. First, it was an integral part of a social and political system that relied upon guilds long after those institutions had lost their vitality in other European countries. Apprenticeship fit into and perpetuated a larger social system rather than being a free-standing institution. Second, largely because it had so integral a place in the social system, apprenticeship was transformed rather than abandoned when Germany industrialized rapidly toward the end of the nineteenth century. Two things happened to apprenticeship at that point. First, it remained the path for entry into the traditional crafts, and many of those crafts were assiduously protected from the encroachment of industry. Consequently one can still easily find there active wood-carvers, violin makers, organ builders, and other traditional craft workers. Second, in the new industries and growing commercial firms, apprenticeship was seen as the best way to train new workers; traditional practices were adapted to modern conditions. Thus apprenticeship programs were created for occupations that had not previously existed, such as auto mechanic and *Industriekaufleute,* along with machine repairer, chemical worker, electrician, and many more. The current system reflects this duality, incorporating both traditional handcraft occupations and modern commercial and industrial occupations, each having its own requirements set by the chambers (*Kammern*), the quasi-public associations that are descended from the guilds.

A major factor in the modernization of apprenticeship was its formal incorporation into the educational system, accomplished by the creation of *Berufsschulen,* part-time vocational schools. The function of these schools was aptly described by Georg Kerschensteiner, one of their chief architects, when in 1910 he contrasted them with then emerging U.S. vocational high schools. *Berufsschulen* he said, were intended to compensate for the limitations of apprenticeship training, while U.S. vocational schools were designed to replace apprenticeship.[43]

The United States' origins as a British colony, persistent shortages of skilled workers, its agrarian character, cheap land, and the absence of strong social controls all combined with its strong democratic ideology to stress school rather than apprenticeship as the principal institution for the socialization of youth. Public schools have, since Horace Mann's day, been promoted as the guarantors of democracy. Yet there is good reason to challenge the common assumption that schools are inherently more democratic than such traditional institutions as apprenticeship.

The United States has no system of apprenticeship capable of sharing these functions, but, as outlined in this chapter, elements of a system may be found in a range of apprentice-like programs that give young people real responsibilities but stress their roles as learners as well as workers, attempt to relate work experience to academic learning, and create opportunities for young people to form close working relationships with adults.

The presence of these opportunities irrefutably demonstrates their feasibility in U.S. education and training. West German apprenticeship cannot be imported whole, but it can be adapted.

4

Academic Schooling

General Preparation for Work

The common schools that spread across the United States in the nineteenth century were intended to prepare children for work, but that was only one purpose. They were also designed to prepare children to read the documents and understand the principles of representative democracy so that they could participate as informed citizens. Children went to school to learn how to read at least the Bible and the news. Instruction in arithmetic prepared them to function as producers and consumers in a market economy, and to perform the measurements and calculations required in shops, on the farm, and around the home.

Schools were also intended to instill in the young attitudes and behavior conducive to productivity and the maintenance of social order: "such norms as punctuality, achievement, competitiveness, fair play, merit, and respect for adult authority."[1] Precepts drawn from democracy, non-denominational Protestant Christianity, and the work ethic were taught explicitly through the moralistic content of McGuffey's Readers and the adoration of such American heroes as George Washington and Benjamin Franklin. They were also taught implicitly in the school's authority structure and the rules governing classrooms.

At the primary school level embraced by the common schools, these multiple purposes were quite compatible; preparation of citizens and of future workers in all walks of life proceeded in the same manner. Completion of primary schooling was less important than attainment of what today is called functional literacy. Girls who finished the primary school course were qualified to become teachers. Only boys preparing for the ministry and the sons of the elite were ordinarily enrolled in secondary school and college. Preparation for specific occupations, even such professions as law and medicine, took place outside of schools, through both formal and informal apprenticeship arrangements.

Conventional histories of American public schools picture them as bastions of democracy, teaching the information, skills, and values essential to preserving and strengthening citizen involvement in government, and offering an avenue of achievement enabling all children to develop their talents to the fullest, regardless of their families' wealth or social connections. This picture's reality has been challenged repeatedly however by recent scholars with a more critical perspective, who have argued that schools have not done enough to reduce race, class, and gender inequality in political and economic spheres.[2]

The school's purposes of preparing young people to be citizens in a democracy and preparing them for work are inescapably contradictory when work's status and rewards are unequal and when access to desirable work is restricted unfairly. The key question is to what extent schools maintain young people in the same social class as their parents, versus supporting their unfettered ascent or descent to the level best suited to their individual talents.[3]

Despite the multitude of Horatio Alger-style myths, it has become increasingly difficult for schools to free students from their socioeconomic heritage. Employment continues to reflect race, class, and gender to an unacceptable degree. As a result, the preparation of youth for work is closely bound up with the perpetuation of a class system from one generation to another as children grow up to assume adult work roles equivalent to those of their parents.

Elementary schools begin the general process of preparing young people for work, with implicit lessons embedded in their structure in addition to the explicit lessons of the curriculum.[4] Schools are formal, hierarchical organizations that tend to treat individuals as members of groups. Like workplaces, schools stress individual achievement. Persons are judged in relation to universal standards. And they must comply with universal rules. Authority is a function of office, not of person. Any teacher, like any supervisor, is to be obeyed, regardless of the student's affection or respect for her or him.[5]

Applying their universalistic standards, teachers and counselors make predictions about young peoples' probable futures.[6] To the extent that schools socialize pupils differently in accordance with these predictions, they also confirm them, thereby contributing to the reproduction of inequality.[7] One way this occurs is through ability grouping in the classroom, a nearly universal practice in the United States.

U.S. elementary schools typically enroll all children in a neighborhood or community and assign them to classrooms according to age rather than ability, except in extreme cases. Differences in ability or performance are recognized by assigning children to subgroups within the classroom. Reading ability is the most common criterion, but mathematics is sometimes taught in ability groups as well.

The rationale behind this practice is that pupils will be able to learn more efficiently with others of similar ability. Most American teachers believe that the range of ability found in a single age-group makes it all but impossible to teach reading to the whole class at once. The empirical basis for this practice, however, is weak. Numerous reviews of research on the effects of ability grouping in elementary school have seriously undermined its justification. One reviewer concluded that the cognitive consequences are at best debatable, but the social consequences are unambiguously negative.[8]

One problem with ability grouping is that the ablest groups move faster, making it difficult for anyone in a lower group to catch up. A second problem is that the children all know who is "best." Social interaction tends to occur within group boundaries, and those in the lower groups feel inferior, which hampers their performance.[9] Group assignment may also be made on inappropriate bases, such as an IQ test rather than a test of ability in the subject matter being taught. Or grouping in one subject, usually reading, may result in inappropriate grouping in another, such as math, simply because of scheduling constraints. Furthermore, when the teacher needs to attend to each group in turn, all the children in the other groups must do seatwork unattended, which is not an efficient form of learning.

Ability grouping is most pernicious when it is based upon and perpetuates racial and social class differences among children. In the most extreme cases, teachers make assumptions about their pupils' abilities based on their social class and then proceed to confirm those assumptions by systematically favoring those whom they expect to perform better and denying opportunities to the presumed lower achievers.[10]

In addition to being treated differently within the same classrooms, children of different social classes often attend distinctive schools, schools that differ not only in their appearance, social climate, and academic emphases, but also in the kinds of attitudes and behavior they promote. A study of four urban elementary schools with pupils from distinctive racial and income groups[11] found that all four schools placed heavy emphasis on proper behavior, but that propriety was defined differently. In the two schools located in middle-income neighborhoods, both black and white, teachers rewarded "nice" behavior, such as demonstrating self-control and having correct posture. In the black and white lower-income schools, proper behavior meant obedience to authority. The lower-income students, especially in the predominantly black school, were being socialized to deference, whereas the middle-income students, especially in the predominantly white school, were being prepared for leadership and responsibility. Moreover, proper behavior in the lower-income schools appeared to be an end in itself rather than the means to establish a climate for learning, as it was in the middle-income schools.

The middle-income schools encouraged students to take initiative and interact with each other through committees and cooperative projects, which were absent in the lower-income schools. Teachers in the middle-income white school preferred students with the highest IQ scores, but those in the lower-income black school preferred students who were submissive even if they had lower IQ scores. The schools in this study were not less effective at teaching low-income children because they operated on a discrepant set of "middle-class values," but because teachers expected less of lower-class students and communicated their belief to these students that they would not amount to much, thereby helping to "perpetuate the very behavior they decry."[12]

A subsequent study using more refined methods produced similar results comparing a first-grade classroom in an upper-middle-class neighborhood with one in a lower-middle-class school. Both were considered good schools and each classroom was selected because of the teacher's solid reputation. The teacher in the upper-middle-class school stressed academic achievement—helping her pupils learn to think and speak, for example, by urging them to extend their verbal statements in class. The teacher in the lower-middle-class school stressed getting the work done, following rules, and retaining facts. The standards of authority in her classroom were externally imposed; the pupils had to comply because she told them to. Standards of authority in the upper-middle-class room were introduced by the teacher as essential to the maintenance of order rather than being imposed arbitrarily. She stressed the reasons for the rules and the benefits to all from adhering to them, thus encouraging the pupils to internalize them. The teacher in the upper-middle-class room frequently called on her pupils to think about the future, in terms of their education and their adult lives. A present orientation dominated the other classroom.

The excellent reputations of both teachers suggested that each was performing in a manner deemed appropriate by parents, a suggestion that was confirmed by parent interviews. Parents and teachers alike expected that the children would achieve educational and occupational levels similar to those of the parents. The two sets of parents' orientations toward the school and their children's performance accurately reflected their different social positions, which were determined by their own employment.

Preparing youth for work is not a neutral task. Work determines social status and material well-being, and parents' own work heavily influences their beliefs about what constitutes high-quality education. Moreover, both grouping practices within classrooms and norms prevailing in schools serving different neighborhoods reflect children's family backgrounds while they contribute to the reproduction of inequality as children learn to fit into the same niche in the socioeconomic structure that their parents occupy. Even in elementary school children are learning general worker virtues, and attitudes and behaviors appropriate to the level in the occupational hierarchy that their family background makes most accessible to them.

Nevertheless, social class mobility does occur. So long as economic growth continues, it is more likely to be upward than downward. However, schools' contribution to social and economic equality has been oversold.[13] Schools necessarily reflect and perpetuate the society they serve. They cannot single-handedly "build a new social order." At best they contribute incrementally to movement toward a society's best hopes.

West German schools, no less than American ones, reflect their society. Democracy is still young in West Germany. A titled aristocracy survives. Marxian socialism is not a foreign ideology but a vital force in politics and culture. Social class divisions are sharper in some respects, but in others they are blurred by the welfare state.

West Germany's *Grundschule* or elementary school enrolls children beginning at age six and includes grades one through four (six in some *Länder*—states). *Grundschulen* (the plural form) are neighborhood schools. Because most city neighborhoods intentionally include a mixture of housing types, many schools include more than one income level. However, some elementary schools have large concentrations of poor, predominantly foreign children while in others only a few Turks may be found among the children of white-collar and professional parents. Large cities have private elementary schools, but of the 3,827,900 children attending *Grundschulen* and *Hauptschulen* (main schools, grades five through nine) in 1985, less than 50,000 (1.2 percent) attended private schools.[14] Christian religious instruction is part of the required curriculum; there are no parochial schools.

Education is one of the most important functions reserved to the 11 states comprising the Federal Republic of Germany. State governments vigilantly maintain their prerogatives, partly in reaction against the extreme centralization imposed by the Nazis. Regular meetings and binding agreements among state education officials promote comparability in curriculum and achievement levels across their school systems.

According to a large-scale study of elementary schools,[15] the greatest variation in available resources and proportions of problem children served by schools was not among but within states. These differences flow from differences in residential patterns but also from the financial bases of West German schools. In general, the states are responsible for salaries but the city, village, or district government pays for the school buildings, equipment, and supplies. Hence a school in a prosperous area may be newly constructed and generously equipped, while a neighboring school with a poorer tax base may be old, poorly maintained, and underequipped, just as in the United States, where local property tax is the principal support for schools, supplemented by state income and sales taxes, at higher levels in some states than in others.

Elementary school curricula are comparable to those found in U.S. schools at the same level. They emphasize the basic skills of language and mathematics but include as well social studies, art, and physical education. *Handwerk* (such as sewing), music, and religion are more prominent than in U.S. classrooms. Instruction is predominantly "frontal"; that is, during 85–90 percent of instructional time the teacher is directing instruction to the whole group in the form of lecture/recitation. Individualized instruction and group work not directly overseen by the teacher are quite rare.[16]

Elementary schools take two approaches to dealing with pupils who lag behind their classmates. One is to create special small classes; the other is remedial instruction occurring both during and outside of regular instruction. Compared to U.S. elementary schools, however, there is a remarkable lack of differentiation during the first four to six years. Instruction is typically directed to the entire class. Ability grouping, so universal in the United States, is present only as a recent innovation. West German elementary school teachers are just as puzzled about how they might teach a class divided into several reading groups as American teachers are about how to teach reading to an entire class at once.

Preparation for work in the United States becomes more explicit at the secondary school level, as does the differentiation among young people that constitutes a major element of that preparation. By the time U.S. young people are in high school, curriculum placement has replaced ability grouping as the major form of differentiation. Whereas elementary school groups are based explicitly on some measure of ability, high school curriculum placement is often represented as a choice. In reality it reflects previous performance to a large extent because those who have not done well in earlier grades are firmly directed into the lower tracks.

Normally there are three main tracks: college-preparatory, vocational, and general. The critical division is between college-preparatory and noncollege tracks. Further divisions may be made between honors or advanced placement college-preparatory tracks and between vocational tracks related to commercial or manual occupations.

Near the end of the nineteenth century, the need to homogenize a dangerously diverse population, business and industry's demand for better trained and more disciplined workers, and the contraction of uneducated youths' employment prospects all contributed to the transformation of the high school from an elite into a mass institution, the majority of whose graduates would not continue their formal education. Publicly supported comprehensive high schools with separate tracks for college-bound youth emerged as a compromise among divergent possibilities, particularly between the private, practically oriented academies and the elite urban Latin schools that were the most prominent types of secondary schools until late in the nineteenth century.[17]

Comprehensiveness, in the sense of teaching all youth under the same roof, maintained the common school tradition. Although European educational systems, especially Germany's, were frequently cited as models in discussions of education at the time, most Americans agreed that a sharply stratified system was inconsistent with democratic principles. The conceit that every boy might grow up to be president was vital enough to serve as an argument against institutional differentiation of secondary education.

One vision of the high school was stated by the Committee of Ten in 1894.[18] Chaired by Harvard's president, Charles W. Eliot, this prestigious group recommended that, in addition to the required core courses, students be allowed to choose a specialization from classical, modern languages, Latin-scientific, or English programs. The idea of electives violated the traditional belief that Greek, Latin, and geometry were exercise machines for the mind, developing the mind's muscles far better than such practical subjects as English and biology. The Committee's recommendation implied that all these subjects had equivalent value, a radical claim at the time.

Recognizing that not all high school graduates would proceed to higher education, the Committee averred that the same courses were equally appropriate for future managers and technicians. Manual workers were not expected to graduate from high school and therefore were beyond the Committee's purview. Had Eliot possessed Mortimer Adler's gift for aphorism, he might have coined the motto of *The Paideia Proposal:* "The best education for the best is the best education for all."[19]

Influential though the Committee of Ten was, the development of U.S. high schools did not follow exactly its prescribed course. The invention of vocational schools, which occurred at about the same time, altered that course, both directly by providing an alternative to academic schooling and indirectly by calling forth a panoply of practices such as IQ testing and guidance counseling specifically designed to identify which youth should be given which form of education.[20] Whereas the Committee of Ten recommended a broad academic education for all who enrolled in high school, the National Education Association's *Cardinal Principles of Secondary Education,* issued in 1918, stressed high schools' role in promoting purposes such as health and citizenship and codified the practice of assigning students to distinctive high school programs in anticipation of their probable futures.

As they now function, U.S. secondary schools continue to exacerbate the differentiation of young people that begins in elementary schools. A recent study of tracking in 25 high schools found that form of instruction as well as content varied according to pupils' track placement. Math and English classes for the high tracks emphasized learning and thinking skills, for the low tracks rote learning and simple skills. High-track English classes studied adult literature and required extensive writing. Low-track classes used only juvenile fiction and emphasized simple writing, such as how to fill out forms. High-track math classes engaged pupils with mathematical ideas; low-track classes taught only computation. Lower-track pupils' attitudes toward school were more negative in high school than in junior high, while higher-track pupils' attitudes remained positive from one level to the next.[21]

Another study, this one of a high school located in a homogeneous white working-class neighborhood, found that tracking was a means of stratifying students from similar family backgrounds into groups with high and low probabilities of upward social mobility. As in elementary schools, grouping by ability resulted in a status hierarchy that was painfully evident to the students. In addition to being conscious of their subordinate status, low-track students spoke of themselves in the same negative stereotypes that high-track students and teachers applied to them. Students also chose their friends primarily from their own track or an adjoining one and participated in extracurricular activities differentially according to track; the majority (more than 80 percent) of college-track students participated in two or more activities, whereas the majority of noncollege-track students did not participate at all, and less than 30 percent took part in two or more activities. Furthermore, college-track students' IQ scores increased from eighth to tenth grade, whereas noncollege-track students' IQ scores declined during the same period.[22]

The study's author described the tracking system as a tournament: "When you win, you win only the right to go on to the next round; when you lose, you lose forever."[23] Most students remained in the same track for all courses all the way through secondary school. Movement from one track to another was quite rare and seven times more likely to be downward than upward when it did occur.

With some exceptions, U.S. secondary schools draw students from their surrounding area, but that area is larger than for elementary schools. Some large cities have instituted specialty or "magnet" schools, which attract commuters, sometimes even from suburbs outside the city school district. Middle schools and junior high schools typically draw pupils from several elementary schools and high schools from several middle or junior high schools. As a result, school size and pupil diversity expand at the secondary level, but secondary schools continue to reflect the population of their surroundings.

High schools in inner city areas may graduate far less than half of the students who enter and send none to college while suburban schools a few miles away send more than 80 percent of their graduates to college. Despite highly visible differences among high schools' facilities, curricula, school climates, and students, it has been surprisingly difficult to document the effects of those differences on students' learning, once the effects of their social class and their previous academic performance are considered.[24] This suggests that the most important differences among U.S. high schools, in general, are *within* schools rather than *between* them.

Even more than elementary schools, tracking within secondary schools and the variations that distinguish secondary schools in different communities channel young people into different kinds of work. Although this channeling is justified as a matching process between individuals' interests and abilities and the labor market, the same process from a more critical perspective ensures that middle-class children maintain their status by coming out ahead of lower-class children.[25]

In sharp contrast to their relatively uniform treatment in elementary school, West German secondary school pupils are strongly differentiated according to academic ability and corresponding expectations regarding future schooling and employment. There are three levels of secondary schools: *Gymnasium, Realschule,* and *Hauptschule.* Pupils are divided at the end of grade four in some states, grade six in others. The early age at which this differentiation occurs and the difficulty of altering school type later make it the most distressing feature of the school system from the perspective of promoting equality.

Those deemed capable of entering the university—seven or nine years hence—are enrolled in the *Gymnasium.* There they receive a broad education in the arts and sciences from grade five (or seven) through grade thirteen, the equivalent of a year or two of college in the United States. *Gymnasien* (plural) in metropolitan areas specialize in, for example, math and science, music, modern languages, or classics. Pupils and their parents choose a *Gymnasium* according to its specialty and reputation. Excellent public transportation facilitates commuting to a *Gymnasium* that may be distant from a pupil's neighborhood.

Those who "possess active minds and eagerness to learn but also have practical skills and interest," as a Bavarian guidebook for parents puts it, are sent to a *Realschule,* where they attend grades seven through ten in preparation for further training in technical and commercial occupations. *Realschulen,* formerly known as middle schools, generally specialize in either commercial or technical fields and are, like *Gymnasien,* located in separate buildings to which pupils often commute.

The least academically accomplished pupils remain in the *Hauptschule,* a neighborhood school often located in the same building as the elementary school. The *Hauptschule* has lost status as a result of increasing enrollment in the two selective secondary schools. Young people with no more than a *Hauptschule* education are increasingly viewed as disadvantaged in the labor market.

All three levels offer a common core of academic subjects, including German, mathematics, social studies, and science—primarily physics and chemistry. Curriculum planners in the various states have attempted in recent years to increase uniformity across school types in these core subjects to facilitate late transitions, reducing the once-and-for-all nature of the differentiation at the end of grade four. Grades five and six, as a result, are designated the "orientation stage" in all three schools. The continuing difficulty of making a late transition is, however, easily imaginable given a selection process that assures faster progress in *Gymnasium* classes than in the *Hauptschule,* regardless of curriculum structure. Moving up a level in the system often requires repeating a year or more; moving down is much simpler and much more common, as in high school tracks in the United States.

During the late 1960s and into the 1970s, secondary school reform was a major item on the West German political agenda.[26] Reformers hoped to attenuate the strict differentiation inherent in the traditional three-level secondary school system. Parents were given a somewhat greater voice in determining which type of school their children attended, though in Bavaria that means nothing more than that they can insist on a three-day trial period in the *Gymnasium* if grades, examination scores, and teacher recommendations do not indicate that their child should be placed there. Transition classes were established to help pupils move to a higher-level school, and pupils in the *Hauptschule* may now enroll for a tenth year, an option taken by about 30 percent of those eligible in 1985.[27] Most dramatically, the second educational path (*der zweite Bildungsweg*) has been expanded, allowing people who did not attend a *Gymnasium* to take college preparatory courses later in life and eventually enroll in a university.

The main focus of these recent reform efforts, however, was on the creation of comprehensive secondary schools to replace the traditional three-level system. Strongly influenced by the United States' comprehensive high schools, reformers pointed to the small proportion of youth pursuing higher education at the university level and argued on democratic grounds for less differentiation, to be accomplished by instituting comprehensive secondary schools. Although the movement was quite successful in a few states with strong leftist political traditions (West Berlin, Bremen, Hesse), it lost momentum by the late seventies.[28] Nationwide only 4.5 percent of secondary school pupils are enrolled in comprehensive schools (*Gesamtschulen*)[29] and half of those schools are in reality the three traditional types of schools housed under one roof.[30]

Rather than structural changes, changes in enrollment patterns have had the strongest effect on opening up the West German secondary schools. In 1952, the *Volksschule* was truly the people's school, enrolling more than 70 percent of 11- to 14-year-olds. By 1975, however, the renamed *Hauptschule* with an added ninth grade enrolled less than half of the 11- to 14-year-olds.[31] The pupils lost to the *Hauptschule* enrolled in *Realschulen* and *Gymnasien*. In 1984, 23.1 percent of 13-year-old males were enrolled in *Realschulen* and 25.5 percent in *Gymnasien*. Among females of the same age, 28.5 percent were in *Realschulen* and 28.4 percent in *Gymnasien*.[32] The fact that female enrollment in *Gymnasien* had surpassed male enrollment by the 1980s is noteworthy as an indication of changing expectations regarding appropriate schooling and occupational prospects for women.

The three types of secondary schools are designed to prepare young people for employment at three different levels of the occupational hierarchy. *Hauptschulen* are for those whose futures lie primarily in manual, clerical, and semiskilled service fields. After completing the *Hauptschule,* males move into vocational training in the skilled and semiskilled trades, especially in the handcraft sector. Females go on to training and employment in semiskilled office work, retail sales, and domestic services. *Hauptschüler* may become carpenters, auto mechanics, office assistants, and saleswomen in bakeries; *Realschüler* become laboratory technicians, precision mechanics, secretaries, and personnel managers.

Increased enrollment in *Realschulen* reflects pupils' and parents' perception of several advantages to the longer and more intensive instruction found there compared to the *Hauptschule.* One is that graduates, who receive a certificate called the *mittlere Reife,* literally "intermediate maturity," are entitled to enter a wide range of full-time vocational schools. A second advantage for *Realschüler* is that they can enter apprenticeships in higher-level occupations and in more desirable firms. Third, if they choose to enter the same occupations that *Hauptschüler* enter, they have a strong advantage in the competition for apprenticeship places. Moreover, holding the *mittlere Reife* allows them to pursue further vocational education after or while they are employed full-time, without supplementary academic instruction, which *Hauptschüler* are required to take before entering the same schools. Increasingly, the *Realschule* is seen as the new minimum standard of educational attainment, required to achieve the same level in the occupational hierarchy formerly attainable by *Volksschule/Hauptschule* graduates.[33] In 1982, half (49.4 percent) of those completing *Hauptschule* and more than one-third (38 percent) of those completing *Realschule* became apprentices.[34]

The *Gymnasium* is by far the most prestigious secondary school for the simple reason that it leads directly to the university, which is the only route to professional status. Obtaining satisfactory grades and passing an examination at the end of grade thirteen confers the *Abitur,* the certificate required for university enrollment. Perhaps the most dramatic change in the paths young people take through the educational system, and the most dramatic proof of apprenticeship's vitality, is the rising proportion of *Abiturienten* (those qualified to enter universities by virtue of holding an *Abitur*) choosing to enter apprenticeship instead. In 1982, 6.8 percent of all apprentices were eligible to attend universities or other *Hochschulen.*[35] This figure is rising as a result of declining job opportunities for university graduates and the increasing popularity of "double qualification," that is, a formerly redundant combination of postsecondary school credentials with apprenticeship certification.[36]

Universities in West Germany are narrower institutions than U.S. colleges and universities. Traditionally they offered only the arts and sciences; in recent years, applied courses of study in such fields as engineering, business, and teaching have gained university status. German universities are more professionally oriented than those in the United States in the sense that entering students are expected to have received their broad general education in the *Gymnasium*. They are admitted, therefore, not to the university as a whole but to what would be called a departmental major in the United States, such as physics or sociology. But the professional orientation goes further. Future doctors and lawyers, for example, are admitted directly from the *Gymnasium* into terminal medical or legal courses of study, which last six or seven years. Thus, German universities can be thought of as offering the third and fourth years of college in the United States along with graduate and professional education, without a separation between undergraduate and graduate programs.

Young people planning to enter upper-level business careers often enroll in a *Fachhochschule*. A *Hochschule,* literally translated as "high school," is an institution of higher education. The term covers the entire range of such institutions, including universities. *Fachhochschulen* are comparable to technical and applied majors in U.S. universities such as business, agriculture, and design. Sometimes they are combined with universities in *Gesamthochschulen,* which look much like public colleges and universities in the United States but are viewed with suspicion by many West German academics who fear they dilute the academic integrity of the universities.

Figure 4–1 schematically represents the main streams in the West German educational system and their relationships to each other. Some possible paths are not represented, most notably the "second educational path," by which skilled workers who have completed their apprenticeship may take courses in an evening *Gymnasium* and then enter a university.

Over the past two decades the *Hochschulen* have grown dramatically. Critics of the West German educational system in the 1950s and 1960s argued that democratic principles and an increasingly technological economy required the abandonment of elitism in higher education, pointing in contrast to the far higher levels of enrollment in the United States and the Scandanavian countries.[37] Sharp increases in the proportion of young people enrolling in *Gymnasien,* combined with a rising birth rate, pushed the total number of pupils in the upper level of the *Gymnasien* from 211,700 in 1960 to 672,100 in 1982.[38] An increasing proportion of *Gymnasium* graduates also chose to enroll in universities over this period—though in recent years that trend has reversed—and, when combined with those seeking university entrance from newly opened alternatives to the *Gymnasium,* they put intolerable pressure on the universities.[39]

The result of that pressure has been that *Gymnasium* graduates no longer have unrestricted choice of where and what they will study. The *numerus clausus,* an admissions procedure based on school grades and examination scores, has been invoked to limit admissions to popular majors and popular universities, and to control the number of doctors, lawyers, engineers, and other professionals who are released on the labor market each year. Although the idea of selecting the best applicants for the most desirable university positions seems perfectly justifiable to Americans accustomed to competitive admissions, the Germans' uneasi-

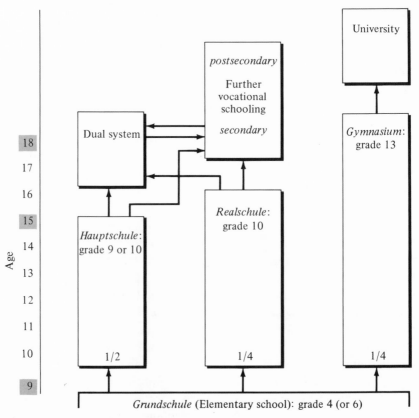

Figure 4–1 The West German Educational System

Adapted from Max Planck Institute for Human Development and Education, *Between Elite and Mass Education: Education in the Federal Republic of Germany,* Albany, NY: State University of New York Press, 1983, p. 68.

ness about it reflects the status of higher education as a basic right, as accessible as elementary and secondary education. The notion of a private university is viewed by many Germans with great suspicion. Only recently have serious attempts been made to found one. Universities and other *Hochschulen* are public, tax supported, and open to all who have satisfied the academic qualifications. There is no tuition fee; government grants and loans are freely available to students from low-income families. The student's right to higher education is so strong that parents who are financially able to pay their children's living expenses while they are enrolled are legally bound to do so. A student whose parents refuse to pay living expenses may apply for an allowance from the university, which the parents are legally bound to repay.

Both German and American observers continue to compare West Germany's rates of enrollment in higher education unfavorably with those in the United States. An unfavorable comparison can only be sustained, however, for the segment of higher education that the Germans classify as belonging to universities. The comparison looks very different if the more narrowly vocational *Fachhochschulen* are included, as they should be because they are comparable to the business and technical courses available in many American four-year colleges and nearly all two-year colleges, and if part-time enrollment is counted, giving an advantage to the German system, which relies heavily upon apprenticeships and internships. In 1983, 45.9 percent of West Germany's 19-year-olds were enrolled in some form of higher education, compared to 40.9 percent of the same cohort in the United States.[40]

Higher education challenges the standard perception that the United States' school system is more democratic than West Germany's. The absence of financial barriers to enrollment in any institution of higher education for any length of time makes this segment more equally accessible than the American system, with tuition fees that increase as a function of the college's or university's prestige. In West Germany, the absence of ability grouping at the elementary level, combined with policies that promote heterogeneous neighborhoods, leaves the secondary schools most vulnerable to the charge of elitism.

Nevertheless, in both West Germany and the United States young people are treated differently in school depending upon their performance, which tends to reflect their social class backgrounds. Elementary schools are more differentiated in the United States by ability grouping and by dramatic differences among neighborhoods. Secondary schools are more differentiated in West Germany and their school system is more sharply focused on preparing youth for specific jobs, beginning at an early age.

One of the most important reasons for such early differentiation in Germany is the apprenticeship system. Because apprenticeship begins between ages 15 and 18, young people likely to become apprentices are separated early from those headed for further schooling. While this separation has some obvious disadvantages, it also meets the needs of noncollege young people far more effectively than U.S. high schools and unsystematic work experience in the secondary labor market. While treating students differently depending upon their school performance and occupational prospects can be discriminatory, it can also provide a clear path to desirable occupational goals.

Radical critics of the schools in both countries charge them with perpetuating social inequality by selectively fostering high achievement among children of the middle classes. According to this line of argument, schools effectively channel more privileged young people into higher-level schools and school tracks, thus assuring that they can maintain or improve their position in society's hierarchy. Defenders argue, to the contrary, that schools merely identify pupils' academic ability, encouraging those with the requisite capacity to make the most of it and offering attainable alternatives for those without. They argue that the identification process does not reflect the social structure perfectly, proving that there is opportunity for upward and downward social mobility, and further that most of the correlation between social class and school performance is attributable to real differences in academic ability, denying the charge that schools practice social class discrimination.[41]

Some of the differences teachers and counselors see among students on the basis of family background and test scores are, no doubt, valid predictors of future academic performance and life chances. However, many strategies supposedly adopted to maximize the learning of all students actually reduce the opportunities and motivation for learning of those identified as less capable. Schools progressively lower some pupils' aspirations so that eventually they accept modest educational and occupational attainment, taking responsibility personally for failing to achieve more and accepting their lower economic and social status as a result of their personal failings.[42] Furthermore, there is an interaction between schooling and family background that enables young people with better educated parents to take greater advantage of what schools have to offer.[43]

The different forms of higher education and different occupational levels for which the *Hauptschule, Realschule,* and *Gymnasium* prepare young people bespeak clear social class differences. West German schools also play a role in assigning pupils to their future social statuses. The question of whether they moderate existing social class distinctions or whether they merely provide the means by which inequality is passed on from one generation to another is even closer to the top of the political agenda with respect to education in West Germany than in the United States. Considering the clear implications of secondary school type for a pupil's adult social status, it is not surprising that there is a strong association between parents' social status and the types of secondary schools their children attend. The *Hauptschule* is filled, for the most part, with working-class young people, the *Gymnasium* with the offspring of the middle class. Table 4–1 makes this point using father's level of education as the indicator of family social status. This relationship holds as well for father's occupation; even among those fathers with only an eighth-grade *Volksschule* or *Hauptschule* education, the higher their level of occupational training, the more likely their children are to attend selective secondary schools.[44] More recent studies have confirmed this relationship, with one important insight, namely that the *Realschule* has come to enroll a cross section of West German society, its pupils representing proportions of working-class, middle-class, and upper-middle-class children roughly equal to those found in the population as a whole.[45] This evenhandedness reflects the *Realschule's* middle position. It is an avenue of upward mobility for working-class children and an acceptable alternative to university preparation for academically less able middle-class children.

Both American and German schools prepare young people for work at two distinct but complementary levels. At the *general* level, they

Table 4–1 West German Secondary School Enrollment, by Fathers' Highest Level of Education

Type of Secondary School	Fathers' Education	
	Hauptschule/ Volksschule	Higher Education
Hauptschule	77	21
Realschule	13	7
Gymnasium	10	72

SOURCE: Based on 1970 census, reported by Luitgard Trommer-Krug, ''Soziale Herkunft und Schulbesuch,'' in Max Plank-Institut für Bildungsforschung, *Bildung in der Bundesrepublik Deutschland: Daten und Analysen*, Vol. 1 (Reinbek: Rowohlt, 1980), pp. 234–235.

teach basic academic skills that are required in nearly all jobs and they teach such worker virtues as punctuality, orderliness, diligence, and acceptance of authority. General preparation for work has the longest history and begins earliest in a child's school career; it is the contribution that recent school reform reports have identified as most critical. At the *specific* level, vocational schools and programs teach knowledge and skills related to particular occupations. A major difference between U.S. and West German schools is that the latter give considerably more weight to specific preparation for work. Specific preparation for work focuses on the knowledge, attitudes, skills, and behaviors needed in a particular occupation or job. General preparation focuses on what workers need to know and be able to do in any job.

In addition to learning, preparation for work also includes the formation of *occupational aspirations* and the acquisition of *occupation-related learning*. General occupational aspiration means aiming toward a *level* in the occupational hierarchy, such as the professions or the skilled trades. Specific occupational aspiration is directed toward a particular occupation, such as lawyer or plumber. Table 4–2 depicts the intersections of general and specific preparation for work with occupational aspirations and occupation-related learning.

Specific career choice or vocational preference has been the mainstay of both research and practice in the field of vocational guidance in the United States.[46] A major limitation of this perspective, however, is that a substantial portion of the youth population does not and cannot make an informed choice of an occupation. Young people who do not attend college seldom select a career from a range of options by finding the best fit with their interests and styles, nor can they be expected to do so. Their ''choice'' is seriously constrained by labor market conditions, and represents an accommodation to economic reality rather than an optimal match between personal characteristics and job demands. Rather

Table 4–2 Aspects of Preparation for Work

General	Specific
Learning	
Basic academic knowledge and skills; worker virtues	Knowledge, skills, and attitudes required for a specific job
Aspirations	
Level in the occupational hierarchy	Particular occupation or field

than choosing a career, they look for work. For them, occupational *level* is a more realistic target for career planning and guidance than occupational title.[47] Aspirations toward a general level in the occupational hierarchy are much more important in preparing noncollege youth for work than the specific side traditionally stressed by researchers and practitioners in vocational guidance.

"Preparation" encompasses the *learning* of knowledge, skills, and attitudes, *socialization* to adult roles, and *development*. Socialization is conventionally defined as "the process by which individuals acquire the knowledge, skills and dispositions that enable them to participate as more or less effective members of groups and the society."[48] The term has been used by social scientists to designate the influence of adult members of society, especially parents, on the young. There is a static bias to its use in many cases; the unstated assumption is that society remains the same and the young merely grow into it. When work and society are in a state of flux, then it is more useful to attend to the knotty question of how young people can be prepared for an uncertain future.

"Development" is a more inclusive term, used by psychologists and educators to mean both the external influences on a growing human being and the internally driven unfolding of physical, emotional, and cognitive maturation. Bronfenbrenner defines development as "the person's evolving conception of the ecological environment, and his relation to it, as well as the person's growing capacity to discover, sustain, or alter its properties."[49] Learning to work, as noted in Chapter 1, is a key element in the process of development. Placing learning in the context of development serves as a reminder that although specific knowledge and skills can be learned, there is no end to learning. Like development, learning to work is a continuing process. Young people need sufficient learning to assume roles as workers, but the best learning is how to keep learning.

John Dewey warned against treating school as "preparation" for life, a warning that applies equally to the issue of preparing youth for work.

A person, young or old, gets out of his present experience all that there is in it for him at the time in which he has it. When preparation is made the controlling end, then the potentialities of the present are sacrificed to a suppositious future. When this happens, the actual preparation for the future is missed or distorted. The ideal of using the present simply to get ready for the future contradicts itself. It omits, even shuts out, the very conditions by which a person can be prepared for his future. We always live at the time we live and not at some other time, and only by extracting at each present time the full meaning of each present experience are we prepared for doing the same thing in the future. This is the only preparation which in the long run amounts to anything.[50]

American schools are less effective at preparing youth for work than they should be because they force youth to wait too long for the promised rewards and obscure for them the relation between what they are doing now and what they will be doing in the future. The present is used "simply to get ready for the future," rather than as a time that is important for itself.

Young people's preparation for work should include socialization in the sense of acquiring such worker virtues as punctuality, responsibility, diligence, and responsiveness to authority. In the terms used in Table 4–2, employers who say they need workers with good work attitudes and the ability to learn[51] are interested primarily in general learning of basic academic knowledge and skills, and worker virtues. They expect to supply the specific job-related instruction and to inculcate the specific attitudes required by the job. Worker virtues are a special concern for disadvantaged youth, who are often considered deficient for not having learned "middle-class values" in their families, schools, and neighborhoods. Unfortunately, when hiring, most employers must rely upon imperfect indicators of the qualities they seek in workers. Those indicators include educational credentials, "proper" speech and dress, and skin color.[52] Effective preparation for work means successfully imparting to all young people the virtues employers seek in all workers and then clearly communicating to employers that applicants possess those virtues.

The primary contribution schools in both countries make to preparing youth for work is at the general level, and encompasses academic learning, the inculcation of occupational aspirations, and of attitudes and behaviors toward work. Schools teach, or attempt to teach, the basic academic knowledge and skills needed for adult competence in work and citizenship. The depth and extent of academic learning achieved in school vary systematically from one school to another, and from one track to another. Students in higher-level schools and tracks are taught to reason and question, and to express themselves; in low tracks they are expected to learn by rote and to obey. Both instructional style and content tend to match the kinds of jobs students' parents have and that they are expected to assume.

School is where young people learn what level in the occupational hierarchy they can reasonably aspire to enter. Those who do well in school know they can remain in school long enough to compete for occupations requiring advanced educational credentials. Poor school performance is a signal for all that a young person will probably have to accept lower-status employment. Hence, young people trim their aspirations to fit the level of the occupational hierarchy attainable with the amount of schooling they believe they will be able to achieve. The kinds of attitudes and behaviors schools inculcate in students also reflect the level of the occupational hierarchy to which students can aspire.

Public school systems support democratic societies by providing avenues of achievement that do not depend solely upon family background. However, young people from better educated families are better able to take advantage of public schooling. Therefore, it is not enough simply to make schooling available for all.

Reforming schools to make them maximally effective with all young people is a critical need in both countries. However, there are limits to what schools can achieve on their own. In addition to changing schools, the United States needs to develop out-of-school educational opportunities that are more effective with young people who are not satisfied or successful in school. Inevitably a large proportion of those young people will come from families in which their parents also did poorly in school.

Apprenticeship is an educational institution that can complement school as a different and often more effective learning environment. It can also contribute to school effectiveness by demonstrating to young people why they need to learn what schools have to offer. Rather than an alternative to school, apprenticeship is a means of improving schools by linking them more directly with the real world of work.

5

Vocational Schooling

Specific Preparation for Work

Vocational schools were first established as part of the secondary school system in the United States during the four decades spanning the turn of the century. In 1880 there were only a few pioneering schools, mostly private, teaching trade skills to young men. The Smith-Hughes Act of 1917 not only signaled broad acceptance of the idea of vocational education but also gave it unique status as the only part of the school curriculum directly subsidized by the federal government.

An exchange of letters between John Dewey and David Snedden published in *The New Republic* in 1915 clearly stated Dewey's rationale for supporting vocational education.[1] His position was that vocational study is a means to broad educational ends. Snedden argued, in contrast, that education is a means to vocational ends. Snedden's view is frequently associated with willingness to tailor schooling to meet labor market demands and to relate educational programs to quite specific vocations, practices that Dewey and those agreeing with him find repugnant.

Calvin M. Woodward was one of the earliest and most effective advocates of vocational skill training in the schools. Speaking to the National Teachers Association in 1883, his encomium of the "fruits of manual training" included:

1. larger classes of boys in the grammar and high schools;
2. better intellectual development;
3. a more wholesome moral education;
4. sounder judgments of men and things, and of living issues;
5. better choice of occupations;

6. a higher degree of material success, individual and social;
7. the elevation of many of the occupations from the realm of brute, unintelligent labor, to positions requiring and rewarding cultivation and skill;
8. the solution of 'labor' problems.''[2]

For Woodward, ''manual training'' was not solely a means of preparing workers; more importantly it was a means of teaching the same knowledge, skills, and attitudes that the common school taught, but in a more immediate and relevant context. It was a new form of pedagogy suitable to all.

It did not remain so. The manual training movement was quickly taken over by Snedden and others and became a movement for vocational education. They prevailed in part because their arguments proved harmonious with growing reliance on secondary schools to help control some of the turbulent economic, social, and political currents of the time. Rapid industrialization was quickly displacing Thomas Jefferson's vision of the United States as a nation of yeoman farmers with what may have been his worst nightmare: a polyglot assemblage of factory hands and clerks crowded into urban tenements. Although some actively opposed this transformation, many leading citizens sought to ameliorate its worst side effects rather than to resist it. The leading citizens were, after all, increasingly industrialists, businessmen, and financiers themselves, or the professionals who served them. This new class included the most notable beneficiaries of the new industrial order and they defined its emergence as progress.[3]

Vocational schools originated as replacements for apprenticeship. Contemporary commentators described apprenticeship as maladapted to modern industry. Unlike a workshop, they pointed out, a factory did not provide free moments for observation and instruction. Moreover, after scientific management principles were applied to factory work, it demanded only the narrowest range of skills from most workers. Even if factories had been capable of providing substantial skill training, craft skills were no longer so necessary to production.[4]

Active opposition to organized labor was another reason for substituting vocational schooling for apprenticeship. The first school in the United States devoted solely to teaching skilled trades was opened in New York City in 1881 with the avowed purpose of replacing apprenticeship. Its founder declared that the school was needed because apprenticeship was controlled by unions and the unions by foreigners. J. P. Morgan agreed so enthusiastically that he contributed half a million dollars to endow the school.[5]

For Snedden, Charles Prosser, and the other founders of vocational education, the school shop was a place where boys who had no prospects of attending college could learn a trade. To secure support from the leaders of business and industry, they stressed the role of vocational schooling in preparing skilled and disciplined workers. In a climate of growing respect for efficiency and commitment to economic progress, this argument carried great weight.

The Smith-Hughes Act, drafted by Prosser, who was also its most effective lobbyist, codified this view of vocational education by supporting only specific trade training, excluding broadly focused efforts to integrate practical and academic studies. This not only separated vocational education from the mainstream of secondary schooling, but validated the practice of differentiating students according to their probable futures and offering them distinctive courses of study.[6] The history of vocational education warns that connecting school too closely with work can exacerbate schools' contributions to maintaining inequality by reproducing in the school society's occupational hierarchy.

Today the most ardent vocationalists affirm the humanistic purposes of education and few of their opponents would argue that young people should learn nothing in school that might be of use in working life. But the strong difference in emphasis on academic versus vocational studies—on general versus specific preparation for work—persists as a critical theme in debates on education in the United States. Ironically, the secondary school reform movement of the 1980s, though driven by the needs of the labor market and initiated by a conservative administration, has opposed vocationalism in the schools. While excoriating Dewey and the progressive education movement he inspired, contemporary conservative critics of education have espoused many of Dewey's ideas.

This seeming contradiction disappears if the ends/means distinction is applied. Dewey did not oppose vocational instruction, but the distortion of education's purposes that result from giving primacy to economic demands. Schools need to meet society's needs, but those needs are for thoughtful citizens and responsible communities as well as productive workers. He advocated forms of manual training as effective methods of enabling young people to understand and act upon the world around them. He was as strongly opposed to teaching vocational subjects for predominantly vocational ends as he was to teaching academic subjects for that purpose. New perceptions of the educational demands of the workplace have made representatives of business and reformers like William Bennett the most vigorous advocates for academic schooling and the harshest critics of vocational schooling because they now see academic learning as more critical to a larger portion of the workforce than it was in the recent past.

Contemporary vocational programs are offered in comprehensive high schools and in two additional kinds of secondary schools: vocational high schools and area vocational centers, both of which are usually able to provide training that is technically superior to that found in comprehensive high schools because of the concentration of students and resources they allow.[7] Specialized vocational high schools are viable only in metropolitan areas with sufficiently large student populations and adequate transportation. They can attract enough students to fill more narrowly defined and less popular vocational specialties and they can, ideally, devote enough resources to vocational instruction to achieve better results. Most vocational high schools offer courses to prepare students for many different occupations; a few are organized around a particular set of occupations, such as aviation or the performing arts.

Absent the concentration of students found in a metropolitan location, area vocational centers have been developed in more sparsely settled locations to secure the same advantages. While specialized vocational high schools offer academic and vocational courses to full-time students, area vocational centers draw their students from surrounding comprehensive high schools, which teach the academic courses. Students typically are transported by bus from their home school to the area center and back for half of each school day.[8]

The standard array of vocational programs includes: agriculture, distributive education (or marketing), health, occupational home economics, business and office, technical, and trade and industry. An eighth category, consumer and homemaking education, is often included in the list even though it does not prepare students for employment outside the home. There is considerable specialization within some of these categories. For example, trade and industry includes a wide range of specific occupations, such as plumbing, printing, and TV repair. Other categories, such as business and office and distributive education (wholesale and retail commerce), frequently have no further subdivisions.

Descriptions of two vocational schools illustrate some of the key features of secondary vocational education in the United States. The first, "Judson Vocational High School," is located in Washington, D.C.[9] Judson enrolls only males and teaches only traditionally male occupations: automobile repair, barbering, building construction, distributive education, drafting, machining, printing, radio and television repair, shoe repair, small engine repair, and tailoring. Auto mechanics is subdivided into a beginning and an advanced course, automatic transmission repair, and auto bodywork. Construction includes "advanced building construction" as well as programs in carpentry, electrical wiring, and masonry.

Each of these areas is taught in a school shop by one or two teachers who have work experience in the field and are certified in pedagogy—often provisionally, because they lack some educational credentials. Every student spends half the day in a shop and the other half in academic classes: English, social studies, science, math, health, and physical education. The school fields athletic teams in the major sports but sponsors few other extracurricular activities.

The main building is an undistinguished two-story brick rectangle. Unlike most U.S. high schools, it lacks a gymnasium or an auditorium. More seriously, the shops are poorly equipped. Tools are few and simple. Machines are outdated. The auto shops in particular are frequent targets of burglaries, so what tools they manage to acquire are often stolen.

Even more than in other U.S. schools, teachers in academic classes tend to emphasize factual information without attending very much to meaning, application, or critical reflection. Because the students lack academic skills, their first challenge is to get across basic information. Finding that challenge so difficult, teachers seldom encourage students to do more with information than give it back in a quiz or exam. Simplification and repetition are considered the best remedial procedures with high school students who read, on the average, at a fifth grade level.

Pedagogical styles are more varied in the shops, where group instruction is interspersed with individual coaching as students work on practical projects. The students' technical achievements and their prospects for obtaining employment related to the field they are studying vary enormously from one shop to another. Some of the shop teachers have not worked in their trade for decades and have been so worn down by the burdens of teaching that they offer very little to their students. Other teachers are in closer touch with their trade and are more demanding. For example, the shoe repair teacher, who consistently receives the least able students, can essentially guarantee a job for each of his graduates. He works with them patiently and firmly, discusses their progress with their academic teachers, and arranges on-the-job training for them through his many contacts with shoe shops around the city, which then hire the graduates he recommends.

The most critical fact about Judson is not that it is a vocational high school but that it serves a poor minority population and lacks the resources to serve them well. Even if they were well trained, the local labor market and unions would not readily accept black plumbers and masons. Judson has a reputation as a "dumping ground." Its students are among the city's least academically capable. Some of the city's other vocational schools, in contrast, are able to select students with higher grades. They function like "magnet schools." More students apply for places than can be accommodated because these vocational schools are viewed as providing higher-quality education than nonselective comprehensive high schools.

Other urban vocational schools can be found that confront similar challenges more effectively, such as the vocational high school in Atlanta vividly and favorably described in two recent studies of high schools.[10] Judson does, however, represent a widespread use of vocational education as an alternative for young people designated unfit for strictly academic education and the kind of employment that requires it, a use advocated by such diverse figures as Booker T. Washington and Arthur Jensen, and continued despite the objection that it is undemocratic.

An area vocational center in upstate New York contrasts sharply with Judson in many ways.[11] It is located in five well-maintained buildings set in a landscaped campus. Students from eight different school districts are transported by bus for half a day's vocational study every day of their eleventh and twelfth grade years. They take academic courses in their home schools. In the center they can learn: auto repair, auto body repair, small engine repair, carpentry, masonry, printing, welding, computer programming, electronics, commercial art, retailing, health care, cosmetology, data processing, and food preparation. The shops are well equipped and well stocked. They have an atmosphere of purposeful busyness. But a closer look reveals that the center's material provisions do not make it an exemplary setting for learning.

Food preparation, a subdivision of occupational home economics, prepares both boys and girls for employment as cooks in restaurants and cafeterias. The instructional facility includes a classroom area for lectures and teacher demonstrations, and a kitchen equipped for institutional cooking. In order to enhance student interest and motivation, the teacher, Mrs. Carter, has the second-year class plan and prepare meals for the faculty cafeteria. She continually emphasizes the work-relevance of what the students do in school, not only in connection with the real job of preparing food for others to eat but as their work affects their immediate and longer-term opportunities for employment. She often reminds her students that employers ask her to recommend students for part-time work while they are still in school and for full-time jobs upon graduation. Mrs. Carter bases such recommendations, she tells them, not only on students' culinary accomplishments but also on their punctuality, reliability, and responsibility. Failure to complete assignments, disruptive behavior, and other expressions of noncompliance are treated as signs of unreadiness for employment rather than simply infractions against class- room norms.

The classroom's modeling of a workplace includes regular rotation of tasks among students so that each has the experience of doing everything from planning the week's menu, ordering the food, and supervising the other student cooks to washing and cutting vegetables and cleaning up. A coffee break provides a respite from class work in a form that both teacher and students regard as realistic.

Mrs. Carter and her aide, Mrs. Lynd, are consistently supportive of the students. Their warmth and concern extend well beyond ordinary expectations of teachers. When one boy began to have school problems because his parents were breaking up, Mrs. Carter invited him to move in with her family temporarily, and he lived there for several months. She and Mrs. Lynd consistently treat mistakes as opportunities for learning rather than grounds for censure. They set deadlines for completion of assignments, but routinely grant exceptions.

The teachers' strong commitment to bolstering students' confidence and preventing them from feeling inadequate had both positive and nega- tive aspects. Several students regularly avoided responsibility by taking advantage of the teachers' solicitous behavior. When students asked for help, one of the teachers would frequently perform the task for them. Classmates were ready to do the same. A boy who lacked confidence to plan a menu, for example, simply asked for suggestions from his friends and then took them to Mrs. Carter, who made some changes to add variety and then "his" menu was complete.

But questions about the long-term value of this type of education go deeper than issues of pedagogical style and classroom interaction. The program is organized around the explicit expectation that students will enter careers in food preparation. Questioned about their future plans, however, only half said they planned such careers. The others thought they might work in the field but hoped to find employment elsewhere. Why were they enrolled then? One reason was that it promised a back- up source of employment in case they could not find work in their preferred field right away. More pervasively, they saw vocational classes in the area center as much more congenial than academic classes in the home school. Demands are lighter; classmates are more socially compat- ible and less competitive academically. Students valued the knowledge and skills being taught because they could be used in the real world and because learning them involved some immediate hands-on activity. As one girl put it,

I think it's 100 percent better than school. You get to come up and you *do* it. You plain and simple *do* it. Down there [in the comprehensive high school] you just read about it, write about it. You *do* it up here. I love that.

A vocational course, in short, is an attractive alternative to academic classes for all; it is career preparation only for some.

For students, vocational education is appealing as a more comfortable means of fulfilling their obligation to earn a high school diploma. It is more comfortable because it seems more real, being tied to employment, because it removes them from the losing competition of the academic classroom, because it involves a more active and more tactile approach to learning. It provides a safe niche for students who do not do well in academic classes.[12]

Reinforcing the idea that schools channel youth toward different levels of the social system, the employment prospects and the values associated with high school vocational education attract young people from lower-class families and then, by reinforcing those prospects and values, perpetuates subordinate socioeconomic status. All but two of the food preparation students came from families in which parents held blue-collar jobs. When they were interviewed, parents expressed a lack of respect for educational credentials and asserted the primacy of employment security over occupational and class mobility. They clearly preferred that their children learn a low-level trade and then be steadily employed to having them aspire to higher levels of education and career. Several spoke disparagingly of college graduates who could find no suitable employment and took jobs like their own, which they performed without distinction. They described this situation as a waste, not because there were too few jobs that require a college degree but because the graduates need not have gone to the trouble and expense of college.

Although Mrs. Carter's food preparation class cannot be regarded as adequately representing the range of secondary vocational programs, her students are representative in many ways of vocational high school students across the country. As in her class, large-scale surveys have found that vocational enrollees tend to have working-class backgrounds.[13] Closely allied with their family backgrounds, vocational students consistently have poorer academic records than those in college preparatory programs.[14] Other studies have also found that many students enrolled in vocational programs have no intention of entering the vocation for which they are ostensibly being trained,[15] which proves to be a significant point because the benefits of secondary vocational education accrue to those who find related employment.

This finding is a recent one and helps to explain the ambiguity of previous studies, which reported mixed employment outcomes for vocational graduates.[16] High school graduates identified by analysis of their transcripts as vocational "concentrators," that is, as students who have taken a coherent series of courses in a single specialty, demonstrate somewhat higher rates of employment and earnings than graduates of the general track, but the advantages are small.[17] More impressive advantages are obtained by vocational concentrators who subsequently find jobs related to their training. These students experience higher labor force participation, lower unemployment, and higher earnings than comparable graduates of the general track. However, only about one-third of vocational graduates find training-related jobs. Furthermore, half of the students who take vocational courses do so unsystematically, failing to acquire vocationally useful training.[18]

The conclusion best supported by available evidence is that secondary vocational schooling can provide education and training that prove useful in the labor market, but that it does not do so consistently for the majority of enrollees. Further testimony to its limited impact comes from skilled workers asked to identify the most important sources of their skills— looking backward in time rather than forward. As noted in Chapter 3, most craftsmen (60 percent) say they learned their skills informally while on the job. Far fewer (11 percent) attribute their skills primarily to formal apprenticeship, and even fewer (8 percent) to vocational schooling, and formal on-the-job training (4 percent). The trend from 1963 to 1976 was toward citing training provided by firms more and that provided by vocational schools less.[19]

If vocational studies in high school have only limited impact on subsequent occupational attainment, they might be justified as a first step toward further education and training. Here the evidence is consistent: vocational graduates are less likely than general graduates to enter higher education. When they do, they are more likely to enroll in technical schools than in four-year colleges.[20] Students who concentrate on vocational courses begin high school with lower educational aspirations than general students, but even after initial differences have been statistically controlled, they are less likely to enroll in postsecondary education.[21] It may be that initial advantages enjoyed by some vocational graduates in the labor market serve more to reduce educational aspirations than to provide lasting occupational benefits. Perhaps it is because they believe their vocational training is all they need that they do not pursue further education that would, in the long run, be more likely to advance their careers.

The evidence makes it difficult to describe secondary vocational education as a successful enterprise. However, its limited effectiveness cannot be explained solely as a fault of the educational system. The youth labor market conditions described in Chapter 2 are also implicated. If employers refuse to hire recent high school graduates, then high schools alone cannot be blamed for the failure of vocational training to confer labor market advantages. The fact that those advantages are selective rather than universal says something about the way the labor market operates. Employers, particularly large firms, often do not expect to hire trained workers but to provide training. They look, therefore, for applicants with the lowest probable training costs. Academic competence and "industrial discipline"—worker virtues—are the two principal characteristics sought under these circumstances. Only when specific job skills are easily transferable, effectively taught in classrooms, and relatively expensive for employers to teach will they be marketable in the sense of giving applicants who have them an advantage.[22] Typing is the exemplar of such a skill. It does not vary from one employer to another as, for example, machinists' equipment and tasks do. It is amenable to classroom instruction. And learning it takes enough time that employers would find it costly to teach. Therefore, employers seek and hire vocational graduates who have learned to type in school.[23]

Because most of the jobs employers are prepared to offer to recent high school graduates require only minimal skills, teenage workers are often unable to use their high school vocational training. Often by the time they are judged mature enough to be hired in positions requiring skill and offering advancement possibilities, their high school skills have faded. Vocational teachers who take an active role in placing their students, like Mrs. Carter, the Food Preparation teacher at the Area Vocational Center, improve the entry rates of their students into related jobs. High school administrative procedures can also help; guidance offices that are accustomed to mailing transcripts to support college applications may be quite unresponsive to local employers' requests for information about vocational graduates, thereby depriving those graduates of formal confirmation that they had obtained relevant training.[24]

The greatest value of vocational education in the youth labor market, with some exceptions, is in providing some hands-on work experience and in convincing some employers that it certifies good work habits, reliability, and capacity to learn. It is notable that if moving students into related employment is the criterion, then the most effective form of secondary vocational education is cooperative education, described in Chapter 3 as embodying elements of apprenticeship. About half of cooperative education students are employed after graduation in the same firm where they had their placement.[25] This finding demonstrates again that employers seek to reduce the risk of hiring young workers. They are more likely to make a longer-term commitment after trying them out in a training role.

If the contribution of vocational schooling to the specific preparation of youth for work cannot be firmly substantiated, what about its contribution to the broad education of youth who do not thrive in academic classrooms? Do those students learn more than they would in regular academic classrooms? This is not a question that has often been addressed, but the study that addresses it most convincingly supplies a negative answer. Academic achievement test scores of males in the High School and Beyond study (a nationally representative sample surveyed repeatedly) were used to assess how much was learned during the three years of high school. Initial differences in test scores were statistically controlled so that the increase in performance could be analyzed separately. Academic graduates gained 0.13 of a standard deviation over their tenth grade mean score, but male vocational graduates gained only 0.04. Males who dropped out in their senior year gained 0.03.[26] Vocational schooling does not appear to teach academic content very well.

This attenuation of academic learning is not a necessary consequence of vocational enrollment. It occurs when vocational courses replace academic courses or when academic courses designed for vocational students are less rigorous. Vocational students who continue to take demanding academic courses and whose vocational courses also include substantive academic content gain in basic skills at a rate comparable to that of nonvocational students.[27]

Secondary vocational schooling effectively prepares some young people for employment, notably office workers, but subsequent occupational attainment is no greater for the majority of vocational students who do not find related employment than for graduates of the general track, and inferior to that of academic graduates. The fact that some vocational graduates succeed in capitalizing on their training is used to justify a system that serves many students as an alternate path to high school graduation while making less rigorous academic demands. Unfortunately, it also teaches less academic content, which is the learning that is most useful in the labor market.

While these conclusions could be used to argue for the abolition of vocational schooling, they could equally well be used to argue for its improvement. Particularly in view of testimony from many vocational students that they would have dropped out rather than remain in the general track and in view of the academic and vocational effectiveness of some programs, vocational schooling has a place in secondary education. Its principal purpose, however, should be to provide an alternate path to general education more than training for specific jobs. Furthermore, it should be closely linked with work experience rather than predominantly school-based.

The United States' commitment to preparing youth for adulthood by means of schools is demonstrated by the recent growth of two-year colleges and other postsecondary schools. Although by definition two-year colleges do not serve the half of the youth population whose schooling terminates with high school, they provide vocational education to large numbers of youth and young adults.

Two-year colleges may be either community colleges or technical colleges. The latter generally serve a larger region and offer a more specifically vocational curriculum. However, most community colleges offer vocational courses. Community colleges generally serve four kinds of students. One kind of student hopes to continue on to a four-year college. For this purpose, the name "junior college" is appropriate. A second set of students seek a terminal two-year degree with a vocational focus. These students might also enroll in a technical college. Some students enroll for certification programs requiring less than two years, for example, in real estate. A fourth group of students take courses without working toward degrees or certification; they might be called recreational learners. The last two categories are combined and labeled "continuing education" students in statistical reports. In addition to public two-year and technical colleges, postsecondary vocational education is offered by private "proprietary" schools.

Two-year colleges have grown explosively in the second half of the twentieth century. In 1953–54, 594 institutions in the United States enrolled just over 600,000 students in courses for credit. Thirty years later, 1,219 institutions enrolled almost 5 million students in courses for credit and nearly the same number of additional students taking noncredit courses.[28] From 1970 to 1983, community college enrollments grew by 113 percent, compared to 22 percent for four-year colleges. In all types of postsecondary institutions, more than 9 million students were enrolled in academic courses in 1982, nearly 3.8 million in vocational courses, and more than 5 million in continuing education.[29]

A study comparing 1972 and 1980 high school graduates found a substantial increase in postsecondary vocational enrollment, from 14.8 percent of the class of 1972 to 17.9 percent of the class of 1980. Much of this increase was accounted for by the increase in high school vocational students continuing their vocational studies at the postsecondary level.[30]

Despite its magnitude, postsecondary vocational education has not been extensively studied in terms of graduates' experience in the workforce. One difficulty in undertaking such an assessment is that the age and attendance patterns of students are highly diverse. Forty-four percent of students at community colleges and half at public technical colleges are over the age of 25,[31] meaning that they have already acquired considerable work experience. Many such students attend school part-time to improve their qualifications in the field where they are already employed full-time.

The kinds of careers two-year college graduates enter overlap considerably with those for which high school vocational programs offer training, for example, welder, mason, typist, drafter, cook, machinist, and cosmetologist. Indeed, some high school vocational graduates continue their training in two-year colleges before entering the full-time workforce. However, a higher rung of careers is also accessible via two-year college vocational programs, including nurse, computer programmer, legal aide, and technicians in such fields as engineering, electronics, aviation, and communications.

Although some community and technical colleges maintain excellent ties with local business and industry, thereby improving their graduates' employment prospects, many of the problems of secondary vocational schooling are found at the postsecondary level too: outmoded equipment; a limited supply of qualified instructors; and employers' preference for training their own workers. Postsecondary vocational schools often take the needs of the local or regional labor market very seriously, but are not always able to meet them. It is the closest the United States comes to a system preparing youth for work, but it fails to bridge school and career as apprenticeship does in West Germany.

West Germany's vocational schools complement apprenticeship rather than standing alone. Schooling is compulsory in West Germany to age 18. However, participation in the dual system of apprenticeship combined with part-time vocational schooling discharges the school attendance obligation.

An array of postsecondary vocational schools (e.g., *Berufsfachschulen*, *Fachoberschulen*) makes it possible for young people to prolong their full-time schooling before entering apprenticeships, return to full-time schooling following completion of an apprenticeship, or enroll in full-time schooling as an alternative to apprenticeship in preparation either for employment or for higher education.[32] Training for some occupations, nursing is an example, occurs exclusively in postsecondary vocational schools—with extensive on-the-job training—but for most occupations and among most parents and young people, the dual system remains not only the traditional but the most desirable bridge from school to career. Its enduring appeal is indicated by the increasing number of *Gymnasium* graduates who choose to become apprentices.

Berufsschulen are the vocational schools that apprentices attend part-time. The word *Berufsschule* translates literally as vocational school, but is applied only to part-time vocational schools. *Berufsschulen* contribute to the preparation of youth for work by providing continuing general education through courses in social studies and German and by providing "theoretical" background instruction as a basis for the more practical knowledge apprentices learn in their workplaces. In addition, *Berufsschulen* for manual workers teach specific skills in school shops.

The system of apprenticeship combined with vocational schooling embodies several dualities.[33] In addition to the dual learning settings— *Berufsschule* and workplace—there is a long-standing duality in German thinking between general education and vocational training.[34] The German word for education (*Bildung*) was traditionally applied only to academic education in the arts and sciences. An educated person, in this view, was one who knew classical literature and history and who could apply its lessons to his own self-improvement. (The masculine pronoun used here reflects traditional assumptions about who could be educated.) Being educated was identical to being cultured. Training (*Ausbildung*) and vocational training (*Berufsausbildung*) were entirely different from education and could not be attempted in "educational" institutions. Hence separate secondary schools were created, with only the *Gymnasium* being a truly educational institution in the sense of the word *Bildung*.

Enunciated most authoritatively by Wilhelm von Humboldt, this principle guided the development of the Prussian school system early in the nineteenth century and spread throughout Germany along with Prussian hegemony. Georg Kerschensteiner, the educational philosopher and reformer who was responsible more than any other individual for the development of the *Berufsschulen*, disagreed with this philosophy and argued instead that vocational schooling could also contribute to character development (*Menschenbildung*).

After the horrors of World War II, Germans had to confront the question of how their culture had contributed to the rise of National Socialism. In order to instill resistance in the next generation to Nazi-style totalitarianism and inhumanity, changes were instituted in the educational system as part of reconstruction. Many leaders of that effort blamed the narrowly technical nature of *Berufsschule* training for the failure of German workers to oppose the Nazis effectively. At the same time, the efficacy of classical education as *Menschenbildung* was called into question by the distressing lack of resistance by graduates of *Gymnasien* and universities. Moreover, an entire generation of young people that had grown up under the pernicious influence of Nazi schools and propaganda now had to be prepared for citizenship in a democracy.

Enrolling the majority of youth, the *Berufsschulen* necessarily assumed a share of this new responsibility, adding courses in social studies that emphasized civic education. Although some employers objected to the diversion of time from technical training and production work, the task of the *Berufsschulen* was broadened to include educating young people for citizenship as well as training them for a vocation. No longer was it assumed that apprentices' absorption on the job of their trade's ethos and ethics was sufficient socialization, along with that provided by family and church, to prepare them to function as adult members of a community and a nation.

However, vocational education continued to be seen as inferior to academic education. Germans successfully resisted strong pressure from the occupying powers, especially the United States and France, to abandon their three-level secondary school system in favor of American- or French-style systems. *Gymnasium* and university continued to be seen as the province of a small elite, with the *Volksschule* and apprenticeship for the masses, though the distinction between general education and vocational training was softened somewhat.

Along with dual locations and the duality of education and training, theory and practice constitute a third duality in the system. The *Berufsschulen* are expected to provide apprentices with the foundations upon which their work is based. *Fachtheorie,* the principles and information basic to one's specialty, is one of the courses taught in *Berufsschulen.* For auto mechanics, it includes such topics as metallurgy, the chemistry of synthetic automobile parts, and the evolution of automobile steering systems. Rather than studying general mathematics, apprentice auto mechanics study *Fachrechnen,* the calculations used by machinists; *Industriekaufleute* study accounting. Social studies classes for both examine legal and economic issues affecting apprentices directly, such as the rights of workers and voting procedures.

Although duality between theory and practice is expressed by emphasis on theory in the *Berufsschulen* and practice in the workplace, the integration of the two is perhaps more striking than their separation. Germans expect tilers, electricians, bakery salespersons, and all other working people to understand the fundamental principles of their trade before being authorized to practice it. Being able to perform the tasks is not sufficient.

Integration is far from perfect, however. Another duality in the system is a separation of control between its two parts. Employers control apprentices' on-the-job training, and organize it to meet the needs of their own firms. The states control the *Berufsschulen* and feel more obligation than employers to address the individual needs of pupils and the society's need for broadly trained workers and well-educated citizens, though they are strongly influenced by the employers' chambers. As a result, coordination between work site and school is less than ideal. Nevertheless, reliance in both workplace and school on a uniform plan, jointly determined by employers, teachers, and unions, and evaluated by a qualifying examination, adds coherence to the apprentice's learning in *Berufsschule* and workplace.

Georg Wanner, the third-year apprentice in a large industrial auto repair firm whose workplace was described in Chapter 3, begins his day in the *Berufsschule* for auto mechanics at 7:30. It is a grey stone building with a new brick addition, located in a downtown neighborhood. Despite careful maintenance, the classrooms and halls are drab. Crucifixes adorn the walls of most classrooms, but not a single flag. Crucifixes are typical of Catholic Bavaria. The absence of flags is typical of West Germany, where National Socialism and the partitioning of the nation have given patriotism and its trappings a bad reputation.

The apprentices from Georg's firm attend *Berufsschule* as a group, without apprentices from other firms. Smaller firms have only a few apprentices and try to arrange their schedules so they attend school on different days because it would disrupt the shop if they were all away at the same time.

The day's first subject is technical drawing. The teacher, Herr Schraeder, spends a few minutes chatting informally with the apprentices. Then he announces that it is time "to attack" (*angreifen*) and switches on the overhead projector to display a technical drawing. The apprentices take out small plastic drawing boards and begin to set them up as he gives an assignment, noting that the lesson is an important one for the qualifying examination.

The atmosphere is relaxed but businesslike. Pupils talk together in low voices, mostly to help each other with the exercise. Herr Schraeder helps as needed. While showing me his notebook filled with overhead transparencies, he comments that technical drawing is an important subject because it enables a mechanic who has an idea to explain it to his supervisor much more effectively than purely in words.

It may be that this rationale for technical drawing is nothing but a rationalization for teaching something that an auto mechanic might well never use in a lifelong career. The assumption is striking, though, that an auto mechanic should be equipped from the beginning to communicate ideas about his work. One of the attractive features of the dual system is that its inclusion of "theory" prepares workers for advancement. Instead of learning only those skills required to get a job done, apprentices are expected to learn enough about the principles and purposes of their work to understand how their daily tasks fit into a larger productive process and to move easily into other and more responsible positions. The best reason to teach a shoe salesperson about inventory, which the dual system does, is that the apprentice is a potential manager and shop owner.

The second notable feature of this class, observed in all classes visited, was its informality. German classrooms no longer conform to the stereotype of Prussian discipline. The traditional authority of the teacher began to be loosened after World War II as part of democratization. Widespread student demonstrations in the late 1960s succeeded in reducing teachers' unilateral authority even further at all levels of the educational system.[35] *Berufsschule* pupils were free to leave the classroom at will and to eat and drink during class. Side conversations during a lesson were frequent and often disruptive. Pupils protested quickly against teachers' demands when they thought them too harsh. Several vocational school teachers volunteered that pupils were no longer so much under their thumbs, always quickly adding that they would not have it any other way. One teacher bolstered this point by saying the adults she had taught were annoyingly passive in contrast.

At 8:35 Herr Schraeder dismisses the class. Georg and half of the other apprentices move to the shop where the next class is held, one of four large shops in the new part of the school building. It is bright and clean and filled with tools and machinery, including a dozen automobile engines, each mounted on a stand and ready to operate. Herr Schraeder comments that automobile and truck manufacturers have donated much of the equipment to help improve instruction for their apprentices.

Fachpraxis (shop) and *Fachtheorie* are taught by different sets of teachers. Shop teachers are closer in education and style to practitioners of the craft; teachers of "theory" are more like academic teachers. In contrast to Herr Schraeder's jacket and tie, Herr Lange wears blue jeans and a sweatshirt under his blue shop coat. Only 10 of the 17 apprentices from the technical drawing class are in Herr Lange's shop class now because they are divided into two groups to make shop class sizes smaller. The topic for the day is brake cylinders, hydraulic devices that transfer the force of a driver's foot on a brake pedal to a vehicle's brakes.

With the pupils lined up in two rows of tablet-arm desks, Herr Lange draws a diagram on the blackboard and asks them to fill in information as he proceeds. Wanner and others ask questions in addition to answering his. One makes a joking comment and Lange tells him he is correct. After half an hour, he moves the class to a pair of tables at the back of the shop, where he shows them an actual brake cylinder with part of its casing sliced off end-to-end to reveal its inner workings. He quickly disassembles it, placing each part on the table as he names it; they are the same parts he had described at the blackboard. He calls attention to one small part, saying the qualifying examination will probably ask them to identify it.

Pointing out that this brake cylinder is an old one, Herr Lange brings out another one that also has part of the casing sliced off. This one, he explains, is a dual cylinder from a truck. The pupils participate in naming the parts and describing their functions as he disassembles it. When two pupils begin to talk to each other, he turns and tells them sharply to stop. One pupil points to a screw-on cap with a spring and asks what it is. Herr Lange asks if any of the pupils can identify it. After several incorrect guesses, he says it is a second valve and explains why there are two. Finally he produces a third cylinder, smaller than the others, from a contemporary automobile. When a pupil idly begins reassembling the first cylinder, Lange encourages him to complete the job and the others to watch. Distribution of homework sheets marks the end of the class.

Pedagogically, this lesson was most impressive. Herr Lange engaged the apprentices in a steady dialogue, calling alternately for brief and extended answers to questions that sometimes elicited recall of facts and sometimes reasoning. His pupils asked him questions frequently, something rarely observed in other classes. He readily adapted his plans to pupils' interests, by incorporating one boy's reassembly of a brake cylinder, for example. The lesson moves briskly and logically from the blackboard presentation to the hands-on demonstration of brake cylinders.

It drew upon knowledge the apprentices had already gained from their other classes and their work experience, but elaborated and deepened that knowledge: previously none of them could have explained why a cylinder has two valves or why its piston has holes in it. Vocational education of this quality is education in the best sense of the word. Georg Wanner and his peers were not only learning facts about brake cylinders but also how to pose and answer questions. They were engaged with the lesson throughout and far more active than in their other classes.

The third class, beginning at ten o'clock, following a 15-minute break for *Brotzeit* (morning snack or coffee break), is *Fachtheorie*. It is held in a regular classroom. The main topic is steering mechanisms, illustrated by a large working model with bicycle wheels and a steering wheel.

Following a question and answer review of previous work, Herr Bohle gives a brief history of steerable wheels, beginning with Egyptian carts. He contrasts the simplest method of turning wheels, the solid front axle that pivots around one point like a child's wagon, with the geometric method invented in France, which allows the wheels to remain in the same location relative to the vehicle. He asks the pupils to recall childhood experiences of tipping over in their wagons when they turned too sharply.

He then explains some of the disadvantages of the geometric system using a diagram on an overhead projector and the model. One pupil's extended answer to his question stimulates a prolonged discussion.

The content of this class illustrates the importance attached to "theory" in the dual system. The apprentices could certainly become adept at repairing steering mechanisms without knowing how they evolved from ox-drawn carts. But they are expected to understand their work more fundamentally. The historical review gave them an understanding of *why* steering mechanisms are designed as they are.

Religious instruction, Wanner's next class, is required in Bavaria but is not included in the qualifying examination. Protestants go to a separate classroom. Non-Christians, mostly Moslems from Turkey, are excused, as are agnostics and atheists.

At 11:30 a gong sounds over the intercom system and Herr Bohle leaves the room. The pupils remain in the room and a few minutes later the religion teacher arrives. The atmosphere changes immediately. The apprentices suddenly become loud and combative.

Herr Kreuzer calls the roll amid loud talking and much coughing, receiving rude responses from several pupils. He then announces that the topic for the day is Paul's letter to Philemon, which was written to be carried by an escaped slave whom Paul had instructed to return to his master. His theme is that Catholic writers and social workers in the early nineteenth century anticipated Marx by introducing the principle that workers should be treated as human beings and advocating what is now called *Mitbestimmung,* the right of workers to participate in management decisions. LaSalle, he says, was a better communist than Marx but called for love rather than class war.

This theme, an example of relating general education to appretices' occupational interests, was lost, however, in Herr Kreuzer's random ruminations on Brotherhood Week, the need for understanding between Christians and Jews, the unpredictability of life, and the inconsistency he perceived in people who demonstrate against nuclear weapons while advocating abortion. Some of the pupils were surely sophisticated enough politically to realize that Herr Kreuzer was propagandizing on behalf of the conservative Christian-Social Union (Bavarian partner of the Christian Democratic party) in opposition to the leftist Social Democrats.

As the time approaches when the class will end, apprentices begin to move about, some even standing. When some begin to leave, Herr Kreuzer demands that they clean up the room first, but no one pauses and the room is quickly deserted. He walks over to tell me that this class is especially rowdy. Their fathers, he says, all work for their training firm—implying that they would not otherwise have achieved such a prestigious apprenticeship and that they believe they need not work hard. But the real problem, he says, is having the class just before lunch. They would be better if he taught them earlier.

Perhaps the timing was a valid explanation for the apprentices' behavior; their fathers did not in fact work in the firm. But a more convincing explanation is that they were reacting against the requirement that they study religion and against Herr Kreuzer's rather sanctimonious manner. One could imagine, while listening to him state his opinions so venomously, that Herr Kreuzer saw himself as a missionary preaching the Gospel to the heathen and, having despaired of saving their souls, persevered in the hope that martyrdom would save his own. However, when he taught the same firm's first-year apprentices, both their behavior and his coherence were markedly better.

Social studies begins after lunch, at one o'clock. Herr Reuter is nearing retirement. He projects liveliness and authority. No one misbehaves as he calls the roll. Calling attention to news broadcasts about the twenty-fifth anniversary meeting of NATO leaders in Turkey, he asks a series of questions. The paucity of responses leads him to quip, "Thought questions are not appreciated. Factual questions are easier." Finally, in answer to the question, "What is new in NATO?" a pupil answers that the United States wants the European countries to pay more for defense. The teacher agrees and says the second thing is that the Americans want to develop a space-based defense. "Both," he adds, "will cost you money."

Questioned about interest rates, pupils are able to offer that they are higher in the United States and that the result is climbing interest rates in Germany. The teacher explains that higher interest rates reduce investment and that means fewer workplaces. He stresses that it is important to understand the connections among things, in this case between increased arms spending, higher interest rates, reduced nonmilitary investment, and shortage of workplaces. "How people could live!" he exclaims, if there were no arms race.

Further discussion of investment leads to a question about how Japanese auto makers became so competitive with Germany for the export trade. He answers that they invested while the Germans consumed. The Germans were too self-satisfied. Although the VW beetle was outmoded, it was not changed. Then suddenly it was displaced in world markets by newer Japanese small cars. But now Volkswagen is strong again and, he says, Japanese experts are visiting German auto plants again.

Herr Reuter writes on the board: "*Strukturkrise*" and "*Konjunkturkrise*" (structural crisis and cyclical economic crisis). As an example of a structural crisis, he says that Germany used to sell complete steel mills to third world countries and now those countries are producing cheaper steel. Germany can compete now in the world market only in those industries where skilled workers and advanced technical knowledge are required, he explains. A pupil offers the opinion that the 35-hour workweek, a current and highly controversial union demand, is not possible because of international competition.

Herr Reuter also teaches German and specialized mathematics (*Fachrechnen*), so the apprentices stay with him the remainder of the afternoon. Though the subjects change, his teaching style remains the same: he provides a rich mixture of facts, opinions, and advice, interspersed with his personal experience, stressing the need for his pupils to think but not really giving them opportunities to do so.

The *Berufsschule* for auto mechanics focuses unrelentingly on one occupation. Such a focus is hardly surprising in the courses specifically teaching vocational knowledge, but even in the general academic courses, teachers frequently refer to the pupils' occupation and draw examples from it, as when Herr Reuter talked about economic competitiveness in terms of the automobile industry. Another social studies teacher gave as an example of an interest group influencing political decisions the continuing ability of the West German automobile clubs to defeat legislation establishing a speed limit on the *Autobahn,* despite polls showing a majority of voters in favor of a speed limit. These illustrations helped apprentices learn academic material, by making it more immediately relevant to their own interests; they also reinforced a sense of occupational identity.

Curriculum and instruction were clearly oriented toward the apprentices' qualifying examination. During nearly every day of classroom observation, at least one teacher called attention to items that were important for the examination, as Herr Lange did. But the influence of the examination is even more pervasive. It dominates the *form* of instruction as well as its content. *"Frontaler Unterricht,"* frontal instruction, and handouts are the norm. With some exceptions, the shop teacher, Herr Lange, being the most exemplary, teachers generally limit pupil participation to answering factual questions, and often answer their own questions because the pupils decline to do so. When Herr Reuter said his class preferred factual questions to thought questions, he was quite right, and teachers either share that preference or accede to it when pupils refuse to answer thought questions.

Other investigators have also noted the dominance of the examination and its constraining effect on instructional styles,[36] but the examination cannot carry all the blame. Studies of elementary school instruction have revealed the same reliance on frontal instruction (see Chapter 4),[37] and, though instruction in U.S. schools is probably somewhat more varied, numerous studies have found teacher-centered didactic instruction to be the dominant mode here too, without the excuse of a qualifying examination for the students.[38]

In the technical subjects, where teachers had expert knowledge that the apprentices needed, the information-giving style was understandable, though not necessarily effective, as preparation for the qualifying examination. It was less appropriate for social studies, where the boundaries between knowledge and opinion are not so clear. In religion it seemed totally out of place.

Most of the differences between the *Berufsschulen* for auto mechanics and for *Industriekaufleute* are predictable from the differences between the occupations and the kinds of young people who enter them. The building in which the *Industriekaufleute* apprentices attend classes is also old, sparse, and a bit dingy, though it is located in a more attractive part of the city. All instruction takes place in classrooms; there is no equivalent of the school shop. Perhaps in the future there will be computer labs, but for the moment only a few computers are available to be wheeled from room to room on carts. The pupils, who are nearly all *Realschule* graduates, speak in class more readily and are noticeably better dressed than the auto mechanics. The presence of approximately equal numbers of young women adds a dimension to social interactions that is absent in the all-male school for auto mechanics.

In addition to their instruction in German, social studies, and religion, apprentice *Industriekaufleute* receive instruction in such subjects as accounting, personnel, organizations, materials management, purchasing and sales, and data processing. There is heavy emphasis on knowing and being able to apply the laws governing various transactions. Additional emphases include being able to fill out appropriate forms, to compose letters properly, and knowing how to do certain mathematical calculations.

The mathematical calculations performed by *Industriekaufleute* are not technically difficult; the challenge is learning what factors must be included and where to find the required figures. In one class, for example, the teacher pointed out differences between the costs considered for bookkeeping purposes and those included in the calculations used to determine the sale price of a product. This *Vorkalkulation* (precalculation) was then contrasted with the *Nachkalkulation* (postcalculation) performed after the product has been delivered, in order to determine whether the sale price was appropriate and what the profit or loss to the company was.

The training of *Industriekaufleute*, in other words, entails a considerable amount of applied economics, not just math. The importance of international trade heightens this need, requiring them to understand the intricacies of currency exchange rates and the *Umsatzsteuer*, the tariff that is charged on imported goods to prevent them from being unfairly competitive with domestic goods for which a value-added tax must be paid.

When asked whether they were, overall, satisfied or dissatisfied with their vocational schools, the 21 interviewed apprentices divided by occupation. Six of the eight auto mechanics said they were satisfied, while nine of the thirteen *Industriekaufleute* said they were dissatisfied. Reasons given for satisfaction reflected the stated purpose of the vocational school: to provide a foundation for and to enlarge upon practical training on the job. A few contrasted the *Berufsschule* favorably with their previous school; they liked attending only part-time and studying practical subjects.

The *Industriekaufleute*, being more dissatisfied, also had more suggestions for improvement. Three agreed that religion should be eliminated and two more said it should be replaced by English. Inconsistencies between school instruction and work procedures were criticized, one saying the bookkeeping practices she learned in school were totally different from the computerized system used at Brandt, the large industrial firm. Several complained, as their teachers had, that the eight-hour school days were too long and that too much information was packed into the available time.

Asked whether what they learned in school was important for their occupation and as adults and citizens, 18 of the 21 apprentices said yes. Three *Industriekaufleute* who said no and others who felt ambivalent complained that too much of what was taught in school was important only for the qualifying examination. An *Industriekaufmann* apprentice at Brandt said school instruction was more important for apprentices in small firms who lacked his on-the-job learning opportunities. His colleague said that instead of using what he learned in school on the job, he found he could answer questions in school based on what he learned while working at Brandt. More than half the interviewees said social studies was useful to them, specifying topics such as voting and understanding contracts. Some apprentices complained about the same kind of general information others found valuable. One auto mechanic whose employer serviced only British and Italian automobiles, for example, said the connection between school and work was loose because his teachers always talked about Volkswagens, never about Rovers and Maseratis. Another auto mechanic, in contrast, said he appreciated learning in school about automobiles that were different from those he serviced.

These interviews and other studies[39] suggest that *Berufsschüler* view their schools in much the same way as comparable high school students in the United States: as a necessary evil. When asked to compare full-time school with apprenticeship, apprentices uniformly report a great sense of satisfaction with their new role as productive workers and compare school unfavorably to work. In this they are like many U.S. high school students who find greater stimulation and satisfaction from part-time jobs than from school. The German word *Schulmüdigkeit* (school weariness) captures the feelings of both groups. There are two differences. One is that the phenomenon of school weariness is recognized as legitimate in West Germany and the institution of apprenticeship is offered for the afflicted. The second is that during the term of their apprenticeship, West German youth become less negative about school, gaining appreciation for what school has to offer after abandoning the role of full-time student.[40]

Adults in the United States frequently have the same experience. Many adults bemoan their lack of seriousness as students and wish they had the opportunity to go on in school with heightened motivation and maturity. Some, especially women, do just that. But in West Germany this mature perspective on school is acquired around age 18 or 19 and post-secondary schooling is tuition-free, making it much easier for youth and young adults to act on their new-found appreciation for school.

Apprentices' critical comments suggest that the *Berufsschule's* greatest strength is also an area in which great improvement could be made: integrating work experience with broader learning. One innovation that has been tried to improve integration is "block instruction," in which apprentices attend *Berufsschule* full-time for five- or six-week periods three times a year rather than one day per week, as is normal. This plan has two advantages. First, it enables the teachers to build their lessons from day-to-day instead of having to help their pupils recall what they did in class a week earlier. Second, especially in its "phased" variant, it makes possible a logical sequencing of instruction in relation to apprentices' work assignments on the job.

When asked about this schedule, those apprentices who had it expressed satisfaction with it, as did their teachers. However, as several teachers explained, most employers, especially in small firms, are opposed to the block plan because it deprives them of apprentices' assistance for too long. It is far easier for them to schedule an apprentice's absence one day each week than several weeks at a time.

A more fundamental concern about *Berufsschulen* than the scheduling of instruction, especially from the perspective of apprentices' political socialization, was the near-absence from the classroom of critical reflection on work, the economy, and the political system. Herr Reuter introduced his own critical observations but did not provide opportunities for the apprentices to develop their own. Most teachers did not do that much.

One incident symbolized the possible role of school as a stimulus to critical reflection upon work experiences. In the *Berufsschule* for *Industriekaufleute,* during a lecture/discussion on the topic of investment, Herr Klebel asked his pupils to list the different forms of investment. The resulting list included such items as investment in the physical plant and investment in training. When an apprentice proposed "investment in quality" (*Qualitätsinvestition*), Herr Klebel took exception, saying that this term was a euphemism used by Brandt for investment in automation (*Rationalisierungsinvestition*). He explained that Brandt employed a term using the positive word "quality" as a means of deflecting criticism for eliminating jobs.

The view that *Berufsschule* teachers should encourage apprentices to question terms, practices, and assumptions they encounter in the workplace would not, of course, find favor among employers, who already believe one weakness of the *Berufsschulen* is that too many teachers belong to the Social Democratic party aligned with the labor unions. However, little partisanship was observed in classes. Furthermore, it is entirely appropriate for public school teachers in a democracy to urge their pupils to question and challenge rather than to accept unreflectively the way the world works. *Berufsschule* teachers could play an even more central role in preparing West German youth for work and citizenship if they found more opportunities to challenge apprentices to think critically about their experiences in the workplace.

The critical difference between West German *Berufsschulen* and U.S. vocational high schools is the one noted by Georg Kerschensteiner. *Berufsschulen* are designed to supplement apprenticeship; U.S. vocational high schools were developed to replace apprenticeship. Evidence on the effects of vocational schooling in this country raises questions about the wisdom of this strategy. Although vocational schooling substantially aids some American youth under some conditions, it is not nearly as effective in facilitating a smooth transition from high school into employment as the West German dual system. Labor market conditions are partly to blame for the inefficacy of U.S. vocational schools, but so is the separation of school learning from work experience. The most effective form of vocational schooling is the one that most nearly approaches apprenticeship, namely, cooperative education.

Yet the vocational education tradition in the United States contains within it some of the elements that make apprenticeship effective. Students enroll in vocational programs and prefer them to their academic classes because they believe what they learn there is important. Many vocational teachers are able to bridge the worlds of school and work, as Mrs. Carter did, patiently teaching young people about the kinds of demands that regular employment will make upon both skills and deportment.

U.S. vocational schooling needs a stronger dose of planned work experience for students; simultaneously it needs increased academic rigor. West German *Berufsschulen,* through their link to apprenticeship, contain the first. In some ways they are more rigorous too, but they have not yet succeeded in achieving an optimal level of integration with work experience, in part because apprentices from different firms bring with them such a diversity of experiences.

Contrary to the recommendations of some recent secondary school reform proposals, and the implicit consequences of others, vocational education should not be banished from U.S. secondary schools. Rather, it should be redirected from specifically vocational to more general academic purposes. In addition, it should be united with the range of apprenticeship experiences described in Chapter 3. Then it may approach the lofty goals stated in 1918 in the *Cardinal Principles of Secondary Education.*

It is only as the pupil sees his vocation in relation to his citizenship and his citizenship in the light of his vocation that he will be prepared for effective membership in an industrial democracy. Consequently, this commission enters its protest against any and all plans, however well intended, which are in danger of divorcing vocational and social-civic education. It stands squarely for the infusion of vocation with the spirit of service and for the vitalization of culture by genuine contact with the world of work.[41]

6

◆

Cloudy Futures

Why the American System Fails

Three major differences emerge from a comparison between U.S. and West German approaches to preparing noncollege youth for work. The process is more carefully planned, more specifically targeted, and occurs at an earlier age in West Germany. In both countries, young people learn basic academic subject matter in school, and learn by comparing their school performance to others' which level in the occupational hierarchy they can hope to achieve. Youth in both countries acquire worker virtues from their work experience, but in the United States that experience is haphazard, gleaned from the youth labor market rather than from formal apprenticeship. Young people's career directions in both countries depend heavily upon labor market conditions prevailing when they are eligible for career-entry jobs, which is in the late teens in West Germany and early twenties in the United States. Specific job training coincides with career entry, occurring about five years earlier for West German youth.

These differences are summarized in Table 6–1 using the framework introduced in Chapter 4 (Table 4–2), which distinguishes aspirations and learning at general and specific levels as aspects of preparation for work. Table 6–1 portrays the influence of school and work on preparation for work. Family, community, and peer group also play an important role, but their influence is heavily conditioned by the nature of schooling and work and by the connections between the two. In addition, the institutions of school and work are more amenable to policy manipulation than family, community, and peer group.

The key point that can be deduced from Table 6–1 is that young

Table 6–1 School and Employment Influences on Preparation for Work
of Noncollege Youth in the United States and West Germany

	United States	*West Germany*
	Learning	
General:		
Basic academic knowledge and skills	Schools (ages 5–18)	Schools and apprenticeship (ages 6–18)
Worker virtues	Youth labor market (ages 16–22)	Apprenticeship (ages 15–19)
Specific:		
Knowledge, skills, and attitudes required for a specific job	On-the-job training at career entry (ages 21–22)	Apprenticeship, including on-the-job training and vocational schooling (ages 15–19)
	Aspirations	
General:		
Level in occupational hierarchy	School track (ages 14–16)	School type (ages 10–12)
Specific:		
Particular occupation or field	Open jobs at end of floundering period (ages 20–22)	Open apprenticeships at end of full-time schooling (ages 15–19)

people's attitudes and behavior are shaped by their beliefs about the
consequences of their actions. Apprenticeship reveals those consequences
more clearly and encourages responsible behavior more directly than
the American combination of extended schooling and casual work experience in the youth labor market.

Despite the attention given in recent years to U.S. high school students'
abysmal performance on tests of basic academic knowledge, to unacceptable rates of dropping out, premature parenthood, drug abuse, and criminality, few new insights have emerged to explain why young people in
the United States seem so much more troubled and poorly educated,
on average, then their age-mates in other industrial countries. The catch-
all explanation is youthful immaturity, which would be more convincing
if other countries' youth demonstrated similar immaturity.

School failure and premature parenthood can legitimately be attributed
to age in the sense that only those who are required to attend school
are at risk of school failure, and only those who are biologically capable
of bearing children but socially defined as immature can become parents

prematurely. But the relation of age to drug abuse and criminality—
which rise through adolescence then fall off in adulthood—is less easily
explained in terms of age. As with the floundering period, some observers
have concluded that youth are like that; they have to sow their wild
oats. But, again as in the case of the floundering period, comparison
with other countries refutes this explanation. West German youth experience far lower rates of serious problem behavior in all these categories,[1]
and West Germany is typical of other developed countries. The United
States is the exceptional case. Youthfulness is not inevitably associated
with the magnitude of problem behavior found here. There is something
about the United States that makes growing up more difficult than it
needs to be.

Growing numbers of leaders and citizens now recognize the peril to
society in such problem behavior, but that recognition thus far has yielded
attacks on schools and teachers for declining standards and legislation
mandating higher standards, which are narrow responses to a broad and
multifaceted problem. Campaigns designed to give young people more
information about drugs and sex will not solve the problem either. Such
responses ignore connections among apparently different problems and
avoid the fundamental changes needed to make it possible for more
American youth to become healthy, contributing adults. Apprenticeship
provides a framework for dealing with a range of problems that have
been treated separately, though they are, in reality, interrelated.

Youth who are in or heading toward college use drugs and get pregnant,
but they are not seriously afflicted so long as they can remain on the
path of higher education. Noncollege youth are involved in a disproportionate amount of problem behavior. One reason is surely because that
problem behavior interferes with school achievement, reducing their motivation and opportunity for higher education. A second is that some of
the same personal characteristics that are associated with problem behavior
make it difficult to pursue higher education (e.g., low self-esteem, absence
of positive role models). A third reason is that schools and the labor
market give noncollege youth insufficient motivation to behave responsibly and to work hard in school.

American schools isolate youth from adults and from workplaces and
other community settings. Weak links between school and work, combined with initial confinement to the secondary labor market, cloud young
people's futures, obscuring their perception of how their current behavior
is likely to affect their prospects for the future. Youth facing poverty
and discrimination are particularly prone to doubt that they can improve
their future prospects materially by working hard in school and behaving

responsibly or, conversely, that they place themselves at substantially greater risk of adult distress by failing in school and by engaging in self-destructive and socially irresponsible behavior. They see themselves as headed for dead-end jobs, unemployment, and welfare regardless of what they do. "Why not get what pleasure you can?" they ask themselves. "Why postpone gratification that may never come again?" The probable returns for avoiding self-destructive behavior and working hard in school do not appear to them sufficient to justify abstinence, responsibility, diligence, and possible alienation from peers.

West Germany's dual system does a better job of representing to noncollege youth the rewards of school achievement and responsible behavior, and the path from school to a rewarding adult career. *Berufsschulen* teach apprentices knowledge, skills, and attitudes they need at work; workplaces are organized to reinforce those lessons and to teach more than the bare necessities for performing a specific job. As apprentices traverse the institutional bridge from school to work that apprenticeship provides, they have a clearer sense of future direction and stronger motivation to perform well in school than most American youth who do not go to college. Daily they work alongside adults who tell them and show them what they must do to become skilled workers. Doing well in school is one of the requirements.

Although most young people do not have a clearly defined vision of the future that explicitly guides their day-to-day decisions, the ideas they have about their likely place in the world, regardless of how well formed, can strongly affect their behavior. In his classic study, *Rebellion in a High School,* Arthur Stinchcombe argued that a high school's claim on students' obedience is based on the presumption that if the student complies with the school's demands then she or he will reap rewards in the future in the form of employment, income, and prestige. Those who reject this relationship, who do not believe they will benefit in the future from current conformity, resist the school's authority and do not attempt to meet its expectations. He pointed out that males, who are less likely than females to improve their future prospects by a fortunate marriage, are more rebellious, as are black youth who believe discrimination will prevent them from using education to better their situation.[2]

The United States is school-bound. We rely too heavily on schools as the primary public institution to prepare youth for work. This reliance is democratically motivated, but it reflects a nineteenth-century world, when young people were, in James Coleman's words, "action-rich and information-poor."[3] He meant that when public schools were first established, young people brought to them a wealth of practical knowledge and experience that continued to accumulate while they were students because they spent relatively little time in school compared to the time spent working, primarily on the family farm, and engaged with family members and neighbors in other forms of constructive activity. By the end of the twentieth century, he argued, this situation has been reversed. Young people are now sufficiently schooled that they are "information-rich and action-poor."

Restoring the balance between information and action serves both pedagogical and socialization purposes. Enriching young people's action experience gives them alternative opportunities to learn and motivates them to learn more in school. It also introduces them more effectively to the world beyond their family, school, and peer group. Most importantly, experience in the larger community creates a vision of what might be in the future that can guide young people's current behavior and planning.

Prolonged schooling and prolonged confinement to the secondary labor market obscure for most American youth the reasons for working hard in school and avoiding problem behavior. Teachers say, "Learn this; you will need it when you are older." But by tenth grade this claim has worn thin. College-bound youth accept the importance of schoolwork because they care about Scholastic Aptitude Tests, or they have figured out how to learn meaningless material long enough to pass examinations. Few of them and none of the noncollege-bound really believe they will ever be called upon to say what Vasco da Gama discovered or to solve problems in solid geometry.[4]

Noncollege youth have solid grounds for skepticism. Many of them have been "exposed to" the same subject matter year after year for five or six years by the time they get to high school. While their more academically able classmates encounter some new material and are challenged by added depth, those in the lower tracks receive a blandly repetitive curriculum of "basic and applied" subjects. Each year their teachers despair over what they failed to learn the year before and strive to make up for their deficiencies with the same ineffective methods and uninteresting content. No wonder so many youth become school-weary. Apprenticeship offers school-weary youth a respectable and rewarding alternative to full-time school attendance. School-weary American youth become dropouts or remain in school unwillingly and unproductively, psychological dropouts who waste their own time and that of their teachers.

Moreover, most high school students have direct evidence to dispute their teachers' claims that learning lessons in school will pay off in the labor market. They are already working. They know from personal experience that school learning is irrelevant to the secondary labor market jobs they have. They have not yet learned how the primary labor market differs from the secondary labor market. Many of their older friends, siblings, and workmates are working in the secondary labor market, further obscuring from their view the kinds of career jobs that require academic knowledge.

Minority youth have a harder time seeing beyond the jobs they and their friends, family, and neighbors have, if they have any job at all. A "job ceiling" has traditionally prevented people like them from achieving visible positions in business and the professions. At least until recently, blacks who succeeded have become doctors and teachers, but not accountants, middle managers, and commissioned salespersons (with the exception of a few businesses like mortuaries and life insurance sales that have traditionally been operated by blacks in black communities). Lacking intermediate-level role models, some young minority people set their sights high but anticipate being unable to achieve their lofty goals.[5] They have said, in effect, "If I can't be a doctor, then maybe I can get a job as a janitor"; "If I don't make it to college and become a teacher, I'll get a job in a grocery store." Affirmative action has improved this situation, but those who benefit from it seldom remain in poor neighborhoods where their achievements are visible daily, and racial discrimination continues to frustrate high aspirations.

Along with all the other barriers to upward mobility, parents tend to pass on to their offspring behavior patterns and attitudes appropriate to their own class position. They do this directly by teaching and advising, but also indirectly by example, particularly by means of the style of interaction they use with their children. Several studies have found that more democratic and affectionate practices favored by middle-class parents are more effective both in securing children's compliance with parents' wishes and in inculcating the attitudes and personal styles associated with middle-class status than the more authoritarian styles common among working-class parents.[6] A recent study extends this association to school performance, indicating that adolescents whose parents use "authoritative" styles do better in school. "Authoritative" means with clear but rational and bounded authority, as distinct from "authoritarian," which is arbitrary and unlimited. Authoritarianism mixed with neglect, which is found most often in families wracked by poverty, is the most dysfunctional style.[7]

Parents' modes of relating to their children reflect their immediate circumstances and their own socialization as children, but also, not so obviously, the nature of their employment. Longitudinal studies have demonstrated that parents' values regarding their children reflect their working conditions. Specifically, parents whose work is more substantively complex and requires them to make independent judgments stress the importance of their children becoming independent and creative. Those whose work is simpler, more repetitive, and closely supervised value obedience and conformity in their children.[8] These findings are consistent with the research on parental styles and mirror the findings of studies that show schools and tracks for middle-class and for lower-class children teach different lessons about appropriate behavior and aspirations.[9]

Overreliance on school and confinement to the secondary labor market during and immediately after completing high school obscure the path from school to desirable careers for youth who do not enroll in higher education. But the problem does not result solely from their limited knowledge of the labor market. Their perceptions are demonstrably valid. School performance is not closely related to employment opportunities during the first several years after high school.

John Bishop found that among youth who did not enroll full-time in college, the correlation between grades and test scores on the one hand and employment and earnings on the other during the first ten years after graduation ranged in different studies from zero to quite modest. However, productivity was consistently and substantially correlated with grades and scores.[10] In addition to confirming young people's belief that working hard in school does not pay off in the labor market, these findings suggest that young workers' productivity is not appropriately rewarded with higher pay.

In other words, although adult earnings are strongly correlated with number of years of schooling completed, earnings and job status are curiously uncorrelated with grades in school. Among people who have completed the same amount of schooling, how well they did in school has little direct connection with how well they do in life.[11] School attainment, measured in years of schooling completed, is an excellent predictor of occupational status, but school performance, indicated by grades, is a poor predictor of occupational success. One explanation for the apparent contradiction between these two findings is that school's impact on work is more general than specific. School attainment opens doors to higher-level occupations, but the kind of performance demanded on the job is different from the performance that earns high grades.

A study of young women moving from high school into clerical jobs supports this interpretation. Rather than finding that school experiences shaped young women's attitudes toward work, as a prominent argument goes,[12] observations and interviews found a sharp discrepancy between attitudes toward school and toward work and between performance in the two settings. While a majority of the young women found school boring and distasteful, most were stimulated by their work experience, took it seriously, and tried hard to do well, exhibiting diligence and responsibility their teachers had never witnessed. Although their school performance limited these young women to low-level occupations, they did not carry over into their new jobs the "poor work habits" they had demonstrated in school.[13]

Some students exhibit problem behavior at home and in the community as well. But a substantial number of youth who do poorly in schools successfully adapt their behavior to the work setting by following instructions and acting responsibly. Many young people who do poorly and create problems in school simply regard the school as unreal and fail to take it seriously.[14] Work, in contrast, is real if only because they are paid for it. Even many successful students consider school unreal but have learned to live with the unreality. They study for tests but forget the answers as soon as the test is over. They can perform mathematical calculations when the problem is laid out for them but they cannot use what they know about math to solve real problems.

Although this assessment is not flattering to schools, its implications are hopeful for the future success of marginal students: many of them are likely to be much more competent and successful in work than they were in school. Indeed, a longitudinal survey of young men, following them from tenth grade to their mid-twenties, found that with growing maturity nearly all accepted the need to work hard, though they had initially expressed diverse attitudes toward hard work.[15] However, if many youth dismiss school as unreal and unimportant, then much of society's investment in schools is squandered. We send our children to school so they will be more effective citizens and workers and better able to control and enjoy their lives. When they sharply divide school from life, then school does not support the transition to adulthood; it becomes nothing more than a place to wait until adulthood arrives. They and we need more from our educational system than that.

Studying the vexing issue of why U.S. youth perform so poorly in school, Bishop repeated a theme sounded earlier in James Coleman's classic study, *The Adolescent Society,*[16] namely, that high school students who work hard achieve by surpassing their peers, confronting them with a choice between achievement and acceptance. Coleman surveyed students in several midwestern high schools during the 1950s about their values and aspirations and was disturbed to find that they were more concerned with recreational activities and peer interactions than with academics, the business of the schools. The majority said they would prefer to be remembered as good athletes or social leaders than as brilliant students. Coleman's observation that American high schools reinforce the peer culture has been confirmed repeatedly.[17]

Peer influence is not always negative. Young people tend to choose friends who are like themselves and who, therefore, share many values with them and with their parents.[18] However, among youth whose race and class limit their expectations of achievement as adults, peer influence often militates against working hard in school. Even among some middle-class black youth, taking school seriously and working hard at it is denigrated as selling out to white values. In order to demonstrate solidarity with other blacks, one must treat school casually, despite parents' entreaties to work hard.[19]

In a black and Hispanic community, John Ogbu found that youth simply did not try to do well in school or on standardized tests, in part because parents gave a double message, extolling the value of working hard while lamenting the fact that discrimination so often renders effort useless. Having concluded that good school performance will not help them get ahead, the youth in this community saw no reason to forego short-term pleasures of free time and peer interaction; they had no motivation to work hard. Ogbu argued that school failure is thus "adaptive" to the reality they perceive. Being denied access to high-status and highly rewarded occupations, minority youth rationally choose to avoid the pain of academic striving, settling for the low-status jobs they can obtain without higher education because they believe they could do little better even if they remained in school and got good grades.[20]

Such willful rejection of school is not limited to American minorities. A comparable phenomenon has been documented among working-class boys in a British secondary modern school who actively opposed the authority of teachers and school administrators and denigrated all work other than manual labor as unworthy of white men. Rather than being powerless pawns in a system manipulated by the dominant classes, the investigator saw the boys as choosing to behave in ways that they believed confirmed their independence from higher authorities and their identities as working-class males. They were not simply relegated to lower-class status by the machinations of the class system, but by their own ostensibly rebellious behavior they actively participated in their occupational and hence social class assignment.[21]

Peers do not necessarily conflict with parents, struggling for dominance over young people's loyalties. Each contributes to preparing youth for adulthood, more often in a complementary than a competitive manner. Disadvantaged youths' peers may contribute to the perpetuation of disadvantaged status, but not necessarily more than parents. The key question is not how to counter peer influence, but how best to channel it to benefit individual young people and society as a whole.

The short answer to this question is that the peer group should, in general, promote the same orientation as adult-dominated socializing institutions, notably family, school, and work. But that answer raises another question, which is how to accomplish this desirable objective. Totalitarian states have answered that question quite effectively, if unacceptably. The *Hitlerjugend* and the Soviet Young Pioneers are two examples of formally organized and orchestrated adult interventions into young people's peer relations designed specifically to mold a new generation to serve totalitarian states. Their effectiveness may have depended upon the nearly absolute authority of the state over individuals, families, and all other institutions. That, at least, is one explanation for the comparative impotence of such organizations as the YMCA and YWCA, Boy and Girl Scouts, which were founded around the turn of the twentieth century in order to give adults more control of adolescents' peer relations, and to promote democratic values. As constructive as these organizations have been for many American youth, they have had nothing approaching the frightening power of their totalitarian counterparts.[22]

But other democratic nations do a better job than we of promoting a positive peer culture. Japan is most notable in this regard, for example, by giving students serious leadership and maintenance responsiblities at school, but West Germany and other European countries also implement policies specifically intended to strengthen constructive peer interaction. It is curious that so many parents and teachers of adolescents bemoan the effects of "peer pressure" without ever considering that under many circumstances peer influence is positive and in a different institutional context it could become a more consistently positive element of socialization.

West German youth, like their American counterparts, are strongly oriented to their peers. Two differences stand out. First, the structure of the school system, as described in Chapters 4 and 5, divides peer groups that often remain intact through the years in U.S. schools. Because young people are sorted into three different levels of secondary schooling after the fourth or sixth grade and then those who become apprentices leave full-time schooling after ninth or tenth grade, attending *Berufsschulen* only one day per week thereafter, only students in the college-preparatory *Gymnasium* attend school with old friends after the age of 16. The others make friends in their *Berufsschulen* and at their workplaces, and they see their old friends from their neighborhood and elementary school only during leisure time.

West German youth spend relatively little time with peers in school or at home. Schools do not sponsor extracurricular activities. Therefore, even when young people go to school with friends, they have fewer opportunities to interact with them socially in school. Because most families live in apartments, homes are also not so accommodating to peer group activities as they are in suburban America. Three kinds of settings are available instead: sports clubs, youth centers, and commercial recreation.

Rather than belonging to school teams, West German athletes belong to sports clubs, which are supported by membership fees and government subsidies. Even neighborhood clubs may have quite elaborate facilities, such as large clubhouses, multiple playing fields, and running tracks, even in city locations where property values are astronomical. Serious athletes like Boris Becker and Steffi Graf join serious clubs. Professional soccer and hockey teams are sponsored by clubs that go big-time.

Youth centers are sponsored by churches and by government. Church and state are not constitutionally separated as they are in the United States; almost all citizens, regardless of their religious affiliation, pay a special tax to support churches. Work with youth in centers and in youth organizations is more professionalized in West Germany than in the United States, with highly developed pre-service and in-service training programs. Though not limited to youth, government-run sports facilities such as swimming pools and ice-skating rinks also serve as youth hangouts.

Lacking large homes for entertainment, German youth and adults both turn more frequently to commercial locations. Every genuine neighborhood has a *Kneipe* or *Lokal,* a tavern that functions as a public sitting room for eating, drinking, and socializing, especially for the regular crowd that gathers at their appointed places *am Stammtisch.* Sports clubs also usually offer at least the chance to buy a beer or soft drink, and sometimes operate a small tavern for members and guests. For young people, discoteques are the most prominent meeting places. As in the United States, movie theaters and shopping malls are also popular gathering places.[23]

Nevertheless, West German apprentices' peer interactions frequently occur in settings where adults are present. More importantly, those youth have many opportunities to interact extensively with adults at work, where they spend far more time than in school. Reliance on school as the dominant institution preparing youth for work has unintentionally left U.S. youth subject to the unmoderated influence of their peers.

Peer influence, to reiterate, is not by itself the source of the problem. Becoming adult includes forming lasting relations with age-mates outside the family, including enduring love relationships. Before they make long-term adult commitments, young people need to enlarge their social networks to include close friends of the same and other gender. Problems arise when peers promote values and encourage behavior that conflict with those of parents and the larger community and/or with those that are most likely to foster the young person's healthy development, notably the acquisition of academic knowledge and skills and of worker virtues and the avoidance of self-destructive behavior. All parents and most adults want young people to grow into competent and responsible adults. Some parents and some communities are better able to support such growth than others. To the extent that young people feel isolated from adults and the larger community, they tend to lose touch with their communities' positive values.[24]

Medieval apprentices lived in their masters' households, subject to their discipline in social and religious as well as vocational matters. If apprentices learned to read and write it was because their masters or their masters' wives taught them. At the age of 14, young people left their parents' home for good but were "bound over" to their masters, who stood in loco parentis. Contemporary apprenticeship is much more narrowly vocational. However, as in medieval times, it is based on a contract of indenture signed by parents and employers that spells out the obligations of each party. Nowadays the apprentice's signature is also required.

Apprenticeship contributes to the dispersal of peer groups into different schools and apprenticeship sites. It also constitutes a new arena for peer interaction, especially in large firms with substantial cohorts of apprentices. Spending time together and sharing intense experiences, apprentices quite naturally form attachments to each other. Having identical vocational aspirations and anticipating spending their careers in the same firm together, apprentice cohorts are, if anything, even closer than school classmates. Particularly among the *Industriekaufleute* in the present study, a group spirit was very pronounced, enriched by the presence of both males and females.

But peer interaction among apprentices is moderated by their extensive interaction with adults. Unlike full-time students, who spend most of their time with peers, apprentices' time with peers is limited mostly to their time in instruction and some informal times, as in the company cafeteria during lunch. Most of their working time is spent in predominantly adult company. Like workers the world over, apprentices find time for conversation and joking, with adults as well as peers.

Apprenticeship is a means of making the community, specifically its workplaces, into learning environments for youth. By means of apprenticeship, West German communities incorporate young people as full members at an earlier age and share with parents and schools the responsibility for socializing them for adult roles. That is a major strength of apprenticeship and a powerful motivation for finding ways to adapt it to the United States.

Apprenticeship increases the number of adults who play important roles in adolescents' lives. When apprentices in the present study were asked to name the five most important adults in their lives, five of the thirteen *Industriekaufleute* listed an adult in their workplace, as did four of the eight auto mechanics. Adults in the apprenticeship setting accounted for 50 percent of the unrelated adults named by *Industriekaufleute* and 89 percent of those named by auto mechanics. The few remaining unrelated adults were associated with the types of leisure settings described above: a youth worker, a minister, two coaches and two teachers. When asked to identify exemplary adults in their workplaces, the positive characteristic they attributed most uniformly to those adults was technical competence, suggesting overlap between the technical training and the socialization functions of apprenticeship.

Figure 6–1 summarizes the contrast in broad terms, emphasizing the positive side of the West German situation and the barriers to effective socialization for adulthood in the United States. Harmony is an apt metaphor to describe the coherence of these influences and to contrast it with the relative dissonance that prevails in the United States.[25] Allowing for the exaggeration that inevitably results from generalizing, the two diagrams suggest some of the weaknesses of socialization in the United States and some of the strengths of the West German approach.

The diagrams indicate how apprenticeship, by linking school, work experience, and career prospects, reinforces parents' socialization goals and contributes to social commitment on the part of youth, which, in turn, helps them to move more readily into careers. Higher rates of problem behavior in the United States, cited in Chapter 1, are partially explainable in terms of youths' perceptions of the costs and benefits of behaving responsibly. When they see a direct connection between current behavior and future rewards, they are more likely to be responsible, as their parents would like them to be. The compartmentalization of school, work, and career prospects for youth in the United States obscures that connection and contributes to problem behavior, which, in turn, interferes with career establishment. The feedback loop represented by the dashed lines in both diagrams indicates the effect of young people's knowledge about what happens to older youth in the labor market on their thinking about their own adult careers.

Any society in flux confronts the enigma of how to use its current knowledge and resources to socialize youth for an uncertain future. Parents and educators are especially challenged by this conundrum. While it is impossible to say with certainty what preparation adults of the future should have to grapple with challenges to come, no better prediction is available than the combination of academic achievement and the worker virtues. Although many Germans fretted a decade ago that current indus-

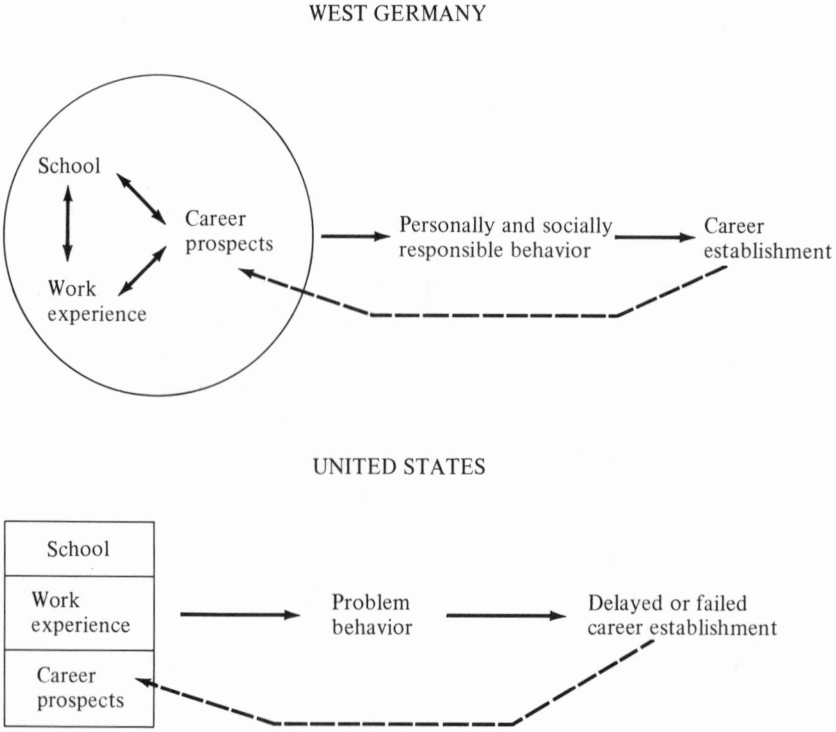

WEST GERMANY

UNITED STATES

Figure 6–1 Socialization for Work in the United States and West Germany

trial conditions had outmoded apprenticeship, recent analyses have concluded that apprenticeship is the ideal method of preparing precisely the kind of highly skilled but highly flexible industrial workers who are critical to new modes of production.[26]

In the United States we do an admirable job of socializing and educating those who do well in school. Our best high schools are excellent and our universities are arguably the best in the world. University training for managers, lawyers, physicians, and engineers is first-rate (though never lacking room for improvement). Schooling for those whose school performance and occupational attainment fall in the middle and lower levels is less than first-rate. Our collective metaphor of life as a contest leaves those who have not made it to the top convinced of their own inadequacy and the rest of society unconcerned about what becomes of them. They belong to a residual category of those who were not good enough to graduate from college and assume one of the privileged professional positions. They are permitted to sort themselves out among the lower-ranking occupational classifications by a process of trial and error. Neither our public educational system nor private employers invest very much in teaching them. They are expendable when economic conditions worsen. Their best hope for the future is that their children will do better in school than they did and thus qualify for the high earnings, security, and prestige that are reserved for college graduates. Sadly, most are poorly equipped to help their children achieve the American Dream.

Apprenticeship, though associated historically with rigid social class stratification, offers a means of directing the resources of an entire community to preparing all young people for rewarding work, compensating at least in part for parents' inability to prepare youth for work they have never known. It gives young people a clear vision of a desirable future and a well-marked path to an adult career, a vision and a path that American youth fail to acquire from school and from work experience.

7

Principles for Practice

Specifications for Reinventing Apprenticeship

Reinventing apprenticeship will meet some of the most serious challenges facing the United States as the twenty-first century approaches. Neither the medieval version of a master teaching the fundamentals of shoemaking to a boy while huddled over a candle-lit workbench nor the contemporary American system for training white males as plumbers, carpenters, electricians, and other tradesmen can do the job. A serviceable apprenticeship system must have the same flexibility, diversity, and openness that characterize our educational system and our labor market.

Changing labor market demands place a premium on academic preparation, social skills, and flexibility, in service as well as in manufacturing jobs. At the same time, the population employers have relied upon in the past to fill positions with those requirements—white middle-class youth—is declining. Even among that relatively privileged group, a litany of problem behavior, including drug use, premature parenthood, delinquency, and suicide, constitutes barriers to successful participation in school and work. If we are to meet increasing global competition and realize our country's democratic ideals, we must find ways to prepare young people from all segments of the population for roles as productive adult workers, citizens, and family members.

Schools alone are inadequate to this task. They have a crucial role to play, but they cannot singlehandedly overcome the disadvantages conferred by poverty, unstable families, racial discrimination, and problem-ridden neighborhoods. Too many young people, particularly those who grow up in such environments, regard school as unreal and unimportant. Because of that perception, they fail to perform well academically. By the time they reach high school, the majority are school weary. Whether they literally drop out or drop out psychologically by putting in their time without learning, their latent talents are wasted along with the resources society ineffectively devotes to their schooling. We all lose.

For all its serious flaws, however, flexibility is a major virtue of the U.S. educational system. The West German system is rigid by comparison. In the United States, a young person who was a mediocre student through most of his or her school career and who took a general rather than college preparatory course may, nevertheless, enroll in a local community college and, for a nominal fee, earn two years of college credit. Although in most cases neither the quality nor the market value of this education is equal to that available in more prestigious four-year colleges, some of these students discover motivation and aptitude sufficient to take them on to four-year colleges and higher-level degrees. Prestigious private universities like Princeton and Stanford educate a disproportionate number of leading professionals, but Kansas State and the City University of New York provide alternative routes to high achievement.

Young people in the United States may change direction quite dramatically after attending college for two or three years. Changes while in high school are easier still. Career changes among high school graduates who do not attend college are the norm, not the exception. Because so many occupations do not require specific skills, entry requires no specific credentials.

Minimal entrance requirements for most manual jobs facilitate movement among jobs according to their availability, pay scales, and workers' emerging interests. In the absence of rigid skill requirements and job definitions, workers can easily take up new occupations with only enough training to enable them to do the work at hand rather than the kind of extensive foundational training required in German apprenticeship. Likewise, new occupations can readily be established and staffed. Photocopy machine repair, for example, is a new field that has grown rapidly as employers trained people to repair only their own machines, without necessarily requiring or imparting a sound fundamental knowledge of optics, mechanics, and electronics.

Closely associated with its greater flexibility is the greater diversity of the U.S. approach. Rather than specifying a single path that all would-be entrants must follow to enter a particular occupation, the United States offers a variety of paths. Some are broader and easier than others, some are more heavily traveled. A team of welders, for example, might include one who learned the trade in a public vocational school, another who paid tuition at a private vocational school, a third who learned informally on-the-job, a fourth who received instruction in the military, and a fifth who took a course taught by his employer. Diversity is also a characteristic of the United States' people and economy. West Germany's rather rigid system would not function well with a heterogeneous population and a free-wheeling economy.

The availability of diverse paths to the same goal gives young people in the United States the sense that many possibilities are open to them. That sense of openness is perhaps as important as the reality. In a society that values individuality and resists placing people in closed categories, all people, and young people especially, have to believe that they can make of themselves all that their talents will allow. Minimizing entrance requirements and maximizing flexibility contribute to maintaining the perception of openness that Americans value.

In order to maintain flexibility, diversity, and openness, an American system of apprenticeship must be designed for general educational and developmental purposes more than for specific job training. Consistent with this orientation, it must be closely articulated with schooling and offer academic as well as job skill credentials. It must assume diverse forms to meet varied needs of youth and varied community and labor market conditions. It must be flexible and open, allowing entry at many points and leading to different schooling and employment options. West German apprenticeship prepares youth for specific occupations, in contrast to schooling in the United States, which offers general preparation for work. Specific forms of preparation for work such as vocational schooling and career counseling are not very effective in the United States. Yet for many vocational students, studying academic material related to a real occupation and being able to learn through hands-on work experience are highly motivating. West German apprentices are motivated even more by having a clear path to adult employment in their training field. Seeing the connection between their apprenticeship and an adult career gives them reasons for learning and for behaving in personally and socially responsible ways.

Can this function of apprenticeship be successfully adapted to the United States, where careers are typically less predictable and where large employers value general over specific preparation? The answer is yes, provided that focusing on a specific occupation remains a means to the end of general preparation rather than becoming the end itself. Means tend to displace ends.[1] Vocational schooling's original advocates in the United States (Chapter 5) saw it as a means to general education, but their vision was supplanted by the goal of training workers to meet labor market demands.

Employers' assertions that they need generally educated workers justify optimism that apprenticeship might be used for general more than specific preparation of youth for work. Changes in the labor market have made employers' needs more congruent with the principles of general education. Already employers expend their own resources to remedy manual and clerical workers' deficiencies in reading, writing, and arithmetic and to provide continuing education for their technical and managerial workers. Apprenticeship offers the prospect that employers will be able to concentrate on education and training that is more closely related to their needs and, because apprentices are motivated to work harder in school, schools will be more effective in imparting basic academics.

Young apprentices' involvement in supervised work experience and their study of academic subjects related to that work should be treated as primarily a means of achieving academic knowledge and worker virtues. Specific job training is more than incidental, however; especially in occupations demanding high levels of technical skill and offering good career prospects, it may be quite functional. But in view of the value employers place on general preparation for work and the match between that emphasis and the volatile U.S. labor market, in which multiple job and career changes are normal and occupational specialties are much less clearly defined, there are fewer occupations for which a West German-style apprenticeship would be appropriate.

The ideal system would offer specific apprenticeships for occupations requiring specific training, such as X-ray technician or legal aide, but also shorter-term apprenticeships that are not so tightly bound to specific occupations, as in Experience Based Career Education. Even programs preparing young workers for specific occupations should be designed so that they serve general preparation purposes, opening up new opportunities rather than limiting the apprentice to a single occupation. For example, an apprentice X-ray technician must learn physics, electronics, and physiology, which would prove useful in other occupations as well.

Tying apprenticeship to schooling helps to maintain its general purposes. Schooling and school credentials are too important in the United States to be replaced by apprenticeship. Rather than replacing schooling, apprenticeship must complement schooling and contribute to the acquisition of school credentials. Apprenticeship complements schooling when it motivates young people to remain in school and to take their school work seriously. In addition, the workplace serves as an alternative environment for learning when apprentices master schoollike tasks there.

German apprentices earn credentials that are transferable from one employer to another and that lead to further education as well as employment. As currently structured, American apprenticeship yields certification as a journeyworker, but that credential has only limited value in the labor market and no value at all for further schooling. With the exception of trades such as barber and electrician, which require examinations to assure mastery of health and safety principles, completion of apprenticeship is usually measured by time served rather than by an assessment of competence. Competency-based certification is more reliable, more flexible, and better suited to generating school credentials.

Assessing apprentices' competence would assure more interchangeability of school-based and work-based training; what counts is performance, not where competence was acquired or how many hours of training were provided. Apprentices should be able to gain credit for previous experience. More adept apprentices should be able to acquire certification in less time. To the extent that work-related competence entails academic knowledge and skill, schools can legitimately give credit as well. For example, machinists need to know higher math. Their demonstrated ability to use trigonometry should qualify them for math credit and for further study in math if they choose.

The United States' size, diversity, and independent spirit make a thoroughly integrated national system of apprenticeship on the West German model inappropriate and unworkable. It is far more likely that an effective apprenticeship system will eventually emerge out of multiple efforts at several levels and in different cities, states, and regions. One advantage of such diversity and experimentation is that young people can participate in different forms of apprenticeship with varying levels of commitment and concentration. Apprenticeships of variable duration and with varying degrees of specificity will give young people more choices as they make their way toward adulthood.

A diverse apprenticeship system that emphasizes general preparation, complements schooling, and leads to school credentials is an institution that is appropriate for all young people in the United States, including those who expect to enroll in higher education. Although the greatest need for apprenticeship lies among those left out of higher education, one of the risks in creating a system solely for that group is that it becomes, by definition, a second choice. Those involved in it are labeled as failures on the ground that they would have enrolled in higher education if they had been intelligent and industrious enough. If apprenticeship is, instead, oriented toward general educational and developmental purposes, if it complements rather than displaces schooling and leads to broadly applicable credentials, and if it may be performed at different levels of specificity with variable time commitments, then there is no reason why it should be limited to noncollege youth. Opening it to all youth would make it more attractive and more effective for those who need it most and give college-bound youth the benefit of a firmer grounding in the working world before they have to make choices about majors and careers.

Making a diverse system of apprenticeship available to all youth means creating a *system,* not just a program. A program, such as the Job Corps or cooperative education, may be part of a system, but a complete system offers an array of diverse opportunities—or programs—and it links them in a coherent whole. Youth then move through sequential stages in the system, selecting the programs that are most appropriate and participating as long as each meets their needs.

In outline, such a system would embody the four essential features of West German apprenticeship: exploiting workplaces and other community settings as learning environments; linking work experience to academic learning; giving youth constructive roles as workers and learners simultaneously; and fostering close relations between youth and adult mentors. However, it would also retain the American virtues of flexibility, diversity, and openness by operating at three levels: exploratory, school-based, and work-based. Work-based apprenticeship includes programs that have traditionally been called apprenticeship. The exploratory and school-based apprenticeships might more properly be called ''apprentice-like experiences.''

Exploratory apprenticeship serves very broad purposes. It gives young people first-hand experience taking real responsibility, making decisions, working cooperatively, and interacting with adults who are neither professional teachers nor their parents. Exploratory apprenticeship introduces young people, as early as the middle school years, to participation in a range of community roles and settings, without expecting that they will remain long or master any of them. Community service and mentoring programs are exemplars of exploratory apprenticeship; neither is necessarily directly related to paid employment or future careers.

School-based apprenticeship may involve paid employment in specific occupations, but retains its primary focus on school-related learning. Cooperative education exemplifies this level by systematically incorporating work experience into the vocational curriculum. Youth-managed businesses offer another promising avenue for learning in work settings that remain closely tied to school. School-based apprenticeships are more demanding and more focused than exploratory apprenticeships, but shorter in duration and less intensively focused on specific occupations than work-based apprenticeships.

Work-based apprenticeship is rooted in traditional apprenticeship, focused on preparation for a specific occupation, but modified by the principles stated above. Focusing on a specific occupation is a means of achieving fundamental knowledge, skills, and attitudes that all adults should possess. Teenagers of both genders and all family backgrounds should have access to such apprenticeships, which should be closely related to schools. In its most elaborate form, work-based apprenticeship trains skilled workers at the level of technician beginning during the junior year of high school and continuing through the completion of a two-year associate's degree at a technical college.

When apprenticeship is directed toward specific occupational training and based in the workplace, then, in addition to the four essential elements of the West German system already identified, five more elements are required: a *contract; earnings;* a carefully planned *progression* of training and responsibility; both *breadth and depth;* and reasonable prospects for *future employment.*

Work-based apprenticeship entails obligations on the part of employer and apprentice, which should be clearly stated in a legally binding contract specifying the amount and quality of training to be provided—stated in terms of competencies, not hours of instruction—and compensation. The apprentice should know what behavior on his or her part will lead to termination on the one hand or posttraining employment on the other. When apprentices are minors, their parents should also sign the contract.

Apprentices who are learning occupational skills will do productive work, for which they should be paid. However, it is essential that work promote rather than displace learning; therefore, earnings should be limited to an appropriate fraction of what a skilled, full-time worker earns in order to be fair to the employer and to protect the apprentice from demands for production that impede learning.

Labor unions are understandably suspicious of a "training wage." However, an apprentice's wages may not necessarily be lower than the minimum wage. Furthermore, clear and conscientiously enforced standards could prevent exploitation. The second potential problem with this arrangement is that young people may be reluctant to accept lower earnings than they could receive for unskilled work. Expanding apprenticeship slowly will demonstrate by a growing number of concrete examples that forgoing current earnings in favor of training is a wise investment. West German apprentices make this choice under the same circumstances because the system is so well-established that they know it is worthwhile.

Progressively increasing skills should be expected of apprentices so that they move step-by-step into more demanding work roles. Sequential progress contributes to efficiency of both learning and production but it also reinforces the apprentice's learning by rewarding achievement. The alternative, a series of work experiences encountered without regard to previous or succeeding placements, is likely to be far less effective and satisfying.

The knowledge and skills imparted to apprentices should be broad in the sense that they are fundamental to the occupation and related fields, thus providing a basis for further education and training. However, they should be specific enough to be usable in a workplace. By balancing these two criteria, apprentices will learn skills that are usable in more than one firm, making the resulting credential transferable.

The West German system demonstrates that guaranteed employment in the training firm to successful apprentices, while desirable, is not necessary so long as there is a reasonable prospect for rewarding employment doing related work. Without such rational grounds for hope, apprenticeship loses much of its motivating power and risks becoming as hollow and meaningless as school is to many youth. Because few U.S. employers are prepared to promise jobs even months in advance, far less years, the most promising strategy will be to develop apprenticeship programs to fill projected shortages. Those programs must then be updated and modified according to changing labor market conditions.

Bearing in mind that the three levels of apprenticeship constitute a spectrum, not a set of discrete categories, there is considerable room for overlap and ambiguity among the levels. The labels provide a framework for an array of apprenticeship opportunities, all of which can currently be found in some form in the United States. A reinvented apprenticeship system should build on those existing programs. Efficiency is one reason for adhering to this principle. Programs that already function effectively need not be recreated. Further, inevitable and justifiable "political" concerns about the allocation of resources and responsibilities cannot be ignored. A new apprenticeship system should enable people and organizations already committed to its goals to work more effectively rather than threatening their turf and turning them into opponents.

Beginning with elements of apprenticeship that already flourish also disposes of the objection that this vision is unrealistic because it is inspired by the West German system. That system cannot serve as a template because too much of it is bound up in German history, culture, and economic structure. However, it can and does serve to identify key elements of apprenticeship that already exist in the United States and to inform the effort to tie those elements together into a system.

Recent developments in the German system address many of the most critical concerns Americans have, indicating that apprenticeship can be adapted to meet contemporary conditions and to remedy its past weaknesses. Because these modifications are emerging in response to new conditions that are similar in both countries, they point in the direction that an American system should take.

Democratization has been a major theme in reforms of the West German educational and vocational training system since the end of World War II. Labor unions have criticized the tripartite secondary school system and apprenticeship for perpetuating social class stratification. However, not even the most fervent critics advocated the abolition of apprenticeship.

Although apprenticeship originated in a sharply stratified social structure, it is not inherently undemocratic. Most workers trained as apprentices do not rise far above the level of journeyworker, but the system's direct connection with career ladders boosts the prestige of less desirable occupations. Having completed apprenticeship, a skilled mechanic can take additional courses and an examination to become a *Meister,* a highly respected title that carries with it the right to operate one's own shop. Further study and examinations qualify a mechanic for the title *Ingenieur,* engineer. American observers have concluded that the strength of West Germany's manufacturing sector results in part from the presence in the highest ranks of corporate management of executives who began their careers as apprentices and worked their way up from the shop floor. Their intimate knowledge of production and expertise in engineering give them key advantages over the managers and accountants who dominated U.S. corporations, and who tend to move readily from one firm to another with little concern for the nature of its products.[2]

The West German system treats as skilled occupations many that are considered unskilled in the United States. Selling shoes in a retail store, for example, requires a full apprenticeship, which includes not only basic customer relations, sizing, and cash register operation, but also instruction in the materials and methods used in making shoes and in bookkeeping. While training such workers so thoroughly might seem excessive, it has two laudable effects. One is that ordinary workers in West Germany are usually quite competent. Retail sales people, for example, are routinely able to provide information and advice that can only be found in the more expensive specialty shops in the United States, if at all. The second is that every person who qualifies to hold a skilled job also obtains the qualifications needed to advance to the next step. The shoe salesperson who is "overtrained" from a U.S. perspective has the basic qualifications to run a shoe store and is prepared to advance to this step if the opportunity arises.

There is an irony here. Americans take pride in the openness of their social structure and view public schools as essential to maintaining that openness. A system like West Germany's appears anachronistically undemocratic because it seems to support rigid distinctions among levels in the occupational hierarchy. Yet, in operation, apprenticeship functions as if every skilled craft worker had the potential to become an independent shop owner and every skilled worker in business and industry could climb the occupational hierarchy. The American habit of undertraining devalues work done by people without college degrees and leaves many of those people with few options for upward social mobility. They might go back to school, but doing so exposes them to the same indignities and frustrations that previously led them to terminate their schooling. The German tendency to overtrain adds status to skilled and semiskilled occupations and provides a solid basis for advancement in the occupational hierarchy through further training that builds upon apprenticeship.

Another source of prestige for the apprenticeship system is its extension to such white-collar occupations as *Industriekaufmann*. Because the system includes so many desirable occupations, apprenticeship remains a desirable form of education and training. German apprentices are far less likely than U.S. vocational high school students to regard themselves as losers, relegated to a lower track compared to college-bound youth.

Nevertheless, the German system still has some aspects that Americans would find objectionable. Although school track assignment is no more dependent on family background than in the United States, differentiation occurs earlier and is more profound in Germany: by grades five or seven young people identified as noncollege bound are assigned to separate school buildings as well as distinctive curricula, exaggerating the magnitude of differences among young people. Although it is possible to move from a lower to an upper level, movement is quite difficult. One apprentice said in her interview that she had advanced from *Hauptschule* to *Realschule* and boasted that she only had to repeat one grade to make the transfer; most who move up, she said, repeat two grades.

Beginning apprenticeship at a young age also perpetuates gender inequality. Even more than in the United States, West German occupations are gender stereotyped. Young women or young men must be exceptionally strong to violate those stereotypes. While some adults have the self-confidence to overcome them, few 16-year-olds are prepared to assume such a burden. The burden has multiple components. A young woman training to be an auto mechanic must be prepared to explain such a bizarre plan to her parents, friends, and anyone else who might ask. She must also cope with being socially out of place on a day-to-day basis.

Auto repair shops are as masculine as a football team's locker room. Some women might find them comfortable and if more women worked in them they would surely change, but they are not the kinds of places most adolescent girls would find appealing. A young woman with anything less than a total commitment to becoming an auto mechanic and to overturning gender stereotypes would find the shop an unpleasant workplace.

West German firms that train women to enter predominantly male occupations have had to admit groups of young women rather than isolated individuals, a sensible strategy but one that is feasible for only the largest employers. Gender inequality in apprenticeship cannot be overcome without a wider movement toward gender equality in all areas of life, backed by affirmative action. Female apprentices are concentrated in a small number of mostly low-status occupations because these are the occupations open to women. As in the United States, higher education and the professions have attracted more women than manual trades. Young women can more realistically aspire to be physicians and lawyers than machinists and carpenters. However, few West German women may be found serving as university professors or among the leaders of business and government. The rapidly declining youth population may have the welcome effect of forcing West Germany to integrate women more thoroughly into the workforce and treat them more equitably.

Parallel to its role in perpetuating gender inequality, West German apprenticeship can legitimately be criticized for perpetuating class distinctions and the disadvantages faced by foreign workers and their children. Rigid occupational entry requirements and the importance of personal connections and personal style in finding an apprenticeship place are barriers to outsiders. However, in both cases it is not apprenticeship per se but the structure of economic and social opportunity that is at fault. Applying affirmative action principles to apprenticeship can alleviate some of the worst inequalities, but the openness of the labor market is most crucial.

The best hope for democratizing West German apprenticeship lies in the workforce demands generated by changing demographic conditions, heightened international competition, and new technology. As in the United States, those demands cannot be met simply by improving the training of current workers' sons. Females and formerly marginal groups must be educated and trained more effectively and then given access to jobs that have heretofore been reserved for German males if prosperity is to be maintained.

Competition from other countries and rapidly changing technology have led representatives of large West German firms to view apprenticeship as the first step in a continuing process of lifelong learning. West Germany's prosperity relies upon exports. As such heavy industries as steel and shipbuilding have declined, auto manufacturing, chemicals, machine tools, and other high-quality finished products have gained prominence. Employers and economic analysts agree that international leadership in producing high-quality goods such as these requires a highly skilled and adaptable workforce. After some debate, they also agree that apprenticeship is essential to maintaining such a workforce.[3]

Several appealing modifications of the West German system have followed from this perception of apprenticeship as the foundation for lifelong learning. One is that increasing numbers of young people enroll in full-time school before and after apprenticeship. More youth enroll in the middle-level *Realschule* rather than the lower-level *Hauptschule,* and a growing proportion of *Abiturienten,* who are qualified to enroll in universities, choose to enter apprenticeship instead. This extension of schooling began as a response to increased competition for jobs. *Realschüler* displaced *Hauptschüler* in competition for occupations formerly considered beneath their qualifications and *Gymnasiasten* entered the elite apprenticeships formerly reserved for *Realschüler.* Although there is a danger of credential inflation in this trend, it has not abated as the outlook for apprenticeship places has improved.

As a result, the *Realschule* diploma has become the new minimum standard of achievement, replacing the *Hauptschule* completion certificate, which formerly enabled its holder to enter most occupations not requiring higher education.[4] Simultaneously, poor job prospects for university graduates encouraged more young people to choose apprenticeship over university studies, but those making that choice retain their access to university courses, and many enroll after completing their apprenticeship. With prolonged schooling, apprentices' average age is increasing. As a result, early choice of an occupation is becoming less critical and further schooling after apprenticeship is becoming more accessible.

The second educational path (*der zweite Bildungsweg*) enables skilled workers who have completed apprenticeship and demonstrated their academic competence to enroll in night school (*Abendgymnasium*), and if successful there, to then enroll in a university. Although free tuition and living allowances increase this option's accessibility, the challenge of attending night school as an adult and of forgoing adult income for four or more years of university study is daunting; only a small proportion of university students enter via the second educational path.[5]

The new phenomenon of double qualification, has become a more prominent form of extended education. Double qualification means acquiring both an apprentice's skilled worker certificate and a diploma from a full-time vocational school. In the past, these two paths were usually distinct. Many occupations could be entered via one path only: nurses must have gone to school; cabinetmakers must have been apprentices. A few, mainly in the commercial sector, were accessible via both routes. The expansion of full-time vocational schooling to absorb young people who were unable to find an apprenticeship gave parents and youth a heightened appreciation of school credentials. Securing two certificates of qualification improves young people's competitive position in the labor market; successfully completing postcompulsory schooling leaves open their path to even higher-level qualification through higher education.[6]

Hermann Stockhausen, who achieved the highest score in his state on the qualifying examination for apprentice plumbers, went on to a full-time *Berufsaufbauschule* (vocational development school) instead of accepting immediate employment as a plumber. He continued in school because he discovered in the *Berufsschule* an interest in and aptitude for physics and math that no one had suspected when he was in *Hauptschule*. He got poor grades there and did not work hard because he was uninterested in the subjects. When math and science were presented in terms of such practical problems as the angle at which a drain pipe functions properly, his interest was piqued and he excelled. His further schooling will make him even more attractive to employers, but he hopes to continue in a *Fachhochschule*, and eventually to become an engineer. Hermann did not need double qualification to get a job, but the availability of vocationally relevant schooling first revealed his proficiency and then offered him an avenue toward higher-level schooling and advanced occupational status.

Treating apprenticeship as the opening phase in a lifelong learning process that enables workers to adapt to new technology and changing economic conditions has reduced some of the West German system's rigidity. One manifestation of this rigidity is dividing occupations into many separate specialties. One apprentice auto mechanic who decided in his third year to switch to auto body repair had to begin both his on-the-job training and his *Berufsschule* course all over again, taking three more years of apprenticeship to qualify for his new career. Others who have had second thoughts about their training occupation but could not tolerate remaining any longer as apprentices have either stifled their doubts and persisted or looked for opportunities to change occupations without undergoing a new apprenticeship.

In response to this problem, the number of occupations offering apprenticeship training has been reduced steadily, from more than 600 in 1971 to less than 400 by 1989. Forty-two different metal-working occupations were recently consolidated into six broadly defined training fields, increasing both the universality of training and the flexibility of the workers who have been trained. Other occupational fields now have a common first-year program to increase flexibility.

Consolidating occupations appears to be an effective reform. Substituting school for workplace training has not succeeded. The vocational preparation year (*Berufsvorbereitungsjahr*) is a year of school added after completion of *Hauptschule* to serve as a first step into vocational training. It is entirely school-based, but the content of instruction is heavily vocational. In theory, the extra school year should count as the first year of apprenticeship, but it seldom has in practice because it was introduced when serious shortages in apprenticeship places turned it into a second-choice alternative. Young people who were unable to find an apprenticeship place were the most numerous enrollees in the vocational preparation year. Any who found a training place during the year immediately quit to begin an apprenticeship, and those who completed the year went back into the labor market to search for an apprenticeship place with no new advantages.[7] This cycle tainted the vocational preparation year in the minds of employers, young people, and parents, all of whom see it more as a waiting station than as a step into serious vocational training.

The basic vocational training year (*Berufsgrundbildungsjahr*) met the same fate except in those regions where an entire industry agreed to rely on it. The implementation of the basic vocational training year demonstrates employers' determination to retain their control of the system, even though control entails paying most of its costs. Resisting the labor unions' preference for a school-based program, employers succeeded in altering the original proposal to create two forms of basic vocational training year: one operated entirely by the schools; the other partly employer-based. The school-based program is much like a full-time vocational school. The employer-based program is similar to apprenticeship except for the consolidation of related occupations. For example, 20 different occupations involving metalwork were combined into one *Metalltechnik* program, a forerunner to the recent consolidation of that field.

An evaluation study directly comparing school-based and employer-based basic vocational training year programs in metal working found the employer-based programs more successful by several criteria, including both practical skill acquisition and attitude formation. Part of the difference was accounted for by the greater attractiveness of the more traditional employer-based program. Young people with a choice preferred it and it proved more effective. The investigators attributed its superiority to the greater amount of time spent learning practical skills and to its resemblance to traditional apprenticeship. Enrollees in the employer-based program knew that if they performed well they would be hired by the employer, a large prestigious firm, upon conclusion of their training. Young people in the school-based program had no such motivation; they expressed doubt about the program's value and felt more pessimistic about their futures. Their behavior and performance suffered as a result.[8] There is no substitute for the motivation youth feel when their diligence in training can lead directly to a good job.

Rigidity, however, still plagues the German system. The consolidation of metalworkers' training represented the culmination of eight years of negotiations among employers, unions, and the government, demonstrating the resistance to change inherent in the complex West German system. When new fields open up, as resulted from the widespread introduction of computers, the system is slow to respond. Large firms like Brandt develop their own programs, filling them with people who have already qualified for more traditional occupations. For example, an *Industriekauffrau* apprentice there was scheduled, upon completion of her apprenticeship, to begin an additional year and a half of training in electronic data processing. Brandt also had a special five-year apprenticeship program that combined training and certification in two occupations, electronics and precision mechanics, qualifying those who completed it to repair industrial robots. But these adaptations are made by large firms acting alone, not by the system as a whole.

Renewed emphasis on quality control has contributed to the adaptation of apprenticeship to changing economic conditions, especially in small and medium-sized enterprises. Concern for improving the quality of training and education dominated reformers' proposals during the 1970s, but then receded when the baby boom cohort flooded the market for apprentices in the early 1980s. Growing international competition during the 1970s led some to conclude that apprenticeship was outmoded. Simultaneously, other critics claimed that too many apprentices were exploited as cheap labor, gaining little of value from their three years of work at low pay. The ultimately unsuccessful movement to create comprehensive high schools was one response to these perceived problems. Another was a tightening of the regulations governing such elements of the system as instructor training and apprentices' firm-based instruction.

Improving quality control is complex because the dual system's governance is complex, involving extended cooperation among numerous stake-holders. The state governments are responsible for education, hence for the *Berufsschulen*. However, in order to assure that apprentices receive comparable training and are able to transfer their credentials across state boundaries, the federal government plays a role and a permanent confer-ence of ministers of culture from all the states meets regularly to set and revise course syllabi.

The *Berufsschulen* assure that apprentices acquire general knowledge of German and social studies and specific knowledge and skills related to their vocation. Their performance is judged primarily on the basis of the examinations all apprentices must pass in order to qualify as skilled workers. The written portion of the examination covers all the subjects taught in the *Berufsschule*. The practical portion relies more heavily on learning from work experience. Apprentice auto mechanics take their practical examination in a shop, where they are given tools, materials, and a blueprint and are required to construct the metal device specified in the blueprint. Experts then judge the product's quality and assign a grade. For aspiring *Industriekaufleute*, the practical examination is admin-istered orally by a panel that assesses their social skills as well as their technical knowledge.

Apprentices take a preliminary examination after a year or two of training. The qualifying examination terminates their apprenticeship, ordi-narily at the end of their prescribed time, but it can be taken and passed early when an apprentice has made exceptional progress. About 90 percent pass the qualifying examination at each administration.[9] An apprentice who fails is allowed to retake the examination twice, lowering the propor-tion who ultimately fail to less than 10 percent. Lacking the skilled worker's certificate that a passing examination grade confers, a young person may seek a new apprenticeship, carrying the stigma of failure and advanced age, or enter the labor market without that all-important certificate. Further schooling is not an inviting option for someone who has failed the most school-like part of apprenticeship.

Apprentices who fail the qualifying examination join youth who have dropped out of their apprenticeship and others who neither started an apprenticeship nor completed further vocational schooling in West Ger-many's equivalent of the secondary labor market (between 5 and 10 percent of youth past the age of compulsory schooling). Most are relegated to unskilled work. Only the most fortunate are able to find jobs that eventually lead to earnings and status approaching a skilled worker's.

The qualifying examinations are uniform nationwide and are written not by the schools or education departments but by joint examination committees sponsored by the chambers responsible for overseeing each occupation or sector. Trade unions, *Berufsschule* teachers, and government education officials are represented on those joint committees, but the majority of members are employers' representatives. Therefore, employers exercise a more powerful influence over the content of the *Berufs-schule* curriculum than any other group.

The chambers are also responsible for enforcing the training guidelines established for each occupation with an apprenticeship. The examinations serve as one source of data for the chambers. Any firm whose apprentices regularly fail the examination is suspected of offering inadequate training. Chamber representatives examine documents such as the firm's training plan and apprentices' individual records of their work experience and firm-based instruction. They may make site visits to inspect training conditions.[10]

The best assurance of quality, however, is employers' investment in training, which reflects their reliance on their own apprentices as future workers. Differences in quality between large and small firms result from this simple fact. Large firms train no more apprentices than they expect to hire. They can afford to invest substantial sums in apprentices' training and to treat them primarily as learners, only secondarily as productive workers. They recoup that investment over the duration of their apprentices' working life in the firm, which they expect will be long. Small firms, especially in the craft sector, consistently take on apprentices even when no permanent places for them are in view. Small shops with a master and two or three journeymen rely on an apprentice or two as helpers, doing routine unskilled work in exchange for training. Although some small shops have excellent reputations for turning out superior workers who are quickly hired by other firms, others do what is required or less, to the detriment of both the apprentices and the system. Any substantial increase in standards or enforcement could compel many small shops to give up training and even to close their doors for want of cheap unskilled labor.

The scope and quality of instruction in the firm is one of the key advantages enjoyed by apprentices in large firms accoring to both apprentices and *Berufsschule* teachers. Large firms employ full-time trainers and provide instructional facilities on site. The result, one *Berufsschule* teacher said, is that *Berufsschule* instruction is most important for apprentices in small firms who get it from no other source; for apprentices from large firms, school classes often accomplish no more than review.

The multifirm training shop (*überbetriebliche Ausbildungsstatt*) is an innovation designed to compensate for this deficiency. Established and operated by a consortium of small and medium-sized firms in the same field, such a shop offers practical instruction to rotating groups of apprentices from participating firms. The government has subsidized the creation of multifirm training shops as a means of raising the quality of apprenticeship training.[11] Because a given region must include enough firms and apprentices to make such a facility viable, its utility is limited to metropolitan centers or to occupations with large numbers of apprentices. As one of the occupations with the largest number of apprentices, auto mechanic is ideal for multifirm training. Less common occupations like coppersmith do not lend themselves so well to the approach.

More than any other recent West German adaptation, the increasing importance of school, especially in the form of double qualification, helps to make some form of apprenticeship a viable option in the United States. Having made a strong commitment to universal schooling and taken steps thereby toward greater equality, the United States will not now set up an alternative path by which some young people bypass school. The emerging West German system, in which the *Realschule* is becoming standard and many apprentices also spend extra years in full-time school, is far more compatible with U.S. traditions than the old system of ending full-time schooling for the majority with ninth grade. It demonstrates that apprenticeship need not replace schooling, even if it does reduce the amount of time young people spend in classrooms.

An American apprenticeship system must be flexible, diverse, and open. It must contribute to school credentials rather than substituting for schooling. And it must be aimed primarily at general preparation for work—in other words, education—more than at specific job training, which is an effective means of preparing youth for adulthood but should not become its sole end. Such a system will embody the essential elements of West German apprenticeship but its foundation has been laid in a variety of programs that already function effectively in the United States.

8

An American-Style
Apprenticeship System

The essential elements of apprenticeship are already in place in the United States. However, they are scattered across the country in programs enrolling small numbers of young people. These programs can be regarded as seeds of a system that will enable every young person to move through a coherent sequence of apprenticeship experiences that are clearly connected to each other and to schooling.

To visualize what such a system would look like, imagine a city, Lakeland, that has established a comprehensive apprenticeship system. By fifth or sixth grade at the latest, every young person in Lakeland is involved in community service. Many projects are sponsored by the schools, but churches, scout troops, 4-H clubs, and other youth organizations emphasize community service too.

Young adolescents should engage in service to their communities primarily because they are citizens and, as such, have an obligation to serve. In addition, community service gives young people opportunities to take real responsibility in the real world that involves them with adults. The worklike tasks young people perform in the name of service foster the development of worker virtues, skills in planning, working with people, and often manual skills as well.

As volunteers, early adolescents have access to settings and responsibilities that would be denied them as workers because of their age. Child labor laws forbid most forms of serious paid employment to anyone younger than 14, restrict it seriously for those between 14 and 16, and still limit the options of anyone under the age of 18. Employers and insurance companies tend to be more lenient with volunteers than with paid employees.[1]

Community service, therefore, gives younger adolescents worker roles with a degree of complexity and level of responsibility that they could not ordinarily find in paid employment. Moreover, voluntary service projects undertaken by *groups* of young people provide experiences in planning and management that are unavailable to them in most work settings. By initiating projects that would not exist without them, youth take control of decision-making processes from which they are normally excluded in adult settings.

The distinction between group and individual community service projects is a useful one. As individual volunteers, young people perform roles in programs that are organized and directed by adults. If the young people were not there, the programs would go on without them. Youth serving as voluntary aides in day-care programs are a good example of this kind of voluntary effort. Adults control the day-care program. They define roles and responsibilities for voluntary aides and then train and supervise the youth who fill those roles. The youth volunteers may meet together as a group, and a few may work together at the same time or place, but essentially they volunteer as individuals. Their influence over the program is limited. They may have a good chance of developing a close one-to-one relationship with their supervisor or adult co-workers.[2]

Foxfire is a good example of the second type of community service project, in which youth as a group jointly define and carry out an activity that would not occur without them. The high school students who write and publish the magazine shape it as they choose, mindful of external demands and constraints but deciding themselves how to interpret and respond to them. In the process, people who are too young to hold a real job sign checks for hundreds of thousands of dollars, reorganize the magazine's subscription system, and repeatedly make difficult decisions about such issues as whether to introduce the local people they interviewed to an advertiser who, on the one hand, might exploit them and, on the other, would pay them more than they could ordinarily earn in a year.[3]

Apprenticeship is more obviously an appropriate label for the first form of community service because of the one-to-one adult/youth relationship. Although group projects often revolve around a single adult adviser, she or he cannot always serve as a mentor to each participant. The group adviser, exemplified by Foxfire's Eliot Wigginton, operates rather like an excellent athletic coach, learning each participant's strengths and needs and, through instruction, encouragement, and the identification of appropriate opportunities, helping him or her progress as part of the group effort.

Though apprenticeship is often identified with one-to-one relations, group experiences are a part of contemporary West German apprenticeship in large firms. Apprentices in the firms described in Chapter 3 received regular group instruction and participated in activities designed specifically to encourage group identity, including a retreat of several days at their firms' residential training facilities.

Lakeland supports both youth-directed community service programs, on the Foxfire model, and voluntary service in adult-directed settings. They are complementary parts of a comprehensive system and every young person is able to experience both.[4]

Young people begin serving Lakeland at an early age and continue as they grow older. High schools sponsor increasingly challenging service opportunities. During the summer, some Lakeland high school students join the Youth Conservation Corps. Many high school graduates spend a year in the full-time Youth Service Corps, improving parks, rehabilitating housing, and helping neighborhood groups build community playgrounds and gardens.[5] Youth corps constitute part of an apprenticeship system when they embody the four essential elements of apprenticeship. Projects are selected not only for their value to the community and to the natural environment, but also for their educational potential. Participants are treated as learners, not just workers. Instruction in job skills is balanced by experience and by instruction in basic principles and broader issues. Work experience is related to academic learning. Ideally, remedial instruction is available for those who need it. Supervisors are mentors, not just foremen.

The balance of exploration, education, and training found in various corps reflects the ages and needs of enrolled youth. Lakeland's Youth Conservation Corps teaches some basic manual skills but offers more exploration than training. The city's Youth Service Corps initiates skill training for some graduates. With these variations, the youth corps approach cuts across the three levels of apprenticeship, offering exploratory community service for younger people but intensive work-based skill training for older youth.

In Lakeland, both youth corps programs intentionally enroll a cross section of youth, not just college students taking a break or the unemployed. This diversity creates opportunities for fostering mutual understanding and respect across lines of social class, race, and ethnicity. Because young people are separated along these lines in many school and work settings, when they are thrown together, their diversity becomes a central focus for learning. They also learn together about the conditions they are trying to improve and their origins in natural and human processes.

Lakeland also makes mentors available for all youth who want one. A mentor gives advice and encouragement, sharing the knowledge and wisdom of experience in a relationship that is personal and enduring. Drawing on conversations with Japanese colleagues, Urie Bronfenbrenner defined a mentor as follows:

> A *mentor* is an older, more experienced person who seeks to further
> the development of character and competence in a younger person
> by guiding the latter in acquiring mastery of progressively more complex
> skills and tasks in which the mentor is already proficient. The guidance
> is accomplished through demonstration, instruction, challenge, and
> encouragement on a more or less regular basis over an extended period
> of time. In the course of this process, the mentor and the young
> person develop a special bond of mutual commitment. In addition,
> the young person's relationship to the mentor takes on an emotional
> character of respect, loyalty, and identification.[6]

Mentors for youth may be described as teachers, challengers, role models, supporters, and companions.[7] A mentor's functions are parental in many respects, but a mentor, by definition, is someone other than a parent who performs such functions voluntarily rather than out of parental obligation. Similarly, although teachers and counselors may become mentors, they do so only when they exceed the formal demands of their roles.

Mentors have been identified as crucial figures in adult development[8] and as contributing to the disadvantages encountered by women in business—because men with the requisite seniority and power to become mentors are more likely to do so for men than for women.[9] Mentors are essential for youth whose parents are unable because of their poverty and lack of experience to help them set and achieve challenging goals. One commonality among young people who have become successful adults despite childhood deprivation is that they had someone other than a parent to turn to for advice, encouragement, and assistance.[10]

Many young people, about half those responding to several surveys, already know an unrelated adult who might qualify as a mentor, typically a neighbor, family friend, or someone like a music teacher or gymnastics coach.[11] Elementary school-age children and younger adolescents who do not know such a person can be matched with one through the Big Brothers/Big Sisters program. Because of the program's emphasis on personal relations, Big Brothers and Big Sisters do not give youth worker roles or explicitly relate work to schooling. However, to the extent that Big Brothers and Big Sisters teach, they create learning opportunities for youth in the community. Even without addressing work directly, mentoring programs demonstrate the power of that relationship and the capacity of ordinary adults without professional training to foster the development of youth.

Middle school and high school youth in Lakeland often find mentors through a Learning Web program, which is clearly exploratory; it gives them a chance to try out a range of adult roles. As they enter their senior year, some join a program patterned after Career Beginnings,[12] which provides mentors who give concrete advice and assistance about higher education and employment. In addition, employers, as a matter of course, assign adult workers as mentors to their youth employees who have special needs, as in the Work-Scholarship Connection, described below. Like youth corps, mentoring begins with the exploratory stage of apprenticeship, but applies across the spectrum.

Experience Based Career Education stands between the exploratory level of apprenticeship and school-based apprenticeship. EBCE was instituted in Lakeland because, as with voluntary community service, young people in EBCE are allowed to take responsibility at a level beyond their presumed capacity, because they are not paid. As learners rather than paid workers they have access to workplaces and occupational levels for which they could not qualify as employees. Middle school and high school students enrolled in EBCE rotate through a number of different workplaces and occupations, giving them a much wider-range view than a traditional apprenticeship in one field.

In Lakeland, secondary vocational education has been redirected from narrowly defined job training to broad preparation for work in the sense of teaching youth the basic academic knowledge and skills they will need for any adult jobs and of fostering worker virtues. High school students' interest in work and their belief that work is real are exploited to accomplish general educational objectives. To the extent that they learn job-related knowledge and skills that serve them well at work, so much the better, but that is in added benefit, not vocational education's primary purpose. Lakeland's vocational programs are no longer evaluated according to how many graduates of the printing program become printers and how many drafting students get jobs as drafters. Instead, they are judged by the same criteria as academic programs, according to gains participants make in academic learning, and graduates' post–high school educational attainment, successful career entry, and progressive advancement thereafter.

Lakeland's vocational curriculum presents students with a series of practical tasks that grow in magnitude and complexity over time and teach both practical skills and related academic lessons. Accomplishment of a task, including in many cases creation of a tangible product, motivates basic learning and skill acquisition. The machine shop takes orders from local industries to produce custom parts, so long as they are challenging enough to teach the students something new but short enough not to become repetitive. Students in the building trades construct a real house. Some specialize in plumbing and others in electricity, but all are involved in reading blueprints, studying building codes, writing letters, and solving math problems as part of the project. Specific job training remains a means to achieving broad educational goals rather than becoming vocational education's principal end.

School-based apprenticeship is a logical extension of current practices in secondary vocational education that bridge school and work. The tradition of cooperative education and on-the-job training associated with secondary vocational schooling is an ideal foundation for building bridges between school and work. Lakeland's vocational teachers play a key role in creating this structure. Many of them have experience in finding appropriate placements for their students, which entails knowing local employers and having their confidence, being able to identify workplaces that will be good learning environments, and being skilled in negotiating agreements that maximize the young person's learning. Not every job placement is conducive to a young person's learning and maturation; selection and oversight must take into account characteristics of both the learner and the site. As in a formal apprenticeship, a contractual arrangement stipulates each party's obligations. The vocational teacher is a guarantor of the student's right to learn and a negotiator between student and employer if either is dissatisfied.

Few secondary school teachers in academic subjects have these skills. Therefore, if apprenticeship is to be broadened to incorporate college-bound youth who use it for longer-range career purposes or for general learning, then vocational teachers must become a resource to all students. They may be charged with arranging all cooperative education placements or they may coach academic teachers in the art of arranging placements. To carry the bridge metaphor further, vocational education is the bridge's abutment on the school side, anchoring the extension of learning into the world of work.[13]

Taking advantage of the cooperative education structure, which is already in place, will require academic teachers to set aside their prejudices against vocational education and vocational teachers. Looking to cooperative education models in higher education may help. Northeastern University and Antioch College have for years operated highly developed cooperative education programs for college students. Because both place students in work settings that are not necessarily related to their future careers and both stress the value of such experience for academic purposes, academic teachers may more readily view them as models than the shop courses taught in another wing of the building where they work. Nonetheless, vocational teachers' experience and expertise are too valuable to be ignored. Staff of community-based youth organizations are another source of assistance because they are more accustomed than most school teachers to locating community resources and using the community as a learning environment.

Youth who enter adult workplaces as learners in cooperative education programs normally have to accept the kind of work they are given and the policies and organizational structures in which their work is embedded. Ideally, they also get to see inside the organization to learn the rationale and the processes behind it, perhaps with the aid of a mentor. But they are unlikely to be consulted about such fundamental matters, much less to participate in deciding them. In order to give more young people opportunities to assume leadership roles and to make critical choices that are out of their hands in ordinary workplaces, Lakeland schools sponsor a range of youth-managed businesses, drawing on the expertise of such organizations as Junior Achievement and North Carolina REAL Enterprises. They include a household chore service, a company that does custom silkscreen designs on T-shirts, and the school's store.

Disadvantaged youth are potentially the greatest beneficiaries of involvement in youth-managed businesses. Experience in their families, neighborhoods, and schools reinforces a view of themselves as suited only to subordinate positions in society. Employment training programs can unintentionally corrobrate this view by throwing together young people who were selected because of their deficits, and then engaging them in menial jobs that offer little independence or responsibility, and require no skills—in short, jobs that represent the lowest level of the occupational hierarchy. The same young woman who might get little more than a pay check out of such a program may emerge from a stint as treasurer of a furniture refinishing business convinced that she has the intelligence and drive to go to college and excel in math.

Entrepreneurial activities introduce youth in dramatic fashion to the challenges and satisfactions of operating a small business. Even though only a few will ever own their own business, the majority will work for a small business during their career, and they may be more sympathetic to their employer's situation if they have experienced it themselves, even without risking their life savings on the venture. Small businesses generate far more new jobs than large businesses and, according to many commentators, are the United States' best hope of meeting international competition because they also tend to be more innovative, inventing and implementing new technologies more rapidly than large corporations with their biases toward caution and their dense bureaucracies.

One model for Lakeland's youth-managed businesses is a Ben and Jerry's ice-cream store franchised to the Learning Web and operated by young people in Ithaca, New York. All employees begin as scoopers, serving customers and performing routine maintenance chores. As they establish their reliability and become interested in other aspects of the store's operation, some become informal apprentices either to an adult manager or to one of the more experienced youth, who teach them how to schedule workers, prepare the payroll, order supplies, and display wares. Committees take responsibility for all aspects of store operation under the leadership of a youth chairperson. Workers are paid hourly for their normal work. Chairpersons receive a stipend that recognizes their extra work but does not reimburse it fully. Committee service, meetings of the entire staff, and training received outside normal work hours are all unpaid; workers are encouraged to view these duties as an investment in learning that will pay off in the future. Those who have performed them responsibly and competently receive recommendations that qualify them for higher-level positions when they move to a new job. Employees who choose not to become involved in management must leave after six months—with job experience and a letter of reference—in order to open positions for others who will also be able to decide whether to treat their job as simply a supportive first work experience or as an opportunity to learn about management.[14]

Exploratory and school-based apprenticeships are less intensive than a formal work-based apprenticeship. They are appropriate for young people anticipating careers in a variety of fields, including those who have no specific career plans and those definitely bound for college. Taking the idea of apprenticeship to its logical conclusion, however, means creating West German-style, work-based apprenticeships that are specific and intensive. In view of prevailing traditions and the labor market in the United States, not as many youth would be involved in such apprenticeships and they would not lead to as many occupations. Only young people with relatively firm career plans would enter a multiyear program. Employers will invest in apprenticeship training only in fields where workers are needed and where they require advanced knowledge and skills.

Jobs with the title "technician" meet these criteria best. Electronics technicians, quality control technicians, robotics technicians, and a range of medical technicians including dental laboratory, X-ray, and EEG all have specialized technological knowledge and skills but do not have a four-year college degree. A 38 percent increase in the number of technicians is projected by the year 2000.[15] Competent and adaptable technicians are crucial to maintaining American competitiveness as new technology continually alters production and communication. The shortage of skilled technicians is severe enough in some industries that technicians' work is done by college-educated engineers, whose advanced training is then inadequately utilized, to their detriment and the economy's.

Technicians need a solid foundation in math, science, and English to go with their technical skills and they need to be able to learn new skills quickly as new technology is introduced. In Lakeland, technicians are trained in a "2+2" apprenticeship. They begin in their junior year of high school by combining vocational courses with academic courses and a work-based apprenticeship. After graduating from high school, they continue with the same combination through two more years of technical college.[16] Programs are planned and evaluated by means of a collaborative agreement among the high schools, the two-year colleges, and local business and industry. Firms add their own classroom instruction when they believe it is needed.

Apprentice technicians' job responsibilities and pay increase sequentially as they gain experience and knowledge. The transition from high school to technical college is a smooth one thanks to articulation agreements between the two institutions specifying that satisfactory completion of the high school portion of the program guarantees admission to the college program. By the end of four years, apprentices have earned a high school diploma, an associate's degree, and a certificate testifying to their possession of high-level skills, all of which are transferable to other employers and may be used for entry into further higher education. Barring unforeseen circumstances, employers in the training firms offer newly trained technicians an appropriate job; they have, after all, been trained to the firms' specifications.

Although some educators expressed concern as the program was being planned that apprentices would have too little time to do their schoolwork, they found that apprentices spend little more time on-the-job than most other students do in part-time jobs unrelated to their schooling. The concentration of school classes into shorter periods of time and the enhanced motivation for learning that apprentices receive from their work experience more than compensate for the hours they put in working.

A second concern during the planning stages was that young people would choose unskilled jobs over apprenticeship positions that paid less during the first two or three years. This proved to be the case for some young people, but others found the promise of a two-year college degree and a career-entry job upon completion of the program sufficient inducement to forgo immediate earnings. In order to assure that initially lower earnings did not prevent low-income youth from becoming apprentices, Lakeland established scholarships to help cover living expenses their parents could not afford.

The 2+2 apprenticeship incorporates all of the best elements of work-based apprenticeship. Although it is challenging to implement because it involves high schools, technical colleges, and employers and longer-term commitments than either employees or employers are accustomed to making, it is a good place to start as well as an ultimate destination for an apprenticeship system. Tying apprenticeship to the relatively prestigious and highly paid occupation, technician, makes all of its variations more attractive.

In addition to starting with a 2+2 program, Lakeland made a second tactical decision in creating its apprenticeship system. Although the planners agreed that the need to prepare disadvantaged youth for work was their strongest motivation, they decided not to address that need by developing programs exclusively for the disadvantaged.[17] If apprenticeship is widely viewed as being for youth who cannot make it without help, then it will not be able to help the youth who need it most. One reason why West German apprenticeship is an effective system is that it is for the majority, not just the needy. Including in the system such selective programs as Brandt's, leading relatively privileged youth to enviable positions, enhances the prestige of the entire system. No one can dismiss it as being a path only for losers. The prestige given to the idea of apprenticeship by an effective 2+2 program enhances the value and attractiveness of other programs of shorter duration, some of which focus more specifically on disadvantaged populations.

In addition to the 2+2 apprenticeship, which assumes a specific career choice by the age of 15 or 16 and a long-term commitment to training by employers, Lakeland created other types of work-based apprenticeship for cases when one or both of these conditions are not met. For high school students who are unable to envision a four-year program with heavy academic demands, they initiated an apprenticeship that begins in high school and concludes a year or two after graduation, without benefit of college enrollment. This program proved effective as a dropout prevention measure. Another apprenticeship program was initiated for young people who had already dropped out, which gave them motivation plus earnings to support their acquisition of a high school equivalency certificate (GED). As has always been the case, high school graduates are also eligible to enter apprenticeships. Using as a model a program sponsored by the International Union of Operating Engineers in the 1970s, Lakeland made possible "dual enrollment" in apprenticeship training and technical college, providing the second half of the 2+2 apprenticeship for young people who did not make a career choice in high school.[18]

All of Lakeland's work-based apprenticeships grew out of their previous apprenticeship programs, but instead of catering primarily to young adult white males, the new programs actively recruit teenagers, females, and members of minority groups. But the greatest changes made in apprenticeship in Lakeland were its extension into new occupations and sponsorship by more employers. Traditional skilled trades constitute too small a part of the labor market to serve all the youth who can benefit from apprenticeship or to meet workforce requirements; if apprenticeship remains primarily within that sector, it will never become a major institution preparing youth for work and adulthood. Lakeland's firms and city agencies accepted the essential principles of apprenticeship training and applied them in the growing segments of the labor market, including technology and middle management.

Employers' use of apprenticeship for purposes beyond training skilled craft workers required them to expand and alter the kind of training they provided, and to make more training available to a wider range of employees. They had to change their former practice of spending most of their training dollars on college-educated employees. Nor could they limit training to the minimum required so that workers could do a specific job. Instead, a larger proportion of training funds had to be invested in fundamental education. Lakeland employers now consider themselves partners with the public schools in the process of preparing youth for adult employment.

As appealing as this vision is, there are limits to what any community, even one so enlighted as Lakeland, can accomplish on its own. Institutions at the state and federal levels must also be involved in the creation of an apprenticeship system.

Military service has traditionally provided young people with extensive education and training, competitive pay and benefits, and generous postdischarge educational assistance. The military is closer to being an institution bridging adolescence and adulthood for noncollege youth than any other now in existence in the United States. It has demonstrated enviable success in providing remedial education and job training to young people who have failed in and been failed by school.[19] The armed forces already sponsor 50,000 apprentices, one-sixth of all those in registered programs.[20]

As the number of youth declines, the military finds itself in competition with private employers and with higher education for competent high school graduates. While this should increase young people's earnings and might motivate more of them to finish high school, competition for bodies may not by itself lead to an overall increase in academic performance and a dramatic reduction in the number of youth who fail in school and at work, which would be the best long-term result for the country. To achieve this goal, we should put to good use the military services' capacity to train, educate, and socialize young people by treating the military as part of a system that prepares youth for work.

However, this would mean changing some of the military's practices. Like private employers, the military tends to hold down training costs by teaching recruits how to do a specific job, without necessarily providing the background they need for understanding what they are doing, why, and how it might be modified under various conditions. As a result, the training promised by recruiters often proves to be of little value in civilian workplaces, because of the distinctive qualities of military hardware and responsibilities, but also because sometimes training is too superficial to be transferable.[21] The military is most effective as an "aging vat," providing youth with a reasonably constructive experience during a time when they are not considered mature enough to begin civilian careers.

In addition to its extensive formal training programs, the military teaches a great deal informally through the same kinds of on-the-job instruction and practice that occur in the private sector. It may be that expanding the notion of apprenticeship could enrich that kind of training by formally linking more and less experienced people in teaching and mentoring relationships. Although increasing the competence of enlistees and thereby of the nation's citizens is a legitimate expectation of the military services, they should not be expected to take on substantially enlarged educational functions until those functions have been duly authorized by Congress and the president and extra funding has been appropriated for those purposes.

Like the military services, the Job Corps removes young people from their home environment and attends to their socialization and education to prepare them for jobs, emphasizing job training and academic instruction. As in military training, the principles of traditional apprenticeship might productively be introduced into the Job Corps, especially after remediation has commenced, as a means of moving participants gradually into regular employment. Cooperative agreements providing apprenticeship placements for Job Corps enrollees after they have achieved a specified level could motivate better performance and increase postprogram employment rates.

The Job Corps should also be expanded. It is essential as an "added-chance" program, enabling young people who have failed at earlier stages to move back into the stream of employment and education. Enrollment, currently frozen at 40,500, has never been able to accommodate more than a fraction of the youth who could benefit from it. As the labor market increasingly requires the contribution of youth who are eligible for the Job Corps, the return on investment, already favorable, will become even greater. It also needs to be tied more closely to other education and training opportunities to fit it into the larger system envisioned here.

An American-style apprenticeship system cannot be created without making substantial changes in schools, communities, and workplaces, and in their mutual relations. The alternative to these changes is not stasis but other, quite possibly less constructive changes; all three institutions will change in response to influences from the national and global economy, from demography, technology, the biosphere, and from government. The issue is whether we can manage change so that it moves in a direction that more effectively promotes the development of all youth into responsible, productive workers who are also active citizens and constructive members of families and other small groups. Stated the other way round, the issue is whether we can allow the changes that will inevitably occur to undermine the maturation process still further, leading to larger proportions of youth who fail in school, become emeshed in irresponsible behavior, and slowly or never find productive work roles.

The first American public schools shared their educational and socialization functions with families, churches, voluntary organizations, and communities. Workplaces often had an educational function that was not limited to teaching apprentices. For example, early factories provided dormitories for their unmarried female workers, who were instructed during their free time in academics, religion, housekeeping, and deportment. Schools assumed more and more functions that had once belonged in the community as larger numbers of people lived in cities rather than towns and villages, and especially as new immigrants were seen as needing "Americanization." In this century, schools have increasingly been asked to take on functions previously assigned to families, social service agencies, churches, and employers: feeding children, giving medical and dental examinations, working with disabled children, preventing health and behavior problems, teaching about values, teaching job skills, and providing afterschool care.

But schools are nearing the limit of what they can accomplish as socializing institutions substituting for deteriorating communities and families. A more rational allocation of these institutions' shared functions is needed in order to fulfill them more effectively. Apprenticeship is a means of accomplishing this reallocation. If schools are to take advantage of apprenticeship for this purpose, they must make some drastic changes. Fortunately, there are others pushing such changes for other reasons. The so-called "second wave" of educational reform—the first having been the reforms ushered in by *A Nation at Risk*—has two themes: concern for at-risk youth; and restructuring. The first theme has already been related to apprenticeship; many restructuring reforms are also compatible with apprenticeship.

Theodore R. Sizer, whose Coalition of Essential Schools is at the forefront of restructuring, has called for a number of changes in the ways schools operate, which are summarized in nine common principles.[22] The first principle is that schools' chief purpose should be to help young people *learn to use their minds well*. School-based apprenticeship has the same purpose. To the extent that technicians and other workers need to learn to use their minds well, work-based apprenticeship will also share this goal, as it does increasingly in Germany. And there is some reason to believe that engaging young people in study, reflection, and problem solving about real issues in the workplace will be a more effective means to this end than classroom instruction, which many see as artificial.[23]

Sizer's fourth principle, *teaching and learning should be personalized,* opens the way for apprenticeship as an alternative approach to learning for those who do not perform well in classrooms. Apprenticeship is better suited to accomplishing social purposes such as this because it puts young people in contact with a larger number and a wider range of adults.

The sixth principle, that a diploma should be awarded for *successful final demonstration of mastery,* enables individual students and different schools to take their own paths to a common goal, again opening the way to apprenticeship as an alternative mode of learning to classroom instruction. The exhibition that Sizer envisions as the final demonstration of a student's readiness for a diploma is much like the practical portion of West German apprentices' qualifying examination. Apprentice auto mechanics and other manual workers take a two-part examination: a multiple-choice test covering both academic and vocational subjects they have studied in the *Berufsschule;* and the construction of a "test piece." When making their test piece, each apprentice is issued a blueprint and a set of materials. They then have eight hours in which to fashion the materials into the object depicted in the blueprint, using the tools at hand. The finished objects are later judged by a panel of masters who rate their quality to determine the apprentice's grade.

Industriekaufleute are not trained to produce goods, but they are expected to learn the social skills required in their occupation. The practical part of their qualifying examination is a half-hour interview by a panel of practitioners who ask them about what they have learned on the job and evaluate them on their self-presentation. Regardless of what is exhibited or how it is evaluated, the principle of awarding a diploma on the basis of demonstrated mastery rather than hours of instruction focuses schooling on its purposes but frees teachers and students to employ diverse means of achieving those purposes.

Sizer's fifth principle is that *the governing practical metaphor of the school should be student-as-worker.* Apprenticeship makes students literally workers, but with implications for pedagogy like those Sizer advocates for the classroom, where "coaching" is the key pedagogical act, a one-to-one process that provokes students to learn how to learn. Coaching is also what mentors do for apprentices at work sites.

If schoolteachers are to exploit their students' apprenticeship experiences for academic purposes, they must learn how to facilitate group discussions and coach individual students effectively. Whole-class lectures, while highly appropriate for some purposes, are not sufficient when students' learning experiences are divergent. A different form of pedagogy is needed to help each one make connections between workplace experiences and academic subjects. Coaching describes part of that pedagogy quite well.

In an earlier book, Sizer made another proposal that is also compatible with apprenticeship. *Places for Learning, Places for Joy,*[24] made the case that academic learning is only one of schooling's three major purposes and that different kinds of learning environments may be more appropriate for each. He proposed different structures, even separate institutions, to accommodate these different purposes. Although Sizer did not incorporate this notion in his descriptions of essential schools, it supports the idea of school and apprenticeship as distinctive but complementary settings for learning.

This insight that different educational purposes may require distinctive environments for learning helps explain a puzzle in recent educational history; that is, the low survival rate of new teaching technologies that have been demonstrated to be effective. Such technologies have repeatedly been introduced into the schools with great fanfare only to be swallowed up by conventional practices.[25] Teaching technologies include procedures as well as machines; they are not limited to programmed or computer-assisted instruction. One reason for their limited impact is that even when they demonstrate effectiveness in terms of the lowest common denominators of learning—performance on standardized tests—they often seem to teachers to be neutral or negative in their other effects. If students do not enjoy programmed learning and therefore fail to carry on or carry over what they have learned, they cannot learn how to apply their skills, to ask questions, or to solve problems.

Flaws such as these are not fatal if new forms of instructional technology are used for limited purposes. The Comprehensive Competencies Program has demonstrated the capacity to boost adults' math and reading by one grade level with 50 hours of carefully planned instruction.[26] No doubt similar approaches could have comparably dramatic effects on standardized test performance by high school students. Although they would not constitute an adequate educational experience by themselves, they could be part of a tripartite instructional system that would be enormously powerful. The second segment would be apprenticeship, with all the advantages already identified. The third would be seminars and classroom projects in which young people exercise their increased academic power to write and talk, not only about what they read, which remains important, but also about what they experience in their apprenticeship. Teachers would lead these seminars in the coaching and facilitating mode, helping with basic academic skills sometimes, recommending remedial work in others, but always urging students to think more deeply about their apprenticeship experiences, and to relate them to their academic learning and to their evolving conceptions of the world and their place in it.

Two distinctive school-teaching roles are implied by this scenario. One focuses on furthering basic skills through a continuing cycle of diagnosis, prescription, and evaluation. This might best be accomplished in an individualized laboratory setting. The other stresses application, integration, and derivation of meaning through critical reflection, writing, and speaking, which is best done in a seminar or project. Some teachers might be more comfortable and more effective specializing in one or the other of these teaching roles. Both types of schoolteachers would be supported by workplace mentors who motivate apprentices to acquire basic skills, give them practice at using them, and supervise the process through which apprentices discover and test information and ideas.

New instructional technologies introduced to teach basic skills more efficiency are often rejected as overly narrow. Their promise of accomplishing some educational objectives is sacrificed because they do not accomplish all. At the same time, discussion-centered classes and writing instruction suffer when improvement in standardized test scores becomes the sole criterion of effectiveness. We need to find ways to teach basic skills efficiently without making the acquisition of basic skills the endpoint. Rather, basic skills should enable young people to learn higher-order skills such as problem solving and to gain understanding along with knowledge and skills. Especially if so unconventional a learning mode as apprenticeship is to be introduced, it is essential that young people acquire the basic tools they need for work as much as for school. There is no necessary conflict between apprenticeship and ''the basics,'' but there is need for better matching of educational purposes with pedagogical techniques.

Apprenticeship could contribute to making schools more vital and more effective, but only if schools change substantially. Profound changes in the ways communities function are also implicit in the implementation of a system of apprenticeship. The Greek word *paideia* best captures the educational quality of communities implied by apprenticeship. Although Mortimer Adler and his associates have used the word as a title for a series of proposals to make schols more rigorous by traditional standards, the word means ''learning community,'' and was applied originally not to a school or other single institution but to the quality of the entire community in all its aspects as an environment for learning.[27]

Apprenticeship intentionally disperses teaching and learning throughout a community rather than concentrating them within a school building. Professional teachers continue to be the specialists, but others are also called upon to teach. Schools continue to be the central institutions of learning, but other institutions and settings also become places for learning. *Paideia,* the idea of a whole community as a learning environment, reverses the specialization of function that characterizes modern societies. It will take time to win widespread acceptance of the ideas that young people can learn outside of school and that ordinary adults can be effective teachers. Starting slowly by expanding and linking components of apprenticeship that are already in place will demonstrate the feasibility of *paideia* more effectively than theoretical arguments.

Transportation may prove to be a bigger barrier to *paideia* than its novelty. Young people living in large cities can move relatively easily from their schools into various community locations by means of public transportation, which is sorely lacking in most suburban and rural areas. Child labor laws and liability are also serious practical barriers. However, the fact that most of the components of apprenticeship already exist on a small scale proves that these barriers can be overcome.

More challenging still than altering schools and communities and the relations between them is the task of convincing employers that apprenticeship is in their best interest. Large numbers of employers will take in apprentices as worker/learners and assign adult employees as their mentors only if they believe this substantial investment of their resources will pay off for them, the sooner the better.

Employers, or more correctly, chief executive officers of large firms representing primary labor market employers, were prominent advocates of school reform in the 1980s because they believed that schools were no longer graduating sufficient numbers of young people who were well-prepared to enter the labor force. In addition to lending their voices to pleas for improvement, some firms joined partnerships with schools that committed their resources to improving schools, such as the Boston Compact and the California Compact. However, partnerships have not yet reached deeply into the workings of schools or accomplished nearly as much as their originators hoped. In Boston, employers have been disappointed with the schools' inability to hold up their end of the bargain: pupils' achievement levels have not increased substantially since the Compact was signed.[28]

Apprenticeship will require far more than good intentions and general promises. Employers will have to invest substantial resources in the education and training of youth even before they are hired. Clearly not all young people who spend time in a workplace as part of an exploratory or a school-based apprenticeship will contribute materially to the firm's productivity and profits. In the absence of Germany's strong traditions and the long-term payoff from training that German employers expect under their larbor market conditions, what will motivate U.S. employers to undertake such an investment?

Fear of disaster has concentrated business leaders' minds on education. Long-term prospects for American prosperity and social stability are not bright unless we can do a better job than we are doing now of preparing all youth for constructive adult lives. At a 1987 conference sponsored by the Education Commission of the States, retired Procter and Gamble CEO, Brad Butler, objected to the conference's title, "The National Forum for Youth at Risk," saying he would have chosen a title that got closer to the heart of the matter: "Will the United States Survive into the Twenty-First Century as a Peaceful and Prosperous Democracy?" People with wealth and power will be unable to enjoy them if substantial segments of the population are unemployable.

Sadly, even as frightening as this apocalyptic vision might be, it is not necessarily sufficient to motivate action on the part of individuals or firms. The threat of a shared disaster does not lead automatically to individual sacrifices. The situation is similar to the use of car pools to conserve fuel. While it is the case that if everyone car pooled everyone would be better off, it is also the case that if some people car pool, then those who do not are even better off: not only do they benefit from the increased supply of fuel, and resulting lower prices, but they continue to enjoy the flexibility and independence of driving their private automobiles. Precisely because the benefits of apprenticeship would be enjoyed by all, any single entity will be reluctant to assume its costs unilaterally. The same conundrum applies to a wide range of societal problems: how can widely shared needs be translated into action by individuals and by individual corporations and communities?

Such situations are the natural province of governments. National defense is another clear example of a situation in which government assumes responsibility for serving shared interests that individuals cannot realistically pursue. Government at all levels must necessarily play a role in supporting apprenticeship, in order to assure that some, at least, of its costs are shared as widely as its benefits.

Federal, state, and local governments can use their taxing power to raise money to support an apprenticeship system. Some of that money need not be new, but can instead be redirected as current education and training programs are altered to include apprenticeship. Tax breaks are a second way of using this power. Firms can already claim training costs as a business expense. Additional tax credits might encourage them to assume what has previously been defined as a public responsibility—enrolling disadvantaged youth—though experience to date indicates that they are an inadequate incentive for this purpose.

Government-funded training facilities would be another use of tax dollars that could be especially useful to firms too small to support their own. It is not clear, however, that these must be new facilities like the new German multifirm training centers. Facilities in existing vocational schools, both secondary and postsecondary, might be adequate to the task, particularly if they are accessible evenings and through the summer.

Governments can also support apprenticeship directly as an employer. Federal, state, and local government employees comprise more than 15 percent of the employed U.S. labor force.[29] All of those employees need skills just as much as employees in the private sector. Therefore, federal, state, and local governments should be expected to participate in apprenticeship training just as much as private employers. Publicly controlled and publicly accountable, governments can provide leadership in developing apprenticeships, just as the West German government does. The military has already been discussed as a trainer of youth. Broadening government's involvement to include the civil service as well is another step.

A related tactic is the use of governments', especially the federal government's, enormous power as a contractor. Just as that power is now exerted to promote such social goods as affirmative action, including provisions favoring minority businesses as suppliers, it could be directed to promoting apprenticeship through requirements or incentives for vendors of goods and services.[30]

Various schemes for providing continuing education accounts could also be brought into play, enabling relatively unskilled employees to pay their employers for training that would make them more valuable.[31] A reverse social security system might be created, funded by payroll taxes and required employee contributions, accessible to young workers just entering the full-time labor force as well as older workers changing careers. Young workers would repay what would in effect be training loans over the course of their working lives.

However, government's role in a market economy is limited; the preferred incentives are those calculated by each firm to maximize its own self-interest. West German firms make such calculations, and despite the strong apprenticeship tradition there, not all invest in training apprentices. Unfortunately, small firms, whose short-term interests are served by having low-paid helpers available, have the most to gain from apprentices and are most likely to train them, with less than optimal quality. In the United States, where most firms traditionally minimize training costs, preferring when they can to hire away trained employees from another firm, incentives to invest heavily in sustained training are even lower, particularly given the labor market volatility that results from employers' readiness to dismiss workers when business slows and workers' readiness to change jobs.[32]

Although no one can forecast business conditions with complete accuracy, employers offering the most expensive formal apprenticeships—those for older youth that focus on quite specific job preparation, such as the 2+2 program for technicians proposed above—could reduce their risk of losing trained apprentices by means of a contractual arrangement. Under this arrangement, a training employer would guarantee a place to a successful trainee and the apprentice would agree to remain in that place for a given number of years. The apprentice would sign a promissory note for a reasonable fraction of the employer's true cost for training, agreeing to repay a declining sum if she or he quit voluntarily before the agreed-upon period of employment. Another employer wishing to hire away that worker could only do so by indirectly paying back the training firm through higher wages or a lump sum payment, which the worker would use to repay the training employer.

This proposal addresses one cost-benefit issue, namely how to protect a training investment against competitors' "raids." It does not address the issue of when the cost-benefit ratios are likely to prove favorable to the training employer. Insofar as these are individual firms' decisions, no single answer can be provided. A wide range of experience and analysis will be needed to make generalizations. The best that can be done now is to cite the experiences of a few employers who are currently providing apprentice-like training. If they have found it in their own interests to pay for training of this sort, other firms will too.

Shearson Lehman Hutton, a leading New York City brokerage house and financial services firm, has grown considerably since its merger with the American Express Company in 1981. Like many other businesses, it has become increasingly dependent on computers. Computers, in turn, make it possible for individual workers to carry out a much wider range of responsibilities than before. As a result, many of the company's jobs require higher levels of education. But the quality of New York City's high school graduates appears to be declining. This problem is epitomized by the oft-told tale of the New York City banks that were unable to fill 250 bank teller positions because the vast majority of applicants, who held high school diplomas, failed an eighth-grade math test.[33] Faced with a shortage of workers qualified to fill such jobs, some other companies have moved many of their operations out of New York City. Yet, as former Shearson chairman Sanford Weill noticed, many youth and young adults in the city were unemployed.

Reflecting on the ironies of this situation, Weill conceived an educational program that would prepare high school students for careers in finance through a combination of course work and on-the-job experience. His idea was realized by Phyllis Frankfort, founding director of the Academy of Finance. The Academy is not a place but a program. Courses in accounting, economics, computer science, and various aspects of finance are offered to high school juniors and seniors, who take these special courses along with their regular required courses. In addition, they take field trips to banks, brokerage firms, the stock exchange, and related businesses, and participate in seminars led by business leaders.

During the summer between their junior and senior years, students serve as interns in some of New York's most prestigious financial services firms. They are paid for their work, but it is primarily a chance to learn firsthand about working in finance. Employers are enthusiastic about the high school students because they are bright, highly motivated, and knowledgeable. Many employers ask their interns to come back and work for them again the following summer.

Without benefit of a sophisticated evaluation design, it is impossible to determine the Academy's impact with precision. However, 90 percent of its graduates enter college, 80 percent with a major related to finance, and the 10 percent who do not enroll in college all take jobs in finance. Such a focused outcome suggests that the Academy succeeds both in stimulating interest in careers in finance and in motivating young people to acquire higher education for that purpose. In addition to the indirect motivation of exposing high school students to desirable jobs that require a college degree, one of the program's finance courses is given at a local college, enabling students to graduate from high school with a college course already under their belts. Outstanding graduates are awarded college scholarships as well.

The key to the Academy's success, according to Frankfort, is the connection it makes among the special courses on finance, regular academic courses, work experience, and success in later life. Graduates of the program are knowledgeable and productive, they take initiative, they are "savvy," and, most importantly, they are responsible. As a result, they move easily either into jobs in finance or on to college. The program has expanded steadily because the industry's demand for interns continues to grow.

There are clearly some selection effects in operation. Students are admitted into the program on the basis of their professed interest in the field, manifested in a pledge to remain in the program for two years. Applicants must have a 75 average in math and English, ruling out the poorest students, but certainly not limiting it to the best. Participating high schools, too, must pass muster as being reasonably well administered and willing to appoint a teacher as coordinator and assign two or three additional teachers to the program's courses. Thus, the Academy is not for the most troubled youth or schools, but neither is it an elite institution available only to young people who already have it made.

Frankfort denies that screening students is a critical element, pointing out that some students are not terribly strong, either academically or in their initial readiness for work. The only criteria the program establishes for sending students out for summer job interviews are that they pass all of their courses and that they be interviewed, neither of which is particularly stringent. What is more important, in her view, is that "carrots" are built in throughout the program to motivate students to be ready for the next step. One of the program's slogans is: "Attendance at school = Attendance on the job." She claims that being reminded to come to school regularly and punctually, and having a reason to do so, leads naturally to dependability at work.

From its origins with 35 students in one school in 1982, the Academy had expanded by 1988 to eight New York City high schools and 21 additional schools in 14 more cities. The total enrollment of 1,069 youth included 352 blacks, 108 Hispanics, and 128 Asians. Shearson and American Express continue to be the core sponsors, but many more firms have added their support by providing internships and donations. Though corporate support has been essential, it has not been as strong as the director would wish. She complains that too many firms are unwilling to make long-term commitments to provide summer internships, each insisting that they must wait to determine their employment needs every year.

An advisory board in each city, made up of business and school representatives, facilitates the program. A carefully crafted curriculum backed by extensive teacher training is another key feature of the program. Participating teachers, who come from business education, social studies, computer science, and other fields, receive special training before they teach Academy courses, and they attend a yearly conference and in-service training session along with program administrators, courtesy of American Express. Some teachers also become summer interns themselves to gain firsthand experience in contemporary finance and business. Allowance is made for local adaptation of the Academy program. Broward County, Florida, for example, stresses real estate more heavily than New York City, because the real estate market is much more active there.

Another secret of the Academy's success is attention to issues of motivation and social relations as well as technical knowledge and competence. From the selection process, which stresses energy and self-direction as well as interest and commitment, to workshops on interview skills and corporate etiquette, students are taught the importance of understanding the social world of the workplace as well as the content of their work. Academy students even attend school in business dress one day each week, and are coached on wardrobe selection and the appropriate use of makeup. All of this is reinforced by the internship, where young people work alongside adults. A Shearson executive commented about the impact of the internship: "It's amazing what happens to these kids. They become very adult. They go back to school and they dress differently. There's a maturity about them."[34] An alumni association helps the Academy retain contact with graduates and supports graduates' continuing efforts to acquire education and work experience.

Several benefits accrue to corporate sponsors. One, of course, is improved public relations. Most corporations like to be known as contributors to the communities in which they are located. Second, and more important, the program provides sponsors with a larger pool of potential employees whom they know well before they must make a decision about permanent hiring. Only a few students go to work full-time immediately after high school, but the companies' willingness to continue offering summer jobs after the formal program has terminated indicates that some of them keep in touch with students after high school graduation. According to Frankfort, it is only the prospect of a "respectable return" on their investment in the form of a more competent workforce that motivates firms to participate. Although they do not apply fixed cost-benefit formulas, firms maintain their involvement when they see young people demonstrating ability and commitment and when some of them become full-time employees.

The Academy of Finance benefits from the prestige attached to working with money, even though students' jobs are far from glamorous. It also demonstrates the use of apprenticeship in a fast-growing white-collar field. Wegmans' Work-Scholarship Connection enjoys neither of these advantages, but demonstrates how the kind of low-skill jobs available to teenagers in the secondary labor market can be enriched with elements of apprenticeship, namely, a connection to school and the provision of mentors.

Wegmans is a supermarket chain based in Rochester, New York, that has been cited by *Fortune* magazine for the quality of its management, in particular its management of personnel. Like most supermarkets, Wegmans employs large numbers of part-time, low-skill workers, many of them teenagers, as cashiers and shelf stockers. Recognizing such issues as the changing demography of youth and the danger that part-time employment may hinder academic achievement, Wegmans made an agreement with the Rochester schools to use part-time jobs to motivate students toward improved school achievement. The program is staffed by Wegmans' employees but housed in the school district headquarters, an arrangement the firm insisted upon as a means of maintaining close contact with the schools.

The Work-Scholarship Connection began in 1987 as part of the city's broad-based effort to improve its schools and to involve local businesses in the process. Teachers and counselors recommend 14- and 15-year-olds for jobs in Wegmans stores who need special motivation to complete high school because of family problems and past failures in school. Wegmans then selects participants and offers them both short-term and long-term motivation. In order to keep their job, participants must maintain a good attendance record in school and at work. Those who remain with the program through high school are awarded a full-tuition scholarship to attend college, up to $5,000 per year, and they are able to continue their part-time job while in college. In the winter of 1989, 51 young people were enrolled in the program.

In addition to the promise of a scholarship, Wegmans gives exceptional personal support. Before they begin work, participants attend a preemployment workshop, supplemented with another after they have started, that stresses the connections between school and work. Each young person in the program is also matched with an experienced adult worker who serves as a mentor. The mentor is responsible for the young person's initial training and for training him or her to move into new jobs as the store's needs and the employee's interests dictate. Mentors are chosen from experienced and competent employees, who are matched with a young person on the basis of likely personal compatibility.

Mentoring extends beyond workplace matters to include advice on life planning, and assistance in solving personal problems. Participants who want one can also be assigned a tutor to help with schoolwork. Tutors will eventually be drawn from former participants who have enrolled in college. Tutors receive special training from the school district. About half of the participants are involved in tutoring at any one time; it is available to them as they need it.

When asked about the company's motivation for offering this program, the director, Allen Johnson, said that Wegmans believes in training their employees, but in this case they are investing in training early, before these young employees have completed their schooling. Their chief hope is that more youth will complete high school, but they also hope that some of them will go on to college and then return to work in the company, bringing with them their educational achievement and strong commitment to the company born of long-term work experience. Wegmans recognizes that only a few are likely to return, he said, but, like other employers, they must show more foresight about preparing their future workforce.

Wegmans' program is a useful exemplar of an apprentice-like program that, nonetheless, lacks one of the key components of a traditional apprenticeship: intensive skill training. None of the jobs done by young people is very challenging. Like many jobs at the lower levels of the service sector, they can be learned quickly and take more persistence than skill. What makes the program noteworthy is that Wegmans has taken jobs that are often disparaged as dead-end and tied them to schooling and personal development by providing a strong incentive and equally strong supports for both diligent work and school achievement.

In view of the reality that the labor market will continue to offer millions of jobs like those in supermarkets and the fact that youth will continue to be prime candidates for filling those jobs, the program illustrates one way of enriching such jobs. In this case the key is not so much that the jobs are made more interesting—the opportunity to learn several jobs is probably the only added interest—as that they are explicitly tied to young people's longer-term future prospects, prospects that are bright and attainable if they can continue in school and demonstrate worker virtues.

The Work-Scholarship Connection and the Academy of Finance involve extensive partnerships between schools and business. Corporate sponsors contribute to the costs of the Academy of Finance, but the schools do too. In both, firms offer jobs for students and make connections between work experience and school. Both programs stress school attendance and achievement. The Academy of Finance has a stronger impact on what schools do, adding courses to the schools' curriculum, and expanding teachers' range of competence. The two programs are notable for the duration of their commitments to youth—from two to four years—and for the fact that they are not job training programs in the narrow sense. Although participants learn to do specific jobs, they are strongly urged to continue their education. Sponsoring companies cannot recoup their investment by hiring participants in career positions until several years later.

A smaller-scale but equally impressive approach is demonstrated by DRT Corporation,[35] which manufactures electronic equipment for commercial use, including computers and printers. In response to a request from a youth center, one of DRT's plants provided a place for Robert Jameson to work as part of a subsidized work experience program. While in ninth grade, Robert met with the other program participants at the downtown youth center twice a week after school to develop employment skills. On the other three days, all reported to their job placements after school to gain work experience.

As his first task, Robert was asked to organize a set of technical drawings that had been stacked in a corner for many months. He quickly and accurately folded and filed them. When someone discovered that a detailed drawing of one part had never been made, they found a drafting board for Robert and asked him to draw it. Having had a drafting course in school, he did that well too.

After demonstrating competence in his first three days of work, Robert got the chance to learn computer drafting, which he did for several months. When the subsidized program ended, he was offered a job with the company working two hours a day after school hours plus vacations, and eventually he got involved in writing computer programs. Gene Barstow, head of the project engineering division, is Robert's supervisor. He explained how Robert got into programming.

I was working with a test program which I inherited, written by someone else in the plant, and I was attempting to explain to Robert a little of what I was going through in order to make some modifications in this program. I said to him, in school, in math class you probably worked in bases other than 10. Base 2 or base 6, something like that. And I said when we work with printers, we work in base 6, which is known as Hex. We send Hex codes to the printer and tell it what to do. Well that's about all he needed to begin to understand the problems that I was looking at and trying to solve. And from there on, he kind of took over that responsibility. He developed quite an understanding of what was happening, plus he remembers things. He can do things in one tenth of the time that I can. Something about age!

A new printer is tested by running it for an extended time to find out what goes wrong. A computer is programmed to operate the printer in specific ways, and to record what happens to it. As the test proceeds and results come in, various problems arise that must be corrected, and the engineers continually ask for alterations in the testing program. As Gene explained,

---

We'll implement one level of this program, and then we get some reaction from the people that are working with it. And then one of our engineers will say, "Why can't it do this?" or "We need to do that." It's been almost every day for a couple of months that we've been putting improvements in it.

When Robert was observed at DRT, he had been there for more than a year and had his own office cubicle, larger than those of some of the regular employees', as he pointed out, complete with nameplate and computer. He explained the day's problems that Gene had put him to work solving.

First, some of the operators in the computer lab had not been changing printer ribbons when they should have, entering a command that reverses the ribbon instead, and some of the tests were ruined as a result. Robert fixed this by programming the computer so that the ribbon cannot be reversed and requiring that operators enter the number of the new ribbon cassette whenever one runs out.

His second problem was to add a subprogram to count the number of dots printed by the dot matrix printer so that the engineers would be able to tell precisely how many times each of the wires in the print head had struck the ribbon.

Third, a long-term problem was to program one computer to operate three printers while making a record of exactly what was happening to each printer. This would enable them to test all three printers simultaneously, while tying up only one computer to drive them. When Robert was observed again two days later, he was working on this problem.

Robert checks a wall chart headed, "Programming Considerations," giving information about Turbo Pascal 4, the programming language he is using. Then he looks at the back of his computer to find the identification number of one of its ports. He types a few lines, says, "It doesn't say," checks a file, and then says, "If that's 956, then this is 957," inferring the needed information from what he has learned.

He continues typing and succeeds in getting printer no. 2 to jam, which produces a message on the screen. He works on, then pauses to explain, "Because one printer can go down while the others continue, I always want to increment the counts of printers that are still running. I have to check whether they are running so I know if I should increment that number. I think I have it figured out."

After making another adjustment to the program, Robert removes the paper from printer no. 1 and manually jams it. The correct messages appear on the screen. "It's doing it right," he comments.

Gene arrives and asks, "How're we doing?"

Robert replies, "I just got it to do counts. Pick one. Hit it. Just hit it!" Gene jams no. 3, then Robert jams no. 1 and they both watch the correct messages appearing on the screen to report what is wrong. They discuss additional problems resulting from operating three printers simultaneously.

Gene concludes by saying, "When you get a breaking point, can you work on printer format counts?" and leaves saying, "Looks good, Robert."

Robert seems quite pleased and exclaims, "He's done," as he leaves his cubicle. To carry out his next assignment, he goes into one of the test rooms where about 20 printers are operating and records the numbers that have been accumulating on these tests. He then enters these numbers on another computer, explaining with a grin conveying sarcasm, "This is the fun part." He quickly completes the routine data entry task and then explains the printout that records how the test of each printer is progressing.

Providing a more detailed account of the testing procedure, he says, "We're doing an extended test, where we accumulate 12 million characters to test how the print head wears. We take the number of failures that we've had and figure out a confidence factor and we also have to figure out how much the printer will actually cost a year for maintenance, and we use it to figure out the selling price."

Gene returns and elaborates the picture of the testing process. He explains to Robert that his boss will want to know how the current test would have gone if they had not had some breakdowns attributable to defects in the prototype, rather than to the design itself. Robert does some calculations, explains them to Gene, who is satisfied. Robert asks, "How'd you know what the boss would ask you?" and Gene explains that his boss had asked a similar question in the previous meeting.

For the remainder of the observation period, Robert worked with Gene and another employee in a joint problem-solving mode, trying to operate printers and programs and helping each other figure out what to do when they did not work as expected.

Although the lone "hacker" has become something of a stereotype, and it is true that some computer users are loners, working with computers is also conducive to cooperation. They are too complicated for most people to know everything there is to know. Therefore, mutual assistance and group problem solving seem to occur naturally.[36] That work tends to be egalitarian because knowledge and skill count more than credentials or age. Some young people, like Robert, are able to understand computers quickly, gaining respect for their demonstrated competence in an area that adults value.

Also notable in Robert's work setting was the closeness of his relationship with Gene. Robert described Gene as "a friend," and said they get together outside of work, to sail, for example. However, Gene is also clearly Robert's supervisor, constantly checking on his work and asking probing questions. Gene, in turn, derives a great deal of satisfaction from the relationship. He said, "I think my family has benefited from it because I go home happy at night, instead of sour-faced. It's very positive for me."

Robert is clearly a very talented young man. As a tenth-grader he is taking twelfth-grade math and finding it "really easy," so easy that his teacher has told him he need not do the homework. Next year he will begin calculus. In addition to his programming and testing work, Gene said he has worked at home to design new parts to improve the printer they have been working on. His talents probably would have been noticed without the aid of this apprenticeship, but being raised by a single parent might have meant missing opportunities to develop them.

The technical and mathematical learning Robert displayed is so impressive that it would be easy to overlook what he was learning about how to function in a work organization. He revealed his awareness of office hierarchies and status symbols by pointing out that his cubicle was larger than some others'. By asking a question, he learned how Gene anticipated his boss's question, a useful skill indeed. He helped Gene prepare an answer. He participated as an equal in the informal give-and-take among employees in the lab.

Unlike the Academy of Finance and the Work-Scholarship Connection, Robert's experience is not part of a well-developed program. It was initiated as part of a small-scale program and then took on a life of its own. However, it indicates how many excellent learning opportunities might be available for young people as apprentices. It also illustrates how apprenticeship can serve employers' self-interest. DRT stands to gain from the arrangement. They are paying relatively little for high-level work and are building in Robert a strong commitment to the corporation. Robert expects to continue working there part-time while he attends college, and perhaps graduate school. In the meantime, he has assisted Gene by helping him get his work done, but probably more importantly by giving him the satisfaction of being able to teach, and sometimes learn from, a younger person.

According to Erik Erikson, the fundamental issue of adult development, comparable to forming an identity during adolescence, is "generativity," meaning, "concern for establishing and guiding the next generation."[37] Its opposite is stagnation. Gene Barstow is surely not the only middle-aged person who could avoid stagnation in work and personal life by assuming a mentor role.

Shearson, Wegmans, and DRT are successful American corporations, guided by people with their eyes on the bottom line. If they can justify investments in training like these, then West German corporations cannot be the only ones whose self-interest is served by apprenticeship.

Americans are pragmatists. Arguments are less potent than demonstrations. Therefore, the next steps toward developing an American-style apprenticeship system should be devoted to demonstrating its viability and utility. The fact that its elements already exist in some form and in some locations makes this task less daunting than it would otherwise be. The strategy of developing demonstrations entails working in selected sites, not attempting to make large-scale changes simultaneously in multiple sites. The rationale for beginning with demonstration projects is that we do not yet know well enough *what works, why,* and *how* to guide a lasting and widespread change in policy and practice. The purpose of demonstration projects, it follows, is to test a new approach, discovering to what extent it has the desired impact and how it may be implemented. Demonstration implies modification. The point is not simply to prove that a proposed strategy works, but to discover whether and under what conditions it works, for whom, and how. Failures to achieve desired goals, as a result, are not necessarily interpreted as failures in the approach; they may be signs indicating where modifications must be made. Nor is it sufficient to assess a demonstration's outcomes. Knowing that something works does not tell how to make it work again under different circumstances.

This seemingly commonsense statement of purpose is remarkably difficult to communicate. When James Coleman and his associates proposed modest experimental demonstrations to test their recommendation of more work and community involvement as part of secondary education, critics took them to task for recommending large-scale changes with too little evidence supporting them.[38] Although the "Second Coleman Report" explicitly stated that sufficient evidence was not available and recommended experimentation, readers were so accustomed to hearing calls for massive change that they overlooked its more modest call. In 1978, the Youth Employment and Demonstration Projects Act (YEDPA) stated its experimental purpose in its title but was, nonetheless, quickly declared a failure because it did not immediately solve the problems it was supposedly designed to explore.[39]

The same pragmatism that makes Americans ready to try out ideas rather than discuss them abstractly also makes them impatient to come up with solutions. Part of the problem lies in the political process. In order to mobilize public opinion to the point of yielding legislative action, a strong case must be made, first, that there is a devastating problem that must be solved and, second, that the proposed action will solve it. Delays in demonstrating the second claim quickly lead to disillusionment and distraction. As difficult as it will be to remain patient, apprenticeship should be developed deliberately.

A second implication of the demonstration strategy is that evaluation is crucial. Here too, impatience has not served the policy process well.

Contrast the quick disappearance of the YEDPA programs with the survival of Headstart and the Job Corps. Early evaluations focusing narrowly on desirable but limited outcomes found both programs wanting; even some supporters pronounced them failures. But grass roots political support was sufficiently strong to keep the programs alive long enough so that they and their evaluations could mature. As a result, subsequent evaluations done with greater care and creativity found later versions of the programs, with many serious refinements, to be effective by a variety of measures.[40]

A truly useful evaluation of a new apprenticeship system will carefully examine how the system operates and how participants respond to it, not just what its outcomes are. Insight into these questions helps to improve the system as it develops and to isolate those aspects of it that are crucial and must be replicated if it is to be adopted elsewhere. Many demonstration projects in West Germany include a "scientific accompaniment" (*wissenschaftliche Begleitung*). This term seems more constructive than evaluation; it does not exclude assessment of outcomes, but broadens the scope of program-related research beyond testing the program's impact.

The portrait of Lakeland, an imaginary city, suggests that a useful strategy would be to create in one community a comprehensive system of apprenticeship. Demonstrating how a coherent system would work is the highest priority because the efficacy of apprenticeship's key elements has already been demonstrated by existing programs. What remains to be determined is whether they can be combined into a system as comprehensive in its own way as the West German dual system. As in Lakeland, such a demonstration would tie together what are now unconnected programs to fill in the gaps and to assure that the same youth have access to all of them. Young people in these communities could count on acquiring extensive experience as community volunteers, in career exploration programs, with cooperative education as part of vocational schooling, and ultimately, if they do not enter higher education, in a formal long-term apprenticeship leading to related employment.

This demonstration would depend upon governments at all levels, the school system, employers, unions, employment training agencies, and social service agencies. In order to achieve its purposes, it would have to be carried on over a period of six to ten years, a length of time virtually unheard of but clearly justified if the purpose is to help young people move from adolescence into adulthood. The system could not be fairly tested by putting only its last stages into effect.

Similarly, offering the system to individuals in random pieces would not truly test its efficacy or reveal its gaps. As unfair as it might seem to favor some youth over others with a concentrated set of special opportunities, no other scheme will adequately test the proposal. Any unfairness in this approach can be alleviated if new resources are used to achieve it, rather than taking services and opportunities away from others. A current example of this approach with younger children is the Beethoven Project, in which a full range of supportive services and education is being offered to residents of a single low-income housing project in Chicago. Widespread interest in this project suggests that there may be a growing consensus that piecemeal programs are not fair tests of new approaches to intractable problems.

The next step would be to involve national institutions in a nationwide effort. But in order to prepare all young people for the future, we must have the collective patience and the political will to eschew both the expectation of a quick fix and unexamined faith in a new approach. Both lead quickly to disillusionment. With patience and thoughtful reflection, we can reinvent apprenticeship as an institution to help young people become adults who are productive workers, active citizens, lifelong learners, and supportive family members.

Reinventing apprenticeship will challenge the capacity of schools, communities, workplaces, and government to work together to create new learning environments for youth. Not accepting the challenge will condemn growing proportions of young people to the margins of society, where they will threaten our stability and prosperity, even our survival. Creating new avenues to adulthood will enable them to achieve their highest aspirations and to contribute their energy and talents to the common good.

Notes

Preface

1. Margaret Mead, *Coming of Age in Samoa* (Ann Arbor, Mich.: Morrow, 1928).
2. Urie Bronfenbrenner with John C. Condry, Jr., *Two Worlds of Childhood: U.S. and U.S.S.R.* (New York: Basic Books, 1970).
3. National Commission on Excellence in Education, *A Nation at Risk: The Imperative for Educational Reform* (Washington, D.C.: U.S. Government Printing Office, 1983).

Chapter 1
The Future of Youth and Work

1. Related by Erik H. Erikson in *Identity: Youth and Crisis* (New York: Norton, 1968), p. 136.
2. Pseudonyms are used in this and following vignettes to disguise individuals and institutions. The case of Vivian is based upon patterns of school-to-work transition found by Jane A. Levine, "The Impact of Early Work Experience on the Vocational Development of Young Workers," Ph.D. dissertation (Ithaca, N.Y.: Cornell University, 1985).
3. Diane N. Westcott, *Profile of the Teenage Worker* (Washington, D.C.: U.S. Department of Labor, Bureau of Labor Statistics, Bulletin 2039, October 1980), p. 41.
4. Richard B. Freeman and David A. Wise, eds., *The Youth Labor Market Problem: Its Nature, Causes, and Consequences* (Chicago: University of Chicago Press, 1982).
5. Paul Osterman has provided the most convincing treatment of the floundering period and the youth labor market in *Getting Started: The Youth Labor Market* (Cambridge, Mass.: MIT Press, 1980). Among the challenges to

the notion that there is a separate youth labor market is an article by Larry J. Griffin, Arne L. Kalleberg, and Karl L. Alexander, "Determinants of Early Labor Market Entry and Attainment: A Study of Labor Market Segmentation," *Sociology of Education 54,* (1981): 206–221. The authors urge dual or segmented labor market theorists to specify their hypotheses more precisely to allow empirical testing. Jerald G. Bachman, Patrick M. O'Malley, and Jerome Johnston document the similarity of dropouts' and recent graduates' jobs in *Adolescence to Adulthood: Change and Stability in the Lives of Young Men* (Ann Arbor, Mich.: Institute for Social Research, 1978).

6. This increase, dramatic by itself, is all the more remarkable because the ratio decreased in every other decade of the twentieth century: James S. Coleman, ed., *Youth: Transition to Adulthood* (Chicago: University of Chicago Press, 1974), p. 47.

7. Youth and America's Future: The William T. Grant Foundation Commission on Work, Family and Citizenship, *The Forgotten Half: Pathways to Success for America's Youth and Young Families* (Washington, D.C.: author, November 1988), p. 27.

8. James R. Wetzel, *American Youth: A Statistical Snapshot* (Washington, D.C.: Youth and America's Future: The William T. Grant Foundation Commission on Work, Family and Citizenship, 1987).

9. Youth and America's Future: The William T. Grant Foundation Commission on Work, Family and Citizenship, *The Forgotten Half: Non-college Youth in America* (Washington, D.C.: author, January 1988), pp. 130–32.

10. Wetzel, *American Youth,* p. 24.

11. William B. Johnston and Arnold H. Packer, *Workforce 2000: Work and Workers for the 21st Century* (Indianapolis, Ind.: Hudson Institute, 1987), p. 95.

12. Wetzel, *American Youth,* p. 1.

13. Robert Taggart, Andrew Sum, and Gordon Berlin, "Basic Academic Skills: Key to Youth's Future," Unpublished paper presented to the U.S. Senate Committee on Labor and Human Resources, January 14, 1987.

14. Charles F. Westoff, Gérard Calot, and Andrew D. Foster, "Teenage Fertility in Developed Nations: 1971–1980," *Family Planning Perspectives 15* (1983): 107.

15. Alan Guttmacher Institute, *Teenage Pregnancy: The Problem that Hasn't Gone Away* (New York: author, 1981).

16. Lloyd D. Johnston, Patrick O'Malley, and Jerald G. Bachman, who conduct these surveys, have made empirical attempts to adjust their findings for heavier use of drugs and alcohol among dropouts and chronic truants. They concluded that including those groups would increase the usage rates reported by about 5 percent: *Use of Licit and Illicit Drugs by America's*

High School Students, 1975–1984 (Washington, D.C.: U.S. Government Printing Office, 1985).

17. U.S. Bureau of the Census, *Statistical Abstract of the United States: 1986,* 106th edition (Washington, D.C.: U.S. Government Printing Office, 1985), p. 182.

18. See, for example, the treatment of "uninvolved youth" by the Carnegie Council on Policy Studies in Higher Education, *Giving Youth a Better Chance: Options for Education, Work, and Service* (San Francisco: Jossey-Bass, 1980).

19. Business Advisory Commission of the Education Commission of the States, *Reconnecting Youth: The Next Stage of Reform* (Denver, Colo.: Education Commission of the States, 1985).

20. Gordon Berlin and Andrew Sum have written of the "silent firing" of hundreds of thousands of young workers, mostly males, who could reasonably have expected to follow their fathers and uncles into highly paid blue-collar jobs. However, since 1974, the proportion of young men employed in manufacturing has declined by one-fourth. Without belittling the plight of adult workers displaced by declining manufacturing, it is plausible to argue that the chief victims have been young high school graduates or dropouts who never had a chance at a good job. Largely as a result of this trend in the labor market, real earnings of young men with jobs *fell* between 1973 and 1984 by 32 percent for whites and 44 percent for blacks: *Toward a More Perfect Union: Basic Skills, Poor Families, and Our Economic Future* (New York: Ford Foundation, 1988), p. 13. See also the interim and final reports of Youth and America's Future, *The Forgotten Half: Non-college Youth,* and *The Forgotten Half: Pathways to Success.*

21. Ronald E. Kutscher, "Overview and Implications of the Projections to 2000," *Monthly Labor Review 110,* no. 9 (1987): 3–9.

22. Ibid.

23. Michael J. Piore and Charles F. Sabel, *The Second Industrial Divide: Possibilities for Prosperity* (New York: Basic Books, 1984).

24. In a series of case studies of industrial computerization, Shoshana Zuboff has made a related point, arguing that computers are too often used to automate production, taking over decisions from skilled workers and building them into control processes when they should "informate," meaning provide detailed information to a wider range of workers, all of whom use that information to improve production: *In the Age of the Smart Machine: The Future of Work and Power* (New York: Basic Books, 1988). See also the brief description of Proctor and Gamble's experience in *Investing in Our Children: Business and the Public Schools,* A Statement by the Research and Policy Committee of the Committee for Economic Development (New York: CED, 1985), p. 16.

25. Chris Argyris, *Integrating the Individual and the Organization* (New York: Wiley, 1964); *Work in America*, Report of a Special Task Force to the Secretary for Health, Education, and Welfare (Washington, D.C.: U.S. Government Printing Office, 1973).

26. Ivar Berg, *Education and Jobs: The Great Training Robbery* (Boston: Beacon Press, 1971); Randall Collins, *The Credential Society: An Historical Sociology of Education and Stratification* (New York: Academic Press, 1979).

27. Russell W. Rumberger, *Overeducation in the U.S. Labor Market* (New York: Praeger, 1981) and his "The Growing Imbalance between Education and Work," *Phi Delta Kappan 65* (1984): 342–346.

28. National Commission on Excellence in Education, *A Nation at Risk: The Imperative for Educational Reform* (Washington, D.C.: U.S. Government Printing Office, 1983).

29. *Investing in Our Children;* Leonard Lund and E. Patrick McGuire, *The Role of Business in Precollege Education,* Research Bulletin No. 160 (New York: The Conference Board, 1984).

30. One of the most comprehensive statements of this critique is by David T. Kearns and Denis P. Doyle, *Winning the Brain Race: A Bold Plan to Make Our Schools More Competitive* (San Francisco: Institute for Contemporary Studies Press, 1988). Kearns, chief executive officer of Xerox, estimates that unless schools are dramatically improved, U.S. businesses will have to spend $25 billion a year on remedial education for employees before they can begin to do specific job training (p. 139).

31. The sense of helplessness can be traced to the "Coleman Report," which was widely misinterpreted as proving that only family background affected students' learning and that nothing under schools' control makes a substantial difference: James S. Coleman, Ernest Q. Campbell, Carol J. Hobson, James McPartland, Alexander M. Mood, Frederic D. Weinfeld, and Robert L. York, *Equality of Educational Opportunity* (Washington, D.C.: U.S. Government Printing Office, 1966). These conclusions were a severe blow to the optimism about schools as guarantors of equality that followed initial steps toward desegregation. New research helped to change the climate of opinion, especially studies documenting the enduring effects of preschool programs like Headstart and the "effective schools" research, which first identified some schools as doing a better job than others of teaching academic material to disadvantaged children and youth and then spelled out what those schools did to achieve their results. See Lawrence J. Schweinhart and David P. Weikart, "Young Children Grow Up: The Effects of the Perry Preschool Program on Youth through Age 15," *Monographs of the High/Scope Educational Research Foundation,* no. 7 (1980); Irving Lazar and Richard Darlington, with Harry Murray, Jacqueline Royce, and Ann Snipper, "Lasting Effects of Early Education: A Report from the Consortium

for Longitudinal Studies," *Monographs of the Society for Research in Child Development 47,* nos. 2–3, Serial no. 195 (1982); Ronald R. Edmonds, "Effective Schools for the Urban Poor," *Educational Leadership 37* (1979): 28–32; Stewart C. Purkey and Marshall S. Smith, "Effective Schools: A Review," *Elementary School Journal 83* (1983): 427–452; Sara Lawrence Lightfoot, *The Good High School: Portraits of Culture and Character* (New York: Basic Books, 1983).

32. Among the more influential statements of this position were Samuel Bowles and Herbert Gintis, *Schooling in Capitalist America: Educational Reform and the Contradictions of Economic Life* (New York: Basic Books, 1976); Martin Carnoy and Henry M. Levin, *The Limits of Educational Reform* (New York: Longman, 1976); and Christopher Jencks, Marshall Smith, Henry Acland, Mary Jo Bane, David Cohen, Herbert Gintis, Barbara Heyns, and Stephan Michelson, *Inequality: A Reassessment of the Effect of Family and Schooling in America* (New York: Basic Books, 1972).

33. Arthur Jensen and Richard Herrnstein were leading spokesmen for this position.

34. For example, Kearns and Doyle, *Winning the Brain Race,* recommend year-round schooling for children from poor families on the basis of findings by Barbara Heyns and others that such children lose far more of their school learning over the summer than do children from middle-class families: *Summer Learning and the Effects of Schooling* (New York: Academic Press, 1978).

35. Seymour B. Sarason, *Schooling in America: Salvation and Scapegoat* (New York: Free Press, 1983). James P. Comer has demonstrated how the systematic and sustained involvement of parents can contribute to improving the school performance of poor and minority children: *School Power: The Implications of an Intervention Project* (New York: Free Press, 1980), and his "Educating Poor Minority Children," *Scientific American 259,* no. 5 (1988): 42–48. The workplace becomes a more critical environment for secondary school students; its involvement in schooling is the focus of this book.

36. Leonard Goodwin, "Poor Youth and Employment: A Social Psychological Perspective," *Youth and Society 11* (1980): 311–351.

37. Mihalyi Csikszentmihalyi and Reed Larson, *Being Adolescent: Conflict and Growth in the Teenage Years* (New York: Basic Books, 1984).

38. Lauren B. Resnick, *Education and Learning to Think* (Washington, D.C.: National Academy Press, 1987).

39. The lack of specificity of this goal is not surprising. Theodore Sizer once remarked that the aims of education must necessarily be stated in general terms in order to muster broad support. The more specific the aims, the more difficult it becomes to secure consensus.

40. John H. Bishop, "Why the Apathy in American High Schools?" *Educational Researcher 18,* no. 1 (1989): 6–10.

Chapter 2
The Perilous Transition from School to Career

1. Noah Lewin-Epstein, *Youth Employment during High School* (Washington, D.C.: National Center for Education Statistics, 1981).

2. Ibid., pp. 22–23.

3. Ibid., pp. 5–8; Ivan Charner and Bryna Shore Fraser, *Youth and Work: What We Know: What We Don't Know: What We Need to Know* (Washington, D.C.: Youth and America's Future: The William T. Grant Foundation Commission on Work, Family and Citizenship, 1988), p. 2.

4. Lewin-Epstein, *Youth Employment,* pp. 21, 24–32. Other studies report similar differences: Ronald D'Amico, "Does Employment during High School Impair Academic Progress?" *Sociology of Education 57* (1984): 152–164; and studies cited in Charner and Fraser, *Youth and Work.*

5. Michael Wachter and Choongsoo Kim, "Time Series Changes in Youth Joblessness," in Richard B. Freeman and David A. Wise, eds., *The Youth Labor Market Problem: Its Nature, Causes, and Consequences* (Chicago, University of Chicago Press, 1982), p. 179.

6. Charner and Fraser, *Youth and Work.*

7. Lewin-Epstein, *Youth Employment;* Charner and Fraser, *Youth and Work.*

8. Diane N. Westcott, *Profile of the Teenage Worker* (U.S. Department of Labor, Bureau of Labor Statistics, Bulletin 2039, October 1980) pp. 37–38; see also Paul Osterman, *Getting Started: The Youth Labor Market* (Cambridge, Mass.: MIT Press, 1980); Michael E. Borus, ed., *Youth and the Labor Market: Analyses of the National Longitudinal Survey* (Kalamazoo, Mich.: W. E. Upjohn Institute for Employment Research, 1984).

9. Paul Osterman, *Getting Started.*

10. In addition, 22 percent required less than 30 days of on-the-job training and another 19 percent less than three months' specific vocational training. Michael E. Borus, "A Description of Employed and Unemployed Youth in 1981," in Borus, *Youth and the Labor Market,* p. 42.

11. Ellen Greenberger, Laurence D. Steinberg, and Mary Ruggiero, "A Job Is A Job Is a Job . . . Or Is It? Behavioral Observations in the Adolescent Workplace," *Work and Occupations 9* (1982): 79–96; Lewin-Epstein, *Youth Employment;* Charner and Fraser, *Youth and Work.*

12. Peter Doeringer and Michael J. Piore, *Internal Labor Markets and Manpower Analysis* (Lexington, Mass.: D. C. Heath, 1971); David M. Gordon, *Theories of Poverty and Underemployment* (Lexington, Mass.: D. C. Heath, 1972);

Bennett Harrison, *Education, Training, and the Urban Ghetto* (Baltimore, Md: Johns Hopkins University Press, 1972).

13. MBA stands for Master of Business Administration, normally a two-year postgraduate degree that is increasingly seen as the starting point for a successful career in business, especially in a large corporation.

14. Both Lewin-Epstein (*Youth Employment*) and Beatrice G. Reubens, John A. C. Harrison, and Kalman Rupp in *The Youth Labor Force, 1945–1995: A Cross-national Analysis* (Totowa, N.J.: Allanheld, Osmun, 1981) dispute the reality of a youth labor market, but they do so by setting overly stringent criteria for what would constitute a separate labor market. It is important to note, however, as Reubens et al. point out, that gender differences in the distribution of jobs are even greater than age differences.

Lewin-Epstein argued against the idea of a youth labor market on the basis of evidence in his data for continuity between young people's first work experience and subsequent employment. Sixty-two percent of the seniors who worked while in school and planned to work after graduation rather than enroll in higher education said they had a job already lined up. Only 31 percent of the seniors without jobs made the same claim. Most of those with jobs lined up planned to continue in the same job after graduation (pp. 108–109).

Although Lewin-Epstein interpreted this finding as indicating that working while a student serves as a means of entering the adult labor market upon graduation, one can also ask what value a high school diploma has in the labor market if those who earn one simply continue to work in the same jobs they held while in school. Continuity of this kind reflects the absence of opportunity after graduation rather than career entry before graduation.

The very term, "labor market," is metaphorical; it cannot survive reification. There is no single market in which all workers compete freely with each other. Rather there are multiple labor markets with somewhat permeable boundaries existing in particular occupations, regions, and firms.

15. Brian E. Becker and Stephen M. Hills, "The Long-run Effects of Job Changes and Unemployment among Male Teenagers," *Journal of Human Resources 17* (1983): 197–211; Brian E. Becker and Stephen M. Hills, "Teenage Unemployment: Some Evidence of the Long-run Effects on Wages," *Journal of Human Resources 15* (1980): 354–372; Francine D. Blau and Lawrence M. Kahn, "Race and Sex Differences in Quits by Young Workers," *Industrial and Labor Relations Review 34* (1981): 563–577.

16. Gloria Shaw Hamilton and J. David Roessner, "How Employers Screen Disadvantaged Job Applicants," *Monthly Labor Review 95*, no. 9 (1972): 14–21; Paul E. Barton, "Youth Transition to Work: The Problem and Federal Policy Setting," in National Commission for Manpower Policy,

From School to Work: Improving the Transition (Washington, D.C.: U.S. Government Printing Office, 1976); Ernest Lynton, Joel R. Seldin, and Sarah Gruhin, *Employers' Views on Hiring and Training* (New York: Labor Market Information Network, 1978); Osterman, *Getting Started;* Leonard Lund and E. Patrick McGuire, *The Role of Business in Precollege Education,* Research Bulletin No. 160 (New York: The Conference Board, 1984); Welford W. Wilms, ''Vocational Education and Job Success: The Employer's View,'' *Phi Delta Kappan 65* (1985): 347–350.

17. Ellen Greenberger and Laurence D. Steinberg, *When Teenagers Work: The Psychological and Social Costs of Adolescent Employment* (New York: Basic Books, 1986).

18. Jerald G. Bachman, Patrick M. O'Malley, and Jerome Johnston, *Adolescence to Adulthood: Change and Stability in the Lives of Young Men* (Ann Arbor, Mich: Institute for Social Research, 1978).

19. Stanley P. Stephenson, ''From School to Work: A Transition with Job Search Implications,'' *Youth and Society 11* (1979): 114–132; Robert H. Meyer and David A. Wise, ''High School Preparation and Early Labor Force Experience,'' in Freeman and Wise, *The Youth Labor Market Problem.*

20. Lewin-Epstein, *Youth Employment.*

21. Stephen F. Hamilton, ''Working toward Experience,'' *Transaction/Society 19,* no. 6 (1982): 19–29; David T. Ellwood, ''Teenage Unemployment: Permanent Scars or Temporary Blemishes?'' in Freeman and Wise, *The Youth Labor Market Problem;* Lester C. Thurow, ''Vocational Education as a Strategy for Eliminating Poverty,'' in National Institute of Education, *The Planning Papers for the Vocational Education Study* (Washington, D.C.: author, 1979); Linda S. Gottfredson, ''Education as a Valid but Fallible Signal of Worker Quality: Reorienting an Old Debate about the Functional Basis of the Occupational Hierarchy,'' in Alan C. Kerkhoff, ed., *Research in Sociology of Education and Socialization,* vol. 7 (Greenwich, Conn.: JAI Press, 1985).

22. Jeylan T. Mortimer and Michael D. Finch, ''The Effects of Part-time Work on Adolescent Self-Concept and Achievement,'' in Kathryn Borman and Jane Reisman, eds., *Becoming a Worker* (Norwood, N.J.: Ablex, 1986).

23. Ernest W. Stromsdorfer, ''An Economic Analysis of the Work Experience and Career Exploration Program'' (Bloomington, Ind.: Indiana University, 1973); Philip A. Cusick, *The Egalitarian Ideal and the American High School: Studies of Three Schools* (New York: Longman, 1983); Greenberger and Steinberg, *When Teenagers Work.* Some studies have failed to find this effect or found no identifiable danger point. See D'Amico, ''Employment during High School''; Larry Hotchkiss, ''Work and Schools: Complements or Competitors?'' in Borman and Reisman, *Becoming a Worker.* However, in addition to the prima facie validity of the argument that working half-

time interferes with full-time schooling, the strongest support for a 15–20 hour per week danger point is its independent rediscovery by developmental psychologists Greenberger and Steinberg a decade after it was reported by economist Stromsdorfer.

24. Greenberger and Steinberg, *When Teenagers Work.* Charner and Fraser cite studies with contrary findings in *Youth and Work.*

25. Ivan Charner and Bryna Shore Fraser, ''Fast Food Jobs'' (Washington, D.C.: National Institute for Work and Learning, 1984).

26. Osterman, *Getting Started,* p. 16.

27. This interpretation challenges the assumptions underlying career guidance, which have been strongly influenced by the theoretical and empirical work of John L. Holland and Donald E. Super, both of whom focus on the match between individual characteristics and the demands of various occupations. Both argue for rational approaches to occupational choice but assume implicitly that choice is possible for all young people, regardless of their educational attainment and the level of the occupational hierarchy to which they can reasonably aspire. See Holland's *Making Vocational Choices: A Theory of Vocational Personalities and Work Environments* (Englewood Cliffs, N.J.: Prentice-Hall, 1985) and Super's *The Psychology of Careers: An Introduction to Vocational Development* (New York: Harper and Row, 1957).

Even without reference to the secondary labor market, the notion of a one-time career choice makes no sense when the average American adult worker has 10 different employers and at least that many different jobs in a lifetime. See Robert Hall, ''The Importance of Lifetime Jobs in the U.S. Economy,'' *American Economic Review, 72* (1982): 716–724; and Kenneth I. Spenner, Luther B. Otto, and Vaughan R. A. Call, *Career Lines and Careers,* Vol. 3, Entry into Careers Series (Lexington, Mass.: Lexington Books, 1982).

28. For more information about the *Berufsschule,* see Chapter 4. Rolf and the other Brandt apprentices followed the ''block plan,'' attending *Berufsschule* full-time for five- or six-week blocks rather than attending one day a week over a three-year period, which is the normal schedule.

29. Joseph A. Limprecht and Robert H. Hayes, ''Germany's World-Class Manufacturers,'' *Harvard Business Review 60,* no. 6 (1982): 137–145.

30. Der Bundesminister für Bildung und Wissenschaft, *Grund- und Strukturdaten, 1986/87* (Bad Honnef: Bock, 1986), pp. 89, 122.

31. Memories of National Socialism effectively quell most expressions of national pride by Germans. If they wished to boast, they might point out that because East Germany is the source of most manufactured products for the entire Eastern bloc, if the export trade of the two Germanys were added together, no other country would even be close.

32. Deutscher Industrie- und Handelstag, *Berufsausbildung in der Bundesrepublik Deutschland: Das duale System* (Esslingen/Neckar: Bechtle, 1982), p. 7.

33. Joachim Münch, *Das duale System: Lehrlingsausbildung in der Bundesrepublik Deutschland* (Bonn: Deutscher Industrie- und Handelstag, 1979), p. 91.

34. M. E. Taylor, *Education and Work in the Federal Republic of Germany.* (London: Anglo-German Foundation for the Study of Industrial Society, 1981).

35. Deutscher Industrie- und Handelstag, *Berufsausbildung,* p. 8.

Chapter 3
Discovering Apprenticeship

1. Stephen M. Hills and Beatrice G. Reubens, "Youth Employment in the United States," in Beatrice G. Reubens, ed., *Youth at Work: An International Survey* (Totowa, N.J.: Rowan and Allenheld, 1983), p. 273.

2. Calvin C. Jones, Susan Campbell, and Pam A. Sebring, *Four Years after High School: A Capsule Description of 1980 Seniors* (Washington, D.C.: U.S. Department of Education, National Center for Education Statistics, 1986). The definition of apprenticeship included programs not recognized by the U.S. Department of Labor's Bureau of Apprenticeship and Training.

3. *Federal Register,* vol. 52, no. 231, Wednesday, December 2, 1987, pp. 45907–45908.

4. Beatrice G. Reubens, *Apprenticeship in Foreign Countries,* U.S. Department of Labor R&D Monograph 77 (Washington, D.C.: U.S. Government Printing Office, 1980), p. 11.

5. Hills and Reubens, "Youth Employment," p. 273.

6. The distinction between apprenticeship programs sponsored by unions and those sponsored by corporations is spelled out by Robert W. Glover in *Apprenticeship Lessons from Abroad,* Information Series No. 305 (Columbus, Ohio: National Center for Research in Vocational Education, The Ohio State University, 1985).

7. Charles Mallar, Stuart Karachsky, and Craig V. D. Thornton, "Evaluation of the Economic Impact of the Job Corps Program," Third Follow-up Report (Princeton, N.J.: Mathematica Policy Research, 1982), p. 13, National Technical Information Service document number PB83-145441.

8. Mallar, Karachsky, and Thornton, "Evaluation."

9. Judith Gueron, *Lessons from a Job Guarantee: The Youth Incentive Entitlement Pilot Projects* (New York: Manpower Demonstration Research Corporation, 1984). The full report was prepared by George Farkas, Randall Olsen, Ernest W. Stromsdorfer, Linda C. Sharpe, Felicity Skidmore, D.

Alton Smith, and Sally Merrill, *Post-program Impacts of the Youth Incentive Entitlement Program* (New York: Manpower Development Research Corporation, 1984). For a summary and critical review of this and many other studies of the Comprehensive Employment and Training Act (CETA) youth programs, see Charles L. Betsey, Robinson G. Hollister, Jr., and Mary R. Papageorgiou, eds., *Youth Employment and Training Programs: The YEDPA Years* (Washington, D.C.: National Academy Press, 1985).

10. Garth Mangum and John Walsh, *Employment and Training Programs for Youth: What Works Best for Whom?* (Washington, D.C.: U.S. Department of Labor, 1978).

11. Barbara Heyns, *Summer Learning and the Effects of Schooling* (New York: Academic Press, 1978).

12. Cynthia L. Sipe, Jean Baldwin Grossman, and Julita A. Milliner, *Summer Training and Education Program (STEP); Report on the 1987 Experience* (Philadelphia: Public/Private Ventures, 1988).

13. Stephen F. Hamilton and Ann C. Crouter, "Work and Growth: A Review of Research on the Impact of Work Experience on Adolescent Development," *Journal of Youth and Adolescence 9* (1980): 323–338; Stephen F. Hamilton and John F. Claus, "Inequality and Youth Employment: Can Work Programs Work?" *Education and Urban Society 14* (1981): 103–126.

14. According to the *National Service Newsletter* (number 53) of October 1988 from the National Service Secretariat, several million youth volunteers donate an average of 50 hours of service per year. A survey found that in 1987, 7,450 18- to 24-year-olds served as full-time volunteers, giving 2,000 hours in the Peace Corps, the California Conservation Corps, and related programs.

15. See the final report of Youth and America's Future: The William T. Grant Foundation Commission on Work, Family and Citizenship, *The Forgotten Half: Pathways to Success for America's Youth and Young Families* (Washington, D.C.: author, 1988.) and the information paper prepared for that commission by Anne C. Lewis, *Facts and Faith: A Status Report on Youth Service* (1988), which cites estimates that between 3.5 and 4 million youth could be productively engaged in full-time service (p. 7). Another recent source on this topic is Charles H. Harrison, *Student Service: The New Carnegie Unit* (Princeton, N.J.: The Carnegie Foundation for the Advancement of Teaching, 1987).

16. Dan Conrad and Diane Hedin, *National Assessment of Experiential Learning Project: A Final Report* (St. Paul, Minn.: University of Minnesota, 1981); Fred M. Newmann and Robert A. Rutter, "The Effects of High School Community Service Programs on Students' Social Development," Report to the National Institute of Education (Madison, Wis.: Wisconsin Center for Education Research, 1983); Stephen F. Hamilton and L. Mickey Fenzel, "The Impact of Volunteer Experience on Adolescent Social Development:

Evidence of Program Effects," *Journal of Adolescent Research 3* (1988): 65–80.

17. Conrad and Hedin, *National Assessment.*

18. Stephen F. Hamilton and R. Shepherd Zeldin, "Learning Civics in the Community," *Curriculum Inquiry 17* (1987): 407–420.

19. Conrad and Hedin, *National Assessment.*

20. Eliot Wigginton, *Sometimes a Shining Moment: The Foxfire Experience* (Garden City, N.Y.: Anchor/Doubleday, 1985).

21. The observations were conducted by Joline Hemminger and Maryellen Horodeck for a study reported by Stephen F. Hamilton, "Adolescents in Community Settings: What Is to Be Learned?" *Theory and Research in Social Education 9* (1981); 23–38.

22. These results are summarized by Thomas R. Owens, "Experience Based Career Education: Summary and Implications of Research and Evaluation Findings," in Dan Conrad and Diane Hedin, eds., *Youth Participation and Experiential Learning* (New York: Haworth, 1982).

23. Ronald B. Bucknam and Sharon G. Brand, "EBCE Really Works: A Meta-analysis on Experience Based Career Education," *Educational Leadership 40*, no. 6 (1983): 66–71.

24. Gene Bottoms and Patricia Copa, "A Perspective on Vocational Education Today," *Phi Delta Kappan 64* (1983): 348–354; John Bishop, "Vocational Education for At-risk Youth: How Can It Be Made More Effective?" Working Paper No. 88–11 (Ithaca, N.Y.: Cornell University School of Industrial and Labor Relations, Center for Advanced Human Resource Studies, 1988).

25. Morgan V. Lewis, and Jeannette L. Fraser, "Increasing Community Involvement in Cooperative Vocational Education." (Columbus, Ohio: National Center for Research in Vocational Education, The Ohio State University, 1982).

26. Cynthia Parsons, "The Bridge: Cooperative Education for All High School Students," Working Paper (Washington, D.C.: Youth and America's Future: The William T. Grant Foundation Commission on Work, Family and Citizenship, 1987).

27. Roger's case is based on the author's observations and included in an unpublished paper prepared for the U.S. Department of Labor, Stephen F. Hamilton and Mary Agnes Hamilton, "Teaching and Learning on the Job: A Framework for Assessing Workplaces as Learning Environments" (1989).

28. Ivan Illich, *Deschooling Society* (New York: Harper and Row, 1970).

29. The observation was done by Walter Frankel as part of a study that included a comparison with another program patterned after Foxfire. See Hamilton, "Adolescents in Community Settings." See also Stephen F. Hamilton, "The Learning Web: The Structure of Freedom," *Phi Delta Kappan 62* (1981): 600–601.

30. Hamilton, "Adolescents in Community Settings" pp. 27–28. Contrast the finding of a small-scale survey of U.S. youth in which only half named one unrelated adult as an important person in their lives: Stephen F. Hamilton and Nancy Darling, "Mentors in Adolescents' Lives," in Klaus Hurrelmann and Uwe Engel, eds., *The Social World of Adolescents: International Perspectives* (Berlin: Walter de Gruyter, 1989).

31. The *Berufsschule* is described in more detail in Chapter 5.

32. Der Bundesminister für Bildung und Wissenschaft, *Grund- und Strukturdaten, 1986/87* (Bad Honnef: Bock, 1986), p. 95.

33. In the United States auto manufacturers franchise local sales and service firms, who receive some supervision and training from the manufacturer but are independently owned. Manufacturers' training of mechanics is reputed to be of high quality, but is available only to a fraction of those doing the work, primarily foremen, and is far shorter than an apprenticeship. West German auto manufacturers own and operate large sales and service shops. Independent shops are typically smaller, though one sizable shop where an apprentice was observed was owned by a firm with a chain of shops repairing Volkswagens. Nearly all repair shops specialize in one or a few makes of automobile. Gasoline stations (*Tankstellen*) are not places to have an automobile repaired.

34. Evelies Mayer, Wilhelm Schumm, Karin Flaake, Heidi Gerberding, and Jochen Reuling, *Betriebliche Ausbildung und gesellschaftliches Bewußtsein: Die berufliche Sozialisation Jugendlicher* (Frankfurt am Main: Campus; 1981).

35. Paul H. Douglas, *American Apprenticeship and Industrial Education,* Studies in History, Economics and Public Law, Vol. 95, No. 2 (New York: Columbia University and Longmans, Green, 1921).

36. Joseph F. Kett, *Rites of Passage: Adolescence in America, 1790 to the Present* (New York: Basic Books, 1977).

37. Bernard Bailyn, *Voyagers to the West: A Passage in the Peopling of America on the Eve of the Revolution* (New York: Knopf, 1986).

38. W. J. Rorabaugh, *The Craft Apprentice: From Franklin to the Machine Age in America* (New York: Oxford University Press, 1986).

39. Recent investigations of the guns produced in Whitney's factory have revealed that the tolerances achieved were insufficient to achieve true interchangeability. Considerable filing and hand fitting was still required. But the principle of mass production was established and the work profoundly deskilled.

40. Mack Walker, *German Home Towns: Community, State, and General Estate, 1648–1871* (Ithaca, N.Y.: Cornell University Press, 1971).

41. Fernand Braudel, *Civilizaton and Capitalism, 15th–18th Century, Vol. 2, The Wheels of Commerce,* trans. Siân Reynolds (New York: Harper and Row, 1982), p. 315 (originally published in French in 1979).

42. Walker, *German Home Towns.*

43. Cited in Douglas, *American Apprenticeship,* pp. 191–192.

Chapter 4
Academic Schooling: General Prepartion for Work

1. Lawrence A. Cremin, *Traditions of American Education* (New York: Basic Books, 1977), p. 51.

2. Michael B. Katz's book, *Class, Bureaucracy and Schools: The Illusion of Educational Change in America* (New York: Praeger, 1975) and Samuel Bowles's and Herbert Gintis's *Schooling in Capitalist America: Educational Reform and the Contradictions of Economic Life* (New York: Basic Books, 1976) are two of the seminal works in what became during the 1970s a large and complex literature on this topic.

3. The reader must recognize that this brief paragraph skims the surface of an enormous body of thought and writing and that other definitions of both democracy and equality are tenable. The Founding Fathers, as their gender suggests, assumed the rectitude of a hierarchy in which mature white male landowners were the true citizens. Among the more egalitarian reactions to this assumption are some Israeli kibbutzim in which all members take turns performing the community's jobs, regardless of interest and aptitude, detaching work completely from both social status and subsistence. The treatment of school, work, and class that follows addresses only issues of equalizing access to desirable work, not of equalizing earnings and status across the job hierarchy.

4. Some have referred to these lessons as the "hidden curriculum," but in view of the multiple purposes of schools listed by Cremin in *Traditions of American Education,* it is not clear from whom they are hidden.

5. Talcott Parsons, "The School Class as a Social System: Some of Its Functions in American Society," *Harvard Educational Review, 29* (1959): 297–318; Robert Dreeben, *On What Is Learned in School* (Reading, Mass.: Addison-Wesley, 1968).

6. The term "probable futures" was used frequently by Harvard president, Charles W. Eliot, an influential school reformer around the turn of the century. It is employed here with conscious irony because of the self-fulfilling prophecy inherent in predicting children's future accomplishments.

7. Bowles and Gintis, *Schooling in Capitalist America.*

8. James E. Rosenbaum, "Social Implications of Educational Grouping," in David C. Berliner, ed., *Review of Research in Education,* Vol. 8 (American Educational Research Association, 1980); see also Thomas L. Good and Susan Marshall, "Do Students Learn More in Heterogeneous or Homogeneous Groups?" in Penelope L. Peterson, Louise Cherry Wilkinson, and

Maureen Hallinan, eds., *The Social Context of Instruction: Group Organization and Group Process* (New York: Academic Press, 1984).

9. Steven T. Bossert, *Tasks and Social Relationships in the Classroom: A Study of Instructional Organization and Its Consequences* (New York: Cambridge University Press, 1979).

10. Ray C. Rist, "Student Social Class and Teacher Expectations: The Self-fulfilling Prophecy in Ghetto Education," *Harvard Educational Review* 40 (1970): 411–451.

11. Eleanor Burke Leacock, *Teaching and Learning in City Schools: A Comparative Study* (New York: Basic Books, 1969).

12. Leacock, *Teaching and Learning in City Schools,* p. 181.

13. One of the first, and still most compelling shocks to the reassuring myth of schools as engines of equality was August B. Hollingshead's classic study, *Elmtown's Youth: The Impact of Social Classes on Adolescents* (New York: Wiley, 1949), which demonstrated to what extent social class determined what happened to young people in school. A lively debate has persisted among sociologists and economists concerned with education, a debate that became heated in the 1970s. One of the most telling studies was done by researchers who were skeptical of schools' ability to reduce class stratification, but found empirical evidence for a higher level of mobility than the "radical critique" allows. See Christopher Jencks, Marshall Smith, Henry Acland, Mary Jo Bane, David Cohen, Herbert Gintis, Barbara Heyns, and Stephan Michelson, *Inequality: A Reassessment of the Effect of Family and Schooling in America* (New York: Basic Books, 1972).

14. Der Bundesminister für Bildung und Wissenschaft, *Grund- und Strukturdaten, 1986/87* (Bad Honnef: Bock, 1986), pp. 26, 37. In the entire country, there were only 311 private *Grundschulen* and *Hauptschulen* (p. 24).

15. Dieter Hopf, Lothar Krappmann, and Hansjörg Scheerer, "Aktuelle Probleme der Grundschule," in Max Planck-Institut für Bildungsforschung, Projektrgruppe Bildungsbericht, *Bildung in der Bundesrepublik Deutschland: Daten und Analysen,* Vol. 2 (Reinbek: Rowohlt, 1980).

16. Hopf, Krappmann, and Scheerer, "Aktuelle Probleme," p. 1130.

17. Theodore R. Sizer, *Secondary Schools at the Turn of the Century* (New Haven, Conn.: Yale University Press, 1964); Katz, *Class, Bureaucracy and Schools.*

18. See Sizer, *Secondary Schools,* for a thorough analysis of the Committee and its report.

19. Mortimer J. Adler, *The Paideia Proposal: An Educational Manifesto* (New York: Macmillan, 1982).

20. Marvin Lazarson and W. Norton Grubb, eds., *American Education and Vocationalism: A Documentary History, 1870–1970* (New York: Teachers College Press, 1974).

21. Jeannie Oakes, *Keeping Track: How Schools Structure Inequality* (New Haven, Conn.: Yale University Press, 1985).

22. James E. Rosenbaum, *Making Inequality: The Hidden Curriculum of School Tracking* (New York: Wiley, 1976).

23. Rosenbaum, *Making Inequality*, p. 40.

24. Christopher S. Jencks and Marsha D. Brown, "Effects of High Schools on their Students," *Harvard Educational Review 45* (1975): 273–324.

25. Jerald G. Bachman, Patrick M. O'Malley, and Jerome Johnston concluded their study of young men's transition to adulthood by admitting that they had expected to find schools operating as "socialization factories," shaping boys to adult standards, but found instead stronger empirical support for the view that schools are sorting mechanisms that do not substantially change pupils, but rather send them off into different directions depending upon the resources they bring with them from their families: *Adolescence to Adulthood: Change and Stability in the Lives of Young Men* (Ann Arbor, Mich.: Institute for Social Research, 1978), pp. 222–225.

26. Claus Offe, *Berufsbildungsreform: Eine Fallstudie über Reformpolitik* (Frankfurt am Main: Suhrkamp, 1975).

27. Der Bundesminister für Bildung und Wissenschaft, *Grund-und Strukturdaten, 1986/87*, p. 8.

28. Wolfgang Mitter, "Education in the Federal Republic of Germany: The Next Decade," *Comparative Education 16* (1980): 257–265.

29. Der Bundesminister für Bildung und Wissenschaft, *Grund- und Strukturdaten, 1986/87*, p. 26.

30. Annegret Körner, "Comprehensive Schooling: An Evaluation—West Germany," *Comparative Education 17* (1981): 15–22.

31. Jens Naumann, "Entwicklungstendenzen des Bildungswesens der Bundesrepublik Deutschland im Rahmen wirtschaftlicher und demographischer Veränderungen," in Max Planck-Institut für Bildungsforschung, *Bildung in der Bundesrepublik Deutschland: Daten und Analysen,* Vol. 1 (Reinbek: Rowohlt, 1980), p. 62.

32. Der Bundesminister für Bildung und Wissenschaft, *Grund- und Strukturdaten,* p. 38.

33. Richard Fauser, "Schulische Qualifikation und Beschäftigungsperspektiven: Zum Einfluß wirtschaftlicher Krisensymptome in der Region auf die Bildungsplanung von Arbeitereltern für ihre Kinder," in Manfred Kaiser, Reinhard Nuthmann, and Heinz Stegmann, eds., *Berufliche Verbleibsforschung in der Diskussion,* Vol. 1 (Nuremberg: Institut für Arbeitsmarkt- und Berufsforschung der Bundesanstalt für Arbeit, 1985).

34. Der Bundesminister für Bildung und Wissenschaft, *Berufsbildungsbericht, 1984, Grundlagen und Perspektiven für Bildung und Wissenschaft* (Bad Honnef: Bock, 1984), p. 42.

35. Der Bundesminister für Bildung und Wissenschaft, *Berufsbildungsbericht*, pp. 43–44.

36. Double qualification is a theme emerging from several chapters in Kaiser, Nuthmann, and Stegmann, *Berufliche Verbleibsforschung*.

37. M. E. Taylor, *Education and Work in the Federal Republic of Germany* (London: Anglo-German Foundation for the Study of Industrial Society, 1981), pp. 173–174. Picht wrote an influential series of articles on the topic for the general public in 1964, recommending that the number of *Gymnasium* graduates be doubled, a goal that was achieved for females but not quite for males.

38. Der Bundesminister für Bildung und Wissenschaft, *Grund- und Strukturdaten, 1983/84*, p. 24.

39. Jill Spence, "Access to Higher Education in the Federal Republic of Germany: The Numerus Clausus Issue," *Comparative Education 17* (1981): 285–292.

40. Dorotea Furth, "Beyond Compulsory Schooling: Problems of the 16–19 Year Olds," *OECD Observer* No. 132 (1985): 7–11, Table 1, p. 8.

41. Emil J. Haller and Sharon A. Davis, "Does Socioeconomic Status Bias the Assignment of Elementary School Students to Reading Groups?" *American Educational Research Journal 17* (1980): 409–418; Robert A. Rehberg and Evelyn R. Rosenthal, *Class and Merit in the American High School* (New York: Longman, 1978). No study has demonstrated that schools differentiate students totally without regard to academic capacity; that would require more valid tests of capacity than have yet been constructed and exceptionally well-controlled studies. The issue cannot be decided one way or another. Empirical investigations yield insights into *how and how much* schooling either contributes to equality or perpetuates inequality.

42. Mary Haywood Metz, *Classrooms and Corridors: The Crisis of Authority in Desegregated Secondary Schools* (Berkeley: University of California Press, 1978).

43. Bachman, O'Malley, and Johnston, *Adolescence to Adulthood*, pp. 208–209, represent this interaction vividly, showing that family socioeconomic status and other attributes are related to the kind of occupation a person acquires both directly and indirectly through their influence on the amount of education the person obtains. Their finding that the indirect influence through schooling was stronger than the direct influence (0.315 compared to 0.239) is consistent with the belief that personal and family characteristics are more important than schooling alone in determining adult status, but it emphasizes the role of schools as both a channel and an enhancer of those factors. School is neither neutral nor impotent.

44. Luitgard Trommer-Krug, "Soziale Herkunft und Schulbesuch," in Max Planck-Institut für Bildungsforschung, *Bildung in der Bundesrepublik Deutschland*, Vol. 1, pp. 235–236.

45. W. Williamson, "Patterns of Educational Inequality in West Germany," *Comparative Education 13* (1977): 29–44; Christoph Führ, *Education and Teaching in the Federal Republic of Germany* (Munich: Carl Hansler, 1979).

46. The major theoretical treatises, which relate personality traits to characteristics of occupations are by John L. Holland, *Making Vocational Choices: A Theory of Vocational Personalities and Work Environments* (Englewood Cliffs, N.J.: Prentice-Hall, 1985) and Donald E. Super, *The Psychology of Careers: An Introduction to Vocational Development* (New York: Harper and Row, 1957). According to their perspectives, individuals, with the help of counselors, should match their interests and personalities to potential occupations and then make plans to prepare for those occupations. Kenneth I. Spenner, Luther B. Otto, and Vaughan R. A. Call, *Career Lines and Careers*, Vol. 3, Entry into Careers Series (Lexington, Mass.: Lexington Books, 1982), p. 169, noted that Holland's and Super's ideas have had an enormous impact on the practice of vocational guidance but have not been taken seriously by many social scientists outside the field.

47. Anne Roe and Marvin Siegelman, *The Origin of Interests* (Washington, D.C.: American Personnel and Guidance Association, 1964). This point is substantiated by the picture of the youth labor market presented in Chapter 2.

48. Orville G. Brim, Jr., "Socialization through the Life Cycle," in Orville G. Brim, Jr., and Stanton Wheeler, eds, *Socialization after Childhood: Two Essays* (New York: Wiley, 1966).

49. Urie Bronfenbrenner, *The Ecology of Human Development: Experiments by Nature and Design* (Cambridge, Mass.: Harvard University Press, 1979), p. 9.

50. John Dewey, *Experience and Education* (New York: Collier, 1938; reprint. 1963), p. 49.

51. Panel on Secondary School Education for the Changing Workplace, *High Schools and the Changing Workplace: The Employers' View* (Washington, D.C.: National Academy Press, 1984; Leonard Lund and E. Patrick McGuire, *The Role of Business in Precollege Education*, Research Bulletin No. 160 (New York: The Conference Board, 1984); and Wellford W. Wilms, "Vocational Education and Job Success: The Employer's View," *Phi Delta Kappan 65* (1984): 347–350.

52. See Linda S. Gottfredson, "Education as a Valid but Fallible Signal of Worker Quality: Reorienting an Old Debate about the Functional Basis of the Occupational Hierarchy," in Alan C. Kerkhoff, ed., *Research in Sociology of Education and Socialization*, Vol. 5 (Greenwich, Conn.: JAI Press, 1987), for a review of the theory of "signaling" in employer selection practices. She claims that the signals employers use to make decisions are fallible, but still rational.

Chapter 5
Vocational Schooling: Specific Preparation for Work

1. *The New Republic 3* (May 15, 1915); 40–43. The exchange was reprinted in *Curriculum Inquiry 7* (1977): 33–39.

2. Quoted in Marvin Lazerson and W. Norton Grubb, eds., *American Education and Vocationalism: A Documentary History, 1870–1970* (New York: Teachers College Press, 1974), p. 61.

3. Robert H. Wiebe, *The Search for Order, 1877–1920* (New York: Hill and Wang, 1967).

4. Paul H. Douglas, *American Apprenticeship and Industrial Education*, Studies in History, Economics, and Public Law, Vol. 95, No. 2 (New York: Columbia University and Longmans, Green, 1921).

5. Arthur G. Wirth, *Education in the Technological Society: The Vocational-Liberal Studies Controversy in the Early Twentieth Century* (Scranton, Pa.: Intext Educational Publishers, 1972).

6. Lazerson and Grubb, *American Education and Vocationalism.*

7. Alan Weisberg, "What Research Has to Say about Vocational Education and the High Schools," *Phi Delta Kappan 64* (1983): 355–359.

8. This is the type of vocational school attended by Roger Parsons, whose cooperative education placement was described in Chapter 3.

9. The author was a teacher of social studies and English at "Judson" from 1968 to 1971. Much has surely changed at Judson since that time, not necessarily for the better. Drug traffic and violence were already endemic then and have become much worse in Washington, D.C. There is no evidence that the city's schools on the whole have improved substantially. Judson will serve, therefore, as an example of a struggling urban vocational high school.

10. Sara Lawrence Lightfoot, *The Good High School: Portraits of Culture and Character* (New York: Basic Books, 1983); Theodore R. Sizer, *Horace's Compromise: The Dilemma of the American High School* (Boston: Houghton Mifflin, 1984).

11. The following description is based on material in John F. Claus's Ph.D. thesis, "Opportunity or Inequality in Vocational Education? An Ethnographic Investigation" (Ithaca, N.Y.: Cornell University, 1986).

12. Sue E. Berryman, "The Equity and Effectiveness of Secondary Vocational Education," in Harry F. Silberman and Kenneth S. Rehage, eds., *Education and Work*, 81st Yearbook of the National Society for the Study of Education (Chicago: University of Chicago Press, 1982).

13. Jeannie Oakes, *Keeping Track: How Schools Structure Inequality* (New Haven, Conn.: Yale University Press, 1984); Joan E. Crowley, Tom K.

Pollard, and Russell W. Rumberger, "Education and Training," in Michael E. Borus, ed., *Tomorrow's Workers* (Lexington, Mass.: D.C. Heath, 1983).

14. Valena White Plisko, ed., *The Condition of Education, 1984 Edition,* National Center for Education Statistics (Washington, D.C.: U.S. Government Printing Office, 1984), p. 105.

15. Paul B. Campbell, Mollie N. Orth, and Patricia Seitz, "Patterns of Participation in Secondary Vocational Education: A Report Based on Transcript and Interview Data of the 1979 and 1980 National Longitudinal Survey New Youth Cohort" (Columbus, Ohio: National Center for Research in Vocational Education, The Ohio State University, 1981), Educational Resources Information Center document number ED 209 476.

16. Many previous evaluations that compared all vocational graduates to graduates of the general track failed to find substantial and reliable labor market advantages attributable to vocational education, though some of these studies found that women with business and office training and men with trade and industrial training earned more and suffered less unemployment than general track graduates. John T. Grasso and John R. Shea, *Vocational Education and Training: Impact on Youth* (Berkeley, Calif.: Carnegie Council on Policy Studies in Higher Education, 1979); National Institute of Education, *The Vocational Education Study: The Final Report* (Washington, D.C.: author, 1981), Educational Resources Information Center document number ED 205 831; Donna M. Mertens, Douglas McElwain, Gonzalo Garcia, and Mark Whitmore, "The Effects of Participating in Vocational Education: Summary of Studies Conducted since 1968" (Columbus, Ohio: National Center for Research in Vocational Education, The Ohio State University, 1980); Robert H. Meyer and David A. Wise, "High School Preparation and Early Labor Force Experience," in Richard B. Freeman and David A. Wise, eds., *The Youth Labor Market Problem: Its Nature, Causes, and Consequences* (Chicago: University of Chicago Press, 1982); Russell W. Rumberger and Thomas N. Daymont, "The Economic Value of Academic and Vocational Training Acquired in High School," in Michael E. Borus, ed., *Youth and the Labor Market: Analyses of the National Longitudinal Survey* (Kalamazoo, Mich.: W. E. Upjohn Institute for Employment Research, 1984); Alan L. Gustman and Thomas L. Steinmeier, "The Relation between Vocational Training in High School and Economic Outcomes," *Industrial and Labor Relations Review 36* (1982): 73–87; Donna M. Mertens, "The Vocational Education Graduate in the Labor Market," *Phi Delta Kappan 34* (1983): 360–361.

17. Campbell, Orth, and Seitz, "Patterns of Participation."

18. Mertens, McElwain, Garcia, and Whitmore, "The Effects of Participating in Vocational Education," cite several studies reporting that about half of vocational graduates find training-related employment. Rumberger and Daymont, "Economic Value," compared the transcripts of 1979 graduates in

the National Longitudinal Survey with their subsequent employment and found that vocational graduates had a much greater likelihood of working in their field of training than graduates of the general track had of finding work in those fields, especially in office and clerical work for women and craft and industrial work for men. Self-selection probably accounts for part of that relationship—some young people who choose a course in food preparation also search for food preparation jobs for identical reasons, and would have done so had they received no training.

The disaggregation of vocational students into "concentrators, limited concentrators, concentrator/explorers, explorers, and incidental/personal" categories was proposed by Campbell, Orth, and Seitz, in "Patterns of Participation." However, the labor market advantages of concentrators, who only account for 14 percent of vocational enrollees, were not impressive in that study. A subsequent study reporting the labor market advantages for concentrators, limited concentrators, and concentrator/explorers who subsequently found training-related employment is referred to in the text: Paul B. Campbell, Karen S. Basinger, Mary Beth Dauner, and Marie A. Parks, "Outcomes of Vocational Education for Women, Minorities, the Handicapped, and the Poor" (Columbus, Ohio: National Center for Research in Vocational Education, The Ohio State University, 1986). This and related studies are usefully synthesized in an unpublished paper by John Bishop, "High School Vocational Education: A Review of Research on its Impacts with Recommendations for Improvement" (Ithaca, N.Y.: Cornell University, New York State School of Industrial and Labor Relations, 1986).

19. Stephen M. Hills, "How Craftsmen Learn their Skills: A Longitudinal Analysis," in Robert E. Taylor, Howard Rosen, and Frank C. Pratzner, eds., *Job Training for Youth: The Contributions of the United States' Employability Development System* (Columbus, Ohio: National Center for Research in Vocational Education, The Ohio State University, 1982); see also Stephen M. Hills and Beatrice G. Reubens, "Youth Employment in the United States," in Beatrice G. Reubens, ed., *Youth at Work: An International Survey* (Totowa, N.J.: Rowan and Allanheld, 1983). Lester C. Thurow, "Vocational Education as a Strategy for Eliminating Poverty," in *The Planning Papers for the Vocational Education Study,* Vocational Education Study Publication No. 1 (Washington, D.C.: The National Institute of Education, 1979), p. 325, cited a 1964 Labor Department study finding that only 12 percent of workers listed formal training as the most important source of their skills, as compared to 60 percent who cited only informal on-the-job training. The remainder attributed their skills to a combination of formal and informal sources.

20. Mertens, "The Vocational Education Graduate"; Plisko, *Condition of Education, 1984.*

21. Grasso and Shea, *Vocational Education and Training.*

22. Thurow, "Vocational Education as a Strategy for Eliminating Poverty."

23. Typing has become so essential as the use of computers has expanded that some have urged universal instruction in "keyboarding" as a fundamental skill for all high school graduates.

24. Bishop, "High School Vocational Education: A Review of Research."

25. Gene Bottoms and Patricia Copa, "A Perspective on Vocational Education Today," *Phi Delta Kappan 64* (1983): 348–354.

26. Ruth B. Ekstrom, Margaret E. Goertz, Judith M. Pollack, and Donald A. Rock, "Who Drops out of High School and Why? Findings from a National Study," *Teachers College Record 87* (1986): 356–373.

27. Suk Kang and John Bishop, "Vocational and Academic Education in High School: Complements or Substitutes," Working Paper 88–10 (Ithaca, N.Y.: Cornell University, New York State School of Industrial and Labor Relations, Center for Advanced Human Resource Studies, 1988).

28. Dale Parnell, *The Neglected Majority* (Washington, D.C.: Community College Press, 1985), p. 85.

29. Valena White Plisko and Joyce D. Stern, eds., *The Condition of Education, 1985 Edition* (Washington, D.C.: U.S. Department of Education, National Center for Education Statistics, 1985), p. 79 and Table 2.2, p. 90.

30. National Assessment of Vocational Education, *Second Interim Report to Congress* (Washington, D.C.: U.S. Department of Education, September 9, 1988), Chapter 6.

31. National Assessment of Vocational Education, *Second Interim Report,* Table 1–1, p. 1–3.

32. More detail on these schools may be found in Russ Russell, "The Institutional Backing for the Transition from School to Working Life in the FRG," Paper No. 84/2e, *Proceedings of the Standing Conference on the Sociology of Further Education* (Blagdon, United Kingdom: Coombe Lodge, 1984); M. E. Taylor, *Educaton and Work in the Federal Republic of Germany* (London: Anglo-German Foundation for the Study of Industrial Society, 1981); and Christoph Führ, *Education and Teaching in the Federal Republic of Germany* (Munich: Carl Hansler, 1979).

33. This is a theme invoked in their critical appraisal by Hansjürgen Daheim, Helmut Heid, Rudolf Laerum, Walter Riester, and Hans-Jürgen Roth, *Sozialisationsprobleme arbeitender Jugendlicher,* Vol. 1 (Munich: Deutsches Jugendinstitut, 1978), p. 23.

34. The historical overview that follows is based largely on information provided by Taylor, *Education and Work in the Federal Republic of Germany.*

35. Maya Pines, "Unlearning Blind Obedience in German Schools," *Psychology Today 15,* no. 5 (May 1981): 59–65.

36. Sabine Sardei-Biermann, *Jugendliche zwischen Schule und Arbeitswelt: Zur Bedeutung der Schule für den Übergang in den Beruf* (Munich: Deutsches Jugendinstitut, 1984); Freya Dittmann-Kohli, Norbert Schreiber, and Frauke

Möller, *Lebenswelt und Lebensbewältigung: Theoretische Grundlagen und eine empirische Untersuchung am Beispiel von Lehrlingen,* Research Report 35, (Constance: University of Constance, 1982).

37. Dieter Hopf, Lothar Krappmann, and Hansjörg Scheerer, "Aktuelle Probleme der Grundschule," in Max Planck-Institut für Bildungsforschung, Projektgruppe Bildungsbericht, *Bildung in der Bundesrepublik Deutschland: Daten und Analysen,* Vol. 2 (Reinbek: Rowohlt, 1980), p. 1180.

38. Larry Cuban, "Persistent Instruction: The High School Classroom, 1900–1980," *Phi Delta Kappan 64* (1982): 113–118; John T. Goodlad, Frances M. Klein, and associates, *Behind the Classroom Door* (Worthington, Ohio: Charles A. Jones, 1970).

39. Dittmann-Kohli, Schreiber, and Möller, *Lebenswelt und Lebensbewältigung;* and Sardei-Biermann, *Jugendliche zwischen Schule und Arbeitswelt.*

40. Sardei-Biermann, *Jugendliche zwischen Schule und Arbeitswelt,* pp. 241–243.

41. National Education Association, *The Cardinal Principles of Secondary Education: A Report of the Commission on the Reogranization of Secondary Education,* U.S. Bureau of Education *Bulletin,* 1918, no. 35, p. 16; quoted in Wirth, *Education in the Technological Society,* p. 129.

Chapter 6
Cloudy Futures: Why the American System Fails

1. Stephen F. Hamilton, "Adolescent Problem Behavior in the United States and West Germany: Implications for Prevention," in Klaus Hurrelmann, Franz-Xaver Kaufmann, and Friedrich Lösel, eds., *Social Intervention: Chances and Constraints* (Berlin: Walter de Gruyter, 1987).

2. Arthur L. Stinchcombe, *Rebellion in a High School* (Chicago: Quadrangle, 1964). David Bakan "Adolescence in America: From Idea to Social Fact," *Daedalus 100* (1971): 979–995, dubbed this dynamic "the promise," saying that youth are asked to conform to adult authority while they are young in return for promised future rewards, and that increasing problem behavior results from young people's declining faith that the promise will be kept. Cheryl D. Hayes, ed., *Risking the Future: Adolescent Sexuality, Pregnancy, and Childbearing,* Vol. 1 (Washington: D.C.: National Academy Press, 1987), p. 178, used the same principle to draw a connection between school performance and teenage sexual behavior.

3. James S. Coleman, "The Children Have Outgrown the Schools," *Psychology Today 5,* no. 9 (February 1972): 72–75, 82. See also his "How Do the Young Become Adults?," *Review of Educational Research 42* (1972): 431–439.

4. John H. Bishop, "Why the Apathy in American High Schools?" *Educational Researcher 18,* no. 1 (1989):6–10, cites the Longitudinal Survey of Ameri-

can Youth (1988) as indicating that less than 25 percent of tenth graders believed that they needed high school-level math and science to obtain their preferred occupation. As a thought-experiment to test the validity of teachers' insistence on the importance of their subjects, consider asking high school teachers to take the examinations given by their colleagues in other disciplines. How many social studies teachers could pass a biology exam? How many math teachers could reconstruct the chronology of the Civil War?

5. John U. Ogbu, *The Next Generation: An Ethnography of Education in an Urban Neighborhood* (New York: Academic Press, 1978).

6. Glen H. Elder, "Parental Power Legitimation and Its Effect on the Adolescent," *Sociometry 26* (1963): 50–65; Robert D. Hess, "Social Class and Ethnic Influences upon Socialization," in Paul H. Mussen, ed., *Carmichael's Manual of Child Psychology,* third edition (New York: Wiley, 1970), Vol. 2; Diana Baumrind, "Early Socialization and Adolescent Competence," in Sigmund E. Dragastin and Glen H. Elder, Jr., eds., *Adolescence in the Life Cycle* (Washington, D.C.: Hemisphere, 1975).

7. Sanford M. Dornbusch, Philip L. Ritter, P. Herbert Leiderman, Donald F. Roberts, and Michael J. Fraleigh, "The Relation of Parenting Style to Adolescent School Performance," *Child Development 58* (1987): 1244–1257.

8. Melvin L. Kohn, *Class and Conformity: A Study in Values,* second edition, (Chicago: University of Chicago Press, 1977).

9. References to young people's and parents' social class must be understood as common usage that is convenient for broad descriptive purposes but inadequate for the analysis of individual cases. There is much to be learned from broad comparisons among people of different income and educational levels, but when the same issues are looked at more carefully, the construct of social class begins to decompose into smaller subgroups in which additional factors such as the nature of the community, the stability of the family, parents' health, the precise nature of parents' work, and individual personal characteristics play a role that is invisible from a distance. Victoria Anne Steinitz and Ellen Rachel Solomon have made this point convincingly in a study of bright "working-class" youth from three different communities around Boston: *Starting Out: Class and Community in the Lives of Working Class Youth* (Philadelphia: Temple University Press, 1986). In West Germany, Sibylle Hübner-Funk and her colleagues provide a parallel study of community-related differences in the transition from school to apprenticeship among young males and females in three communities, one urban, one on the edge of a large city, and one rural: "Major Career Transitions of Youth: The Status Passage from School to Work in Neighborhood Context," *Journal of Adolescent Research 3* (1987): 143–160.

10. Bishop, "Apathy in American High Schools."

11. David C. McClelland, "Testing for Competence Rather than for 'Intelligence,'" *American Psychologist 28* (1973): 1–14; Christopher Jencks, Marshall Smith, Henry Acland, Mary Jo Bane, David Cohen, Herbert Gintis, Barbara Heyns, and Stephan Michelson, *Inequality: A Reassessment of the Effect of Family and Schooling in America* (New York: Basic Books, 1972); Ivar Berg, *Education and Jobs: The Great Training Robbery* (Boston: Beacon, 1970). In an extensive community study, Havighurst and his colleagues came to the opposite conclusion: "Instead of finding work to be an alternative pathway to the school for growth to adulthood, we face the stubborn fact that work and school are sections of the same pathway, and a poor school record tends to guarantee a poor work record." See Robert J. Havighurst, Paul Hoover Bowman, Gordon P. Liddle, Charles V. Mathews, and James V. Pierce, *Growing Up in River City* (New York: Wiley, 1962), p. 142. However, it is not clear that they were measuring school performance in the same way or that they followed their subjects long enough to see them develop more mature behavior at work.

12. Samuel Bowles and Herbert Gintis, *Schooling in Capitalist America: Educational Reform and the Contradictions of Economic Life* (New York: Basic Books, 1976).

13. Linda Valli, *Becoming Clerical Workers* (London: Routledge and Kegan Paul, 1986).

14. Claude E. Buxton, *Adolescents in School* (New Haven, Conn.: Yale University Press, 1973).

15. Jerald G. Bachman, Patrick M. O'Malley, and Jerome Johnston, *Adolescence to Adulthood: Change and Stability in the Lives of Young Men* (Ann Arbor, Mich.: Institute for Social Research, 1978).

16. James S. Coleman, *The Adolescent Society* (New York: Free Press, 1961).

17. James S. Coleman, ed., *Youth: Transition to Adulthood* (Chicago: University of Chicago Press, 1974); Philip A. Cusick, *Inside High School: The Student's World* (New York: Holt, Rinehart and Winston, 1973); and Cusick, *The Egalitarian Ideal and the American High School: Studies of Three Schools* (New York: Longman, 1983).

18. Maureen T. Hallinen, "The Peer Influence Process," *Studies in Educational Evaluation 7* (1982): 285–306; Francis A. J. Ianni, *The Search for Structure: A Report on American Youth Today* (New York: Free Press, 1989).

19. Sygnithia Fordham and John Ogbu, "Black Students' School Success: Coping with the Burden of 'Acting White,'" *Urban Review 18* (1986): 176–206.

20. Ogbu, *The Next Generation*.

21. Paul E. Willis, *Learning to Labour: How Working Class Kids Get Working Class Jobs* (Lexington, Mass.: Lexington Books, 1977), p. 107.

22. See Urie Bronfenbrenner, with John C. Condry, Jr., *Two Worlds of Child-*

hood: U.S. and U.S.S.R. (New York: Basic Books, 1970), for an account of Soviet child rearing, and Christa Wolf, *Kindheitsmuster* (Berlin: Aufbau-Verlag, 1976) for a personal view of childhood under Hitler. Joseph F. Kett, *Rites of Passage: Adolescence in America, 1790 to the Present* (New York: Basic Books, 1977) contains good information on the history of U.S. youth organizations.

23. The 21 apprentices interviewed for this study mentioned sports most frequently when listing leisure activities, followed by going to taverns and discos, working on cars or motorcycles (the auto mechanic apprentices), studying, watching TV or movies, reading, going to a youth center or church group, shopping, doing household chores, and listening to music. They talked about activities with friends far more than activities with family members.

24. Coleman, *Youth: Transition to Adulthood.*

25. This theme is further developed in Stephen F. Hamilton, "The Interaction of Family, Community, and Work in the Socialization of Youth," Working paper (Washington, D.C.: Youth and America's Future: The William T. Grant Foundation Commission on Work, Family and Citizenship, 1987).

26. Horst Kern and Michael Schumann, "Limits of the Division of Labour: New Production and Employment Concepts in West German Industry," *Economic and Industrial Democracy 8* (1986): 151–170.

Chapter 7
Principles for Practice: Specifications for Reinventing Apprenticeship

1. Robert K. Merton, *Social Theory and Social Structure,* enlarged edition (New York: Free Press, 1968), p. 253.

2. Joseph A. Limprecht and Robert H. Hayes, "Germany's World-class Manufacturers," *Harvard Business Review 60,* no. 6 (1982): 137–145.

3. West German participants at two recent conferences have been unanimous on these points. One was organized by Peter Katzenstein at Cornell University, April 16–18, 1987, the other by Ernest Lynton at the University of Massachusetts-Boston, April 5–7, 1989.

4. Richard Fauser, "Schulische Qualifikation und Beschäftigungsperspektiven: Zum Einfluβ wirtschaftlicher Krisensymptome in der Region auf die Bildungs-planung von Arbeitereltern für ihre Kinder," in Manfred Kaiser, Reinhard Nuthmann, and Heinz Stegmann, eds., *Berufliche Verbleibsforschung in der Diskussion,* Vol. 1 (Nuremberg: Institut für Arbeitsmarkt- und Berufsforschung der Bundesanstalt für Arbeit, 1985).

5. Less than 3 percent of students in all forms of higher education, including further vocational schools (*Fachhochschulen*), received their entrance credential from either an *Abendgymnasium* or a *Kolleg,* a full-time continuation school for adults (over 19): Der Bundesminister für Bildung und Wissen-

schaft, *Grund- und Strukturdaten, 1986/87* (Bad Honnef: Bock, 1986), p. 158. The author was a guest at a seminar at the Free University of Berlin taught by a distinguished sociologist, Prof.-Dr. Wolfgang Lempert, who, like the seven students in the seminar, had followed the second educational path. It is possible, in other words, for apprentices to graduate from a university, but it is difficult.

6. See Johann Jürgen Meister, ''Übergangsqualifikationen im Wandel,'' and other chapters in Kaiser, Nuthmann, and Stegmann, *Berufliche Verbleibsforschung*, Vol. 1.

7. Walter Heinz, Helga Krüger, Ursula Rettke, Erich Wachtveitl, and Andreas Witzel, *Hauptsache eine Lehrstelle: Jugendliche vor den Hürden des Arbeitsmarkts* (Weinheim: Beltz, 1985).

8. K. Sonntag and E. Frieling, ''New Ways of Vocational Training in the Federal Republic of Germany: An Empirical Research Comparing Training Systems,'' *International Review of Applied Psychology 32* (1983): 289–306. See also, Karlheinz Sonntag, *Berufsgrundbildung: Ein Reformkonzept und seine Realisierung* (Munich: Verband der Lehrer an beruflichen Schulen in Bayern e.V., 1983).

9. Bundesminister für Bildung und Wissenschaft, *Berufsbildungsbericht 1986* (Bad Honnef: Bock, 1986).

10. The complexity of the dual system's governance structure and its reliance on close cooperation among parties that rarely communciate with each other in the United States make it difficult to understand. A useful overview may be found in a volume about German schools prepared by the Max Planck Institute for Human Development and Education, *Between Elite and Mass Education: Education in the Federal Republic of Germany* (Albany, N.Y.: State University of New York Press, 1983). A more detailed portrait is available in Joachim Münch, *Das duale System: Lehrlingsausbildung in der Bundesrepublik Deutschland* (Bonn: Deutscher Industrie- und Handelstag, 1977).

11. According to Dr. Rainer Ruge, at the Boston conference cited above (note 3), the government will contribute more than DM 300 million between 1989 and 1992 to support multifirm training shops.

Chapter 8
An American-Style Apprenticeship System

1. This passing reference to child labor laws scarcely does justice to the complex issues of legality and liability that accompany schemes to introduce young people into community and work settings. I lack both interest and expertise to shed much light on the subject beyond two points. First, as the examples in this chapter illustrate, the issues have been met and resolved in many different locations; they are not insoluble. Second, my proposal entails a

depth of commitment from many different sources, including schools, government agencies, and private employers, that includes changing any laws and practices that render sound educational practices impossible. In this, too, West Germany's example may be useful. Their worker protection laws are comprehensive for all workers and particularly for young workers without excluding youth from work opportunities.

2. The Early Adolescent Helper program developed by Joan Schine and her associates at the City University of New York is an excellent example of this kind of service. The principles guiding the design of this program were those established by the National Commission on Resources for Youth: *New Roles for Youth in the School and the Community* (New York: Citation Press, 1974).

3. Eliot Wigginton, *Sometimes a Shining Moment: The Foxfire Experience* (Garden City, N.Y.: Anchor/Doubleday, 1985).

4. Fred M. Newmann, *Education for Citizen Action: Challenge for Secondary Curriculum* (Berkeley: McCutchan, 1975) included both forms—an internship and a group community action project—in his outline for the curriculum of a full-year civic education course based on experiential learning. Stephen F. Hamilton, "Adolescents in Community Settings: What is to be Learned?" *Theory and Research in Social Education 9* (1981): 23–38, contrasted the two forms in a study of the Learning Web and a Foxfire-inspired program.

5. The Civilian Conservation Corps (CCC), which employed more than three million young men in the Depression years 1933 to 1942, retains a favorable aura that has helped to stimulate numerous subsequent youth corps programs. The Neighborhood Youth Corps and the Job Corps, both initiated in 1965 as part of the War on Poverty, were inspired by the CCC, though both were modified considerably to adapt them to a different population and new labor market conditions. Subsequently, the Youth Conservation Corps and the Young Adult Conservation Corps, established in 1977 as part of the Youth Employment and Demonstration Projects Act, reached back to the rustic locales and conservation purposes of the CCC. Although neither survived in the Reagan administration, 14 state and 12 city conservation corps have since sprung up and loom large in discussions of national service. Michael W. Sherraden, "Youth Employment and Education: Federal Programs from the New Deal through the 1970s," *Children and Youth Services Review 2,* nos. 1/2 (1980): 17–39, provides a historical overview of youth employment programs. Current Youth Corps programs are described in Youth and America's Future: The William T. Grant Foundation Commission on Work, Family and Citizenship, *The Forgotten Half: Non-college Youth in America* (Washington, D.C.: authors, 1988), p. 62. Richard Danzig and Peter Szanton have written an incisive analysis of the prospects for a national youth service, *National Service: What Would It Mean?* (Lexington, Mass.: D. C. Heath, 1986).

6. Personal communication.

7. These definitions were developed in the course of a study of mentors and youth by the author with Urie Bronfenbrenner, Dale Blyth, Kathy Voegtle, Nancy Darling, and others.

8. Daniel J. Levinson, with Charlotte N. Darrow, Edward B. Klein, Maria H. Levinson, and Braxton McCee, *Seasons of a Man's Life* (New York: Knopf, 1978).

9. Rosabeth Moss Kanter, *Men and Women of the Corporation* (New York: Basic Books, 1979).

10. Bernard Lefkowitz, *Tough Change: Growing Up on Your Own in America* (New York: Free Press, 1987); William Julius Wilson, *The Truly Disadvantaged: The Inner City, the Underclass, and Public Policy* (Chicago: University of Chicago Press, 1987).

11. Stephen F. Hamilton and Nancy Darling, "Mentors in Adolescents' Lives," in Klaus Hurrelmann and Uwe Engel, eds., *The Social World of Adolescents: International Perspectives* (Berlin: Walter de Gruyter, 1989); James Garbarino, Nancy Burston, Suzanne Raber, Robert Russell, and Ann C. Crouter, "The Social Maps of Children Approaching Adolescence: Studying the Ecology of Youth Development," *Journal of Youth and Adolescence 7* (1978): 417–428; Dale Blyth, John P. Hill, and Karen Smith Thiel, "Early Adolescents' Significant Others," *Journal of Youth and Adolescence 11* (1982): 425–450; Joseph J. Galbo, "Adolescents' Perceptions of Significant Adults: Implications for the Family, the School, and Youth Serving Agencies," *Children and Youth Services Review 8* (1980): 37–51.

12. The Career Beginnings program was initiated by the Commonwealth Fund and operates in 25 cities, with coordination and support provided by Brandeis University's Center for Human Resources.

13. Cynthia Parsons has made good use of the bridge metaphor in advocating the expansion of cooperative education: "The Bridge: Cooperative Education for All High School Students," Working Paper (Washington, D.C.: Youth and America's Future: The William T. Grant Foundation Commission on Work, Family and Citizenship, 1987).

14. North Carolina REAL Enterprises promotes the establishment of small businesses by schools that are then "spun off" as independent firms in order to provide jobs for graduates and contribute to economic development in small communities.

15. Bureau of Labor Statistics, *Occupational Outlook Quarterly*. Cited in Nancy J. Perry, "The New, Improved Vocational School," *Fortune* (June 19, 1989), p. 132.

16. Dale Parnell, in *The Neglected Majority* (Washington, D.C.: The Community College Press, 1985) has proposed a "2+2 Tech/Prep" program for the same four-year period and for similar purposes, but without apprenticeship.

The present adaptation of his proposal places apprenticeship rather than schooling at the center of the process.

17. Wilson concurs with this point in *The Truly Disadvantaged.*

18. A. Michael Collins, "Dual Enrollment as an Operating Engineer Apprentice and an Associate Degree Candidate," Final Report to the Manpower Administration, U.S. Department of Labor (Washington, D.C.: National Joint Apprenticeship and Training Committee for Operating Engineers, December 31, 1975). There are other models as well. For example, Monroe County Community College in New York State offers an associate's degree program for apprentice auto mechanics.

19. Thomas G. Sticht, William B. Armstrong, Daniel T. Hickey, and John S. Caylor, *Cast-Off-Youth: Policy and Training Methods from the Military Experience* (New York: Praeger, 1987).

20. Statement of James Van Erden, Director of the Bureau of Apprenticeship and Training, U.S. Department of Labor, during a conference organized by Ernest Lynton at the University of Massachusetts-Boston, April 5–7, 1989.

21. Toni Joseph, "Many Veterans Find Military Jobs No Road to Civilian Success," *Wall Street Journal* (October 9, 1985): 1, 22.

22. Sizer's most extensive analysis of high schools is contained in *Horace's Compromise: The Dilemma of the American High School* (Boston: Houghton Mifflin, 1984). The principles are stated in his "Coalition of Essential Schools: Prospectus, 1984 to 1994" (Providence, R.I.: Education Department, Brown University, 1984) and other Coalition documents. Other educational innovations are also compatible with apprenticeship, including Benjamin S. Bloom's Mastery Learning: *Human Characteristics and School Learning* (New York: McGraw-Hill, 1976); and Cooperative Learning, advocated by Robert E. Slavin, *Cooperative Learning: Student Teams,* second edition (New York: Longman, 1987). Perhaps most promising are high-intensity instructional methods using tutoring and programmed instruction with adult learners. See Robert Taggart, Andrew Sum, and Gordon Berlin, "Basic Academic Skills: Key to Youth's Future," Unpublished paper presented to the U.S. Senate Committee on Labor and Human Resources, January 14, 1987.

23. Lauren B. Resnick, "Learning in School and Out," *Educational Researcher 16,* no. 9 (1987): 13–20.

24. (Cambridge: Harvard University Press, 1973).

25. Larry Cuban, "Persistent Instruction: The High School Classroom, 1900–1980," *Phi Delta Kappan 64* (1982): 113–118.

26. Taggart, Sum, and Berlin, "Basic Academic Skills."

27. Lawrence A. Cremin has used the term in his majesterial treatise on the history of American education in all its aspects. For an overview of the

three-volume study, see his *Traditions of American Education* (New York: Basic Books, 1977).

28. See, for example, Bernard J. McMullan, Phyllis Snyder, and others, "Allies in Education: Schools and Businesses Working Together for At-Risk Youth" (Philadelphia: Public/Private Ventures, 1987); and Dale Mann, "Business Involvement and Public School Improvement," *Phi Delta Kappan 69,* Part 1 (October 1987); 123–128; Part 2 (November 1987): 228–232.

29. In 1985, 107,150,000 people were employed in the civilian labor force. 16,690,000 of these were employed directly by government. See Table 612, p. 368 and Table 462, p. 282 of U.S. Bureau of the Census, *Statistical Abstract of the United States: 1988,* 108th edition (Washington, D.C.: U.S. Government Printing Office, 1987).

30. Construction contractors currently register their apprenticeship programs in large part because such registration authorizes them to pay a reduced wage to apprentices employed in government projects. Incentives such as this can be abused; they must be combined with enforcement to assure that high-quality training is provided.

31. Chapter 6 of Youth and America's Future, *The Forgotten Half: Non-college Youth in America* discusses such schemes. See also Robert Sheets, Andrew Hahn, Robert Lerman, and Erik Butler, "Who Will Train and Educate Tomorrow's Workers? The Financing of Non-college-Bound Young Workers' Recurrent Education," Working paper (Washington, D.C.: Youth and America's Future: The William T. Grant Foundation Commission on Work, Family and Citizenship, 1987).

32. Although West German workers' commitments to their employers are not as strong as in Japan, job changing is far less frequent than in the United States. The English-derived term, *"jobben,"* is used to describe the practice of working briefly for many different employers, and it is a prejorative term. One source of employee loyalty is the firm's obligation. Unlike the United States where thousands of employees are routinely laid off when business slows down, West German employers are forbidden by law to lay off workers except in the most desperate circumstances. Instead, they change production or marketing tactics in response to market changes. For example, when the 1974 oil crisis reduced demand for luxury automobiles, Mercedes (Daimler-Benz) manufactured fewer automobiles, shifting workers to lines producing trucks, which were sold on the international market. When market conditions improved in the 1980s, their workforce was intact. As attractive as this approach is for employees, who enjoy something akin to tenure after several years, its disadvantage is that employers do not take on new workers when the economy turns up because they do not wish to assume the obligation. The West German economy creates few new jobs as a result.

33. One source of this story was a special report on the need for investment

in human capital in *Business Week* magazine, September 19, 1988, which also cited the case of New York Telephone having to test 60,000 applicants to find 3,000 qualified workers.

34. Philip T. Sudo, "School Program Builds Bridges to Wall Street," *American Banker,* March 22, 1988, p. 63.

35. This is a pseudonym, as are the names of the people involved. The observations and interviews on which this section is based were done by Mary Agnes Hamilton in preparation for writing a paper for the U.S. Department of Labor, Stephen F. Hamilton and Mary Agnes Hamilton, "Teaching and Learning On-the-Job" (1989).

36. See Shoshanna Zuboff's accounts of this kind of work environment in industrial plants, *In the Age of the Smart Machine: The Future of Work and Power* (New York: Basic Books, 1988).

37. Erik H. Erikson, *Identity: Youth and Crisis* (New York: Norton, 1968), p. 138.

38. James S. Coleman, ed., *Youth: Transition to Adulthood* (Chicago: University of Chicago Press, 1974). A compendium of comments on this report, several critical, may be found in *School Review 83,* no. 1 (1974).

39. Richard Elmore's paper, "Knowledge Development under the Youth Employment and Demonstration Projects Act, 1977–1981," in Charles L. Betsey, Robinson G. Hollister, Jr., and Mary R. Papageorgio, eds., *Youth Employment and Training Programs: The YEDPA Years* (Washington, D.C.: National Academy Press, 1985) traces the history of the demonstration side of YEDPA.

40. Irving Lazar and Richard Darlington, with Harry Murray, Jacqueline Royce, and Ann Snipper, "Lasting Effects of Early Education: A Report from the Consortium for Longitudinal Studies," *Monographs of the Society for Research in Child Development, 47,* nos. 2–3, Serial no. 195 (1982); Lawrence J. Schweinhart and David P. Weikart, "Young Children Grow Up: The Effects of the Perry Preschool Program on Youth through Age 15," *Monographs of the High/Scope Education Research Foundation,* No. 7 (1980); Charles Mallar, Stuart Karachsky, and Craig V.D. Thornton, "Evaluation of the Economic Impact of the Job Corps Program," Third Follow-up Report (Princeton, N.J.: Mathematica Policy Research, 1982), National Technical Information Service document number PB83-145441.

Index

A Nation at Risk, 12, 61, 166
Ability grouping, 70–71, 74, 83
Abitur, 30, 80
Abiturienten, 80, 146
Academic learning, 14–16, 44, 45, 47, 51, 61, 68, 88, 101, 136, 140, 155, 157, 167, 168
Academy of Finance, 173–176, 178, 182
Adler, Mortimer J., 76, 169
Antioch College, 158
Apprenticeship now in the U.S., 39–40
Area vocational center, 96–98
Aspirations, 9, 84, 86–89, 99, 119, 124–126, 130, 185
Auto mechanic/auto repair, 55–60, 61–63, 67, 106–114, 144–145, 147, 152

Barstow, Gene (supervisor of Robert Jameson), 179–182
Bennett, William J., 12, 93
Berufsschule(n), 30, 32, 51, 61, 67, 104–116, 122, 128, 129, 147, 150, 151
Bishop, John, 125, 126
Black youth, 6, 8, 20, 21, 71–72, 122, 124, 127
Block instruction, 115
Board of Cooperative Educational Services (BOCES), 48
Boston Compact, 170
Brandt (large West German industrial firm), 29–31, 36, 52, 53, 60, 62, 114, 115, 149, 162

Bronfenbrenner, Urie, ix, xii, 87, 156
Butler, Brad, 170

California Compact, 170
Cardinal Principles, 76, 117
Career, 3–5, 17, 19, 22–24, 27, 28, 32, 34, 40, 44, 46, 47, 49, 50, 60, 63, 64, 86, 87, 98, 103, 104, 107, 119, 122, 124, 131–133, 136–138, 143, 147, 157–160, 162, 163, 178, 184
Career Beginnings, 157
Career education, 40, 46, 50, 138, 157
Carter, Mrs. (U.S. vocational teacher), 96–98, 100
Chambers (West German quasi-public organizations), 33, 55, 67, 106, 150, 151
Choice, 13, 27, 28, 30, 59, 75, 82, 86, 91, 126, 139, 141, 146, 148, 149, 162, 163, 166
Citizen, obligations and rights of, 2, 13, 66, 70
Citizenship education, 12, 76, 88, 105, 116, 117
Coalition of Essential Schools, 166
Coleman, James S., 122, 126, 127, 183
Committee for Economic Development, 12
Committee of Ten, 75, 76
Community, 13, 16, 17, 26, 40, 43–46, 49–51, 61, 71, 102, 103, 105, 119, 121, 123, 126, 127, 130, 131, 133, 136, 140, 153–155, 157, 159, 163, 165, 169, 183, 184

Community colleges, 102, 103
Community service, 17, 40, 43, 44, 46,
    51, 140, 153–157
Competence, 12, 14, 15, 29, 44, 65, 88,
    100, 131, 139, 146, 156, 164, 175,
    178, 181
Competencies, 32, 141, 168
Competency-based certification, 139
Comprehensive Competencies Program,
    168
Comprehensive high school, 98
Cooperative education, 40, 47–49, 51, 100,
    116, 140, 158–159, 184
Craft skills/workers, 10, 16, 32, 39, 40,
    53, 55, 63–67, 92, 108, 144, 163
Crime: see Problem behavior

Demographic conditions, 1, 145
Demonstration project to test apprentice-
    ship in U.S., 182–185
Development (definition), 87
Dewey, John, 15, 45, 87, 91, 93
Differentiation of students: see Tracking
Disadvantaged youth, 7, 9, 14, 19, 41–
    43, 88, 121–122, 159, 162, 171
Disconnected youth, 8, 9
Diversity, 77, 116, 135–137, 139, 140,
    155
Double qualification, 80, 146, 147, 152
Dropout(s): see Problem behavior
DRT Corporation, 178
Drug (ab)use: see Problem behavior
Dual system, 2, 32, 33, 103, 104, 107,
    109, 116, 122, 149, 184
    institutional participants in, 32–35

Eliot, Charles W., 45, 75, 76, 154
Employers
    investment in dual system, 35–36, 151
    motivations for investing in U.S. appren-
        ticeship, 170–182
Employment of high school students, 19–
    21, 24–27
Erikson, Erik H., 182
Experience Based Career Education
    (EBCE), 40, 46–47, 50–51, 138, 157
Experiential learning, x, 44, 47
Exploitation, 35, 53, 61, 141, 154

Exploratory apprenticeship, 44, 140

Fachhochschule, 81, 147
Family, 11, 13, 16, 20, 22, 28, 63, 65,
    73, 76, 84, 85, 89, 97, 98, 105, 119,
    123, 124, 128, 130, 135, 141, 144,
    156, 176, 181, 185
Flexibility in U.S. education and training
    system, 16, 135–140, 148, 152, 171
Flexible workers, 10, 12, 16, 133, 135
Floundering period, 3–4, 6, 24, 121
Foxfire, 40, 44–46, 51, 154, 155
Frankfort, Phyllis, 173, 174, 176
Franklin, Benjamin, 64, 69
Freud, Sigmund, 2
Future, the, 1, 10, 11, 14–17, 24, 33, 34,
    46, 47, 57, 60, 69, 72, 76, 78, 81,
    84, 87, 88, 97, 113, 121, 122, 123,
    126, 131–133, 140, 141, 151, 159,
    160, 177, 178, 185

GED (General Educational Development
    certificate/high school equivalency),
    7, 41, 162
Gender inequality, 70, 144–145
General preparation for work, 63, 69–89,
    93, 119–120, 137–140, 152, 157–158
Glenn, Vivian (U.S. floundering period),
    2–3, 19
Governmental activity
    involvement in West German apprentice-
        ship, 34–35, 52–53, 149–152, 171–
        172, 185
    support for U.S. apprenticeship, 171–
        172
Greenberger, Ellen, 26, 27
Griffith, Judy (Learning Web), 50–51
Grundschule, 73, 78
Guilds, 52, 65–66
Gymnasium(ien), 78–82, 84, 85, 95, 104,
    105, 128

Hauptschule, 78–80, 84, 85, 144, 146–148
Heberer, Anna (German Industriekauffrau
    apprentice), 4, 29
Higher education, ix, 9, 24, 28, 32, 75,
    79, 81, 83, 84, 99, 103, 121, 125,
    127, 139, 145–147, 157, 158, 161,

164, 174, 184; *see also* Postsecondary education, University/ies
Hispanic youth, 6, 8, 127
History
   of apprenticeship, 63–67
   of U.S. schools, 69–70, 75–76, 91–93
Hochschule(n), 81, 83
Humboldt, Wilhelm von, 104

Illich, Ivan, 49
Industrialization, 64–66, 92
Industriekaufleute/mann/frau, 52–53, 60, 61, 67, 105, 112–115, 130, 131, 144, 149, 150, 167
Inequality, 13, 70, 73, 84, 85, 93, 144, 145

Jameson, Robert (U.S. "apprentice" in DRT Corporation), 178–182
Jefferson, Thomas, 92
Job Corps, 40–43, 51, 140, 164, 165, 184
Johnson, Allen, 177
Judson Vocational High School, 94–96
Junior Achievement, 159

Kemmler, Rolf (*Industriekaufmann* apprentice), 29–32, 51, 52, 53
Kerschensteiner, Georg, 67, 104, 116
Key features/essential elements of apprenticeship, 40, 42, 46, 51, 61–63, 94, 140, 153

Labor force participation, 19, 20, 99
Labor market, 2–4, 6, 7, 11, 15, 16, 19, 21–28, 36, 40, 41, 51, 77, 78, 82, 84, 86, 91, 93, 95, 99–101, 103, 116, 119–121, 123–125, 132, 135, 136, 138, 139, 142, 145, 147, 148, 150, 160, 163, 165, 170, 172, 176, 177
   youth labor market, 21–28
Lakeland, 153–163
Learning Web, 49–51, 157, 160
Levels of apprenticeship, 140–142, 160
Lifelong learning, 146, 147
Luft-tek (small West German industrial firm), 53–55, 60

Magnet schools, 96
Manual training, 91–93
Manufacturing, 1, 3, 4, 9, 10, 12, 15, 21, 25, 36, 55, 135, 143, 146
Marland, Sidney, 46
Master/*Meister,* 16, 56, 57, 62, 65–66, 135, 143, 151
Mead, Margaret, ix
Mentor(ing), 17, 31, 32, 49–51, 62, 63, 140, 154, 156–157, 159, 164, 170, 177, 182
Middle class, 7, 9, 14, 66, 72, 77, 85, 88, 124, 125, 127, 135
Military service, 5, 163–164
Minority youth, 3–9, 20, 22, 37, 40, 95, 124, 127, 163, 172
Morgan, J. P., 92
Motivation/motivate, 16–17, 46, 61, 84, 96, 115, 121, 122, 127, 131, 136, 149, 161, 162, 164, 168, 170, 174–177
Multifirm training shop, 151–152, 171

Northeastern University, 158

Oettinger, Karl (apprentice auto mechanic), 56–57
Ogbu, John U., 127
Organized labor, 92; *see also* Unions
Osterman, Paul, 27
Overtrained/overeducated workers, 11, 143–144

Paideia, 76, 169
Parents, 4, 5, 23, 42, 47, 51, 62, 63, 70, 72, 73, 78–80, 83–85, 87–89, 97, 98, 104, 120, 124, 125, 127, 128, 130–133, 140, 141, 144, 147, 148, 156, 162
Parsons, Roger (cooperative education), 47–49
Peers/peer group, ix, 16, 26, 42, 50, 109, 119, 122, 123, 126–131
Poor youth, 1, 3, 6, 8, 20, 37, 41, 73, 95, 124; *see also* Disadvantaged youth
Postsecondary education, 5, 32, 55, 80–83, 99, 102, 103, 115, 171; *see also* Higher education, University/ies

Poverty, 6–8, 13, 40, 121, 124, 135, 156
Primary labor market, 3, 24, 26, 28, 36, 124, 170
Probable future, 70, 76, 93
Problem behavior, 7, 8, 17, 120–121, 123, 126, 131, 132, 135
   crime, 8, 41, 121
   dropout(s)/school failure, 3, 7, 8, 15, 40, 120, 123–124, 136, 162
   drug (ab)use, 7, 120–121, 135
   premature motherhood/parenthood, 7, 120
Prosser, Charles, 93

Qualifying examination for apprentices, 150–151

Raab, Petra (*Industriekauffrau* apprentice), 53–56
Race, 14, 20, 70, 111, 127, 155
Racial differences, 71
Racial discrimination, 6, 7, 13, 124, 135
Realschule, 30, 78, 80, 84, 85, 113, 144, 146, 152
Recent changes in West German apprenticeship, 142–143, 145–152
Reforming schools, 89, 165–169
Rigid(ity), 32, 133, 136, 137, 144, 147, 149

School failure: *see* Problem behavior, dropout(s)/school failure
School reform, 1, 13–15, 28, 79, 86, 93, 116, 170
School weariness (*Schulmüdigkeit*), 114, 123, 136
School-based apprenticeship, 140, 157, 158, 166, 170
Second educational path, 79, 81, 146
Service jobs/sector, 3, 21, 55, 99, 177
Shearson Lehman Hutton, 173
Sizer, Theodore R., 166, 167
Smith-Hughes Act, 91, 93
Snedden, David, 91–93
Social class, 127, 133, 143–145, 155
   and U.S. schools, 70–73, 89, 121–126, 133

   and West German schools, 73–74, 77–85, 89, 144
Social skills, 1, 10, 15, 21, 24, 60, 135, 150, 167
Socialization, 11, 67, 87, 88, 105, 115, 123, 124, 128, 131, 164, 165
Specific preparation for work, 12, 17, 46, 49–50, 86–88, 91–117, 119–120, 137–142, 150, 152, 160–165
Steinberg, Laurence D., 26, 27
Stinchcombe, Arthur L., 122
Stockhausen, Hermann (apprentice plumber), 147
Summer Training and Education Program (STEP), 42, 43, 51, 99, 141, 143, 146, 148, 172, 174, 185
System, x, 2, 4, 5, 9, 15–17, 24, 29–33, 35–37, 40, 49, 51–53, 59, 61, 63, 65, 67, 68, 70, 75, 77–81, 83, 84, 91, 98, 100, 101, 103–107, 109, 114–116, 119, 122, 126–128, 133, 135–144, 146–149, 151–155, 162–165, 168, 169, 171, 172, 182, 184

Technical colleges, 102, 103, 162
Technical skills, 10, 24, 161
Technician, 138, 141, 160–162
Tracking (differentiation)
   in U.S. secondary schools, 74–78, 84, 88, 98, 123, 125, 129, 133
   in West German secondary schools, 77–80, 83–85, 144
2 + 2 apprenticeship, 161–163, 172
Two-year colleges, 22, 83, 102, 103, 161

Unemployment, 3, 5, 6, 23, 41, 99, 122
Unions, 14, 33, 40, 64, 110, 111, 163; *see also* Organized labor
United States system of education and training (characteristics), 135–139, 152
University/ies; *see also* Higher education, Postsecondary education
   in U.S., 133, 136, 158
   in West Germany, 29, 30, 66, 67, 78–83, 85, 105, 145, 146

Vocational education/schooling, 5, 12, 17,
    32, 46, 47, 80, 91–117, 137, 147,
    150, 157, 158, 184
  in U.S.: effects, 99–102; postsecondary,
    102–103; purpose, 102, 116–117,
    157–158
  in West Germany (*see also Berufs-
    schule*): postsecondary, 103; pur-
    pose, 104–106, 150
Volksschule, 79, 80, 85, 105

Wanner, Georg (apprentice auto me-
    chanic), 58–59, 106–112
Wegmans (supermarket chain in Rochester,
    N.Y.), 176, 177, 182
Weill, Sanford, 173
White youth, 5–9, 20, 127, 135
White-collar apprenticeship, 55, 59–60,
    144, 176
Whitney, Eli, 64
Wigginton, Eliot, 45, 154
Woodward, Calvin M., 91, 92

Work experience, 16, 17, 21, 23–28, 42,
    43, 47–49, 51, 52, 61, 62, 68, 84,
    95, 100, 102, 103, 109, 115, 116,
    119, 120, 126, 131, 133, 136–138,
    140, 150, 151, 155, 160, 161, 174,
    175, 177, 178
Work-based apprenticeship, 140, 141,
    160–162, 166
Worker virtues, 14, 15, 17, 24–26, 58,
    61, 73, 86, 88, 100, 119, 130, 132,
    138, 153, 157, 178
Work-Scholarship Connection, 157, 176–
    178, 182

Youth Employment and Demonstration
    Projects Act (YEDPA), 183–184
Youth-managed business, 159–160
Youth organizations
  Big Brothers/Big Sisters, 156
  Boy Scouts/Girl Scouts, 43, 153
  4-H, 43, 153
  YMCA/YWCA, 128